ARCHITECTURAL PROGRAMMING

ARCHITECTURAL PROGRAMMING

Information Management for Design

Donna P. Duerk

JOHN WILEY & SONS, INC.

New York   Chichester   Weinheim   Brisbane   Singapore   Toronto

To all my students,
past, present and
future.

Library of Congress Cataloging-in-Publication Data:

Duerk, Donna P.
Architectural programming: information management for design /
Donna P. Duerk
    272 p. 28 cm.
    Includes bibliographical references and index.
    ISBN 0-471-28468-8
    1. Architectural design—Programming.   I. Title.
NA2750.D83   1993
720'.28—dc20   93-10180

Printed in the United States of America

20 19 18 17 16 15 14

Contents

Foreword

There is a large body of research that makes it clear that the planning, design, and management of our physical environments affect the behavior, performance, and satisfaction of individuals, groups, and whole organizations. Depending upon how well or poorly we plan, make, and use our environments, there can be benefits or there can be costs, or more probably both. The benefits or costs are, of course, strongly related to how well a place functions, but are also related as strongly to the psychodynamics of the place; its symbolic and aesthetic capacity; peoples' social interactions and their opportunities for choice; the group's or organization's culture; and the happiness, health and well-being of people who live in, work in, and visit the place. Without support for *all* these criteria designed into the physical environment, the full effectiveness and richness of places-designed-for-purpose will not be met.

If information is gathered about the people who will use a place and about their interests, needs, aspirations, behaviors, interactions, and tasks; and the necessary environmental requirements to support these expectations are developed and documented; and if information is wisely used in the planning and design process, the place can become a tool, one that can help us achieve our purposes. But the substantial benefits of place-as-a-tool can only be realized if a set of clear objectives and detailed guidelines are established, prior to planning, for what the new place must be like and do, and then only if these planning directives have been purposefully developed to produce benefits.

This "prior-to-planning" process is called *pre-design programming*. It is a form of design research, a disciplined process of data collection, analysis, and organization of information through which all the influences on the proposed environment are explored. It is disciplined but it is not science, for it deals with real people in real settings, in all their complexity.

Because programming really examines what people and organizations need functionally, economically, spiritually, and symbolically, it places their needs at the center of the act of planning and design. This is in itself an attitude, an ideology of what place-making should be for in our lives. But an information-rich design process does not displace other ideologies about design. A good pre-design program is no constraint for the designer concerned with form as narrative, form as critique, form as Techne, or form as any of the remarkable things it can be. My own experience in many projects indicates that design teams covet a good pre-design program as an enriching framework for exploration and creativity.

The use of a thoughtful pre-design program focuses the act of design on the important issues and makes the design team more resourceful. A thoughtful pre-design program is not a set of commands but a set of explanations for suggestions. It presents the rationale for why certain requirements are selected and which of them are priorities. Thus, it enables the designer to explore a range of solutions to any requirement (or sets of requirements that interact) and allows the designer to "interrogate" the program (and often the programmers themselves) so as to make wise trade-offs when all requirements cannot be met.

Although there are a few other books about pre-design programming, none of them is as open, accessible, and malleable as this one. Even so, this one is rigorous and thoughtful, a true "how-to" book, useful for doing your first pre-design program and many after that. What makes it particularly useful is the approach of *issue-based programming*, where issues are concerns that demand a design response and

thus become the units of analysis in the programming process. Issues come up in the design and use of every building and are generic like privacy and communality, mood and image, flexibility and stability, and openness and security. Issues are not facts, but rather are spectrums, continuums, and dialectics, the very stuff of the choices we must make in design.

In addition to describing Issues, the method also helps you develop and describe Facts, Values, and Performance Requirements. Facts are the important "givens" in the project — the site's characteristics, local climate, applicable building codes, demographics of the users, local road systems, and traffic. Within a framework of knowledge about Facts, Values are invoked that guide our choices about Issues. First they help us decide about which Issues are most important and then they help us decide where on the spectrum (say, of security versus openness) our requirements for a solution should fall. Of course, in design projects, there are often conflicting values and this book suggests ways to make decisions among them, or, better yet, to seek a wise compromise based on those values that are shared.

Performance Requirements describe what the design *solution* must *do*, or how it must perform in use, not what it must specifically *be* (its dimensions, shape, and location). With performance-based guidelines, the creativity of the design team is sought, welcomed, and respected, rather than deeply constrained. The book shows how Performance Requirements can generate design concepts and even how they might be presented. Of course, we do not always know what we need to know in order to make "wise-enough" decisions in the design process, so Duerk shows us how to find out by doing some research, and she provides an overview of many of the important Issues in design and behavior research. Doing all this obviously increases the amount of information in the design-decision process, so information management strategies are offered.

My own experience in developing pre-design programs for a very wide variety of buildings indicates that developing such programs really saves time and effort in the design process, that architects and designers are very pleased to have a good program to work with, and that ultimately clients get a better place to be in and to use. There are also hidden but enriching benefits gained from the client's own engagement in the process. Clients become more resourceful, sensitive, and knowledgeable because of their increased understanding of themselves and what they really need from their environments. They get a picture of themselves that they seldom have, both as a whole and with parts, and they develop with the designer a set of jointly agreed-upon expectations about what the new place should accomplish. This process-gained knowledge enables the client to be a *much* wiser user of the place after it is built. After a period of occupancy, the program's goals and performance requirements can form the basis for an evaluation of how well the place and its parts work. This evaluation permits the place to be further improved and, if done perhaps annually, can help design become a continuous learning process, as well as be an ongoing diagnostic checkup so the places' users can maintain a good fit between their environment and their needs.

Michael Brill, April 1993

This text was developed on a Macintosh IIcx using Pagemaker 4.2a, Word 5.0, Freehand 2.0, Superpaint 3.0, Photoshop 2.01, Canvas 3.0.3, DeskScan II 1.61, and Type Reader 1.0. The body of the text is 10 pt Galliard with 12 pt headings. Captions are 9 pt Helvetica.

Acknowledgments

Writing this book has been a very gratifying experience. One of the most satisfying lessons I learned is that being an author is really a team sport. First on the list for acknowledgment are those people who have given me my intellectual foundation in architectural programming: Professor Henry Sanoff of North Carolina State's School of Design, Willie Peña of CRS-Sirrine in Houston, and Professor Sandy Howell of Massachusetts Institute of Technology. I would also like to express my gratitude to all my friends and colleagues of the Environmental Design Research Association for all those thought-provoking conversations enjoyed over the years, especially with Bob Hershberger and Kent Spreckelmeyer. I have also learned a lot from my colleagues in the College of Architecture and Environmental Design here at California Polytechnic State University in San Luis Obispo. This book could not have been written without all of my students who asked good questions and challenged me to present my ideas clearly.

Contributions for the text contents came from many corners. My thanks go to all the people who gave me permission to use portions of their work, especially to students Wayne Rizzo, Steve Lampert, Jane Geddes, Gary Hitesman (who did most of the work for the example program in Chapter 12), and Jay Farbstein (who allowed me to use major portions of one of his program documents as the second example program in Chapter 12).

Technical support came also from many directions. Ross Parsons designed the page layout and created the final graphics from my sketches. Many thanks go to him for being so easy to work with. Stephen Narron and Joseph Kasparovitz helped me with scanning the work covered by permissions.

The acknowledgments are not complete without thanks going to my personal cheerleaders: my daughter Stephanie; my confidants Jerry Dagna, Claire Guest, and Greg Peck; my support team Carol Pimentel, Allen Root, Brenda Drechsler, Mike Oliviera, and Stuart Clyde; and all the rest of my friends and family who lightened my load when things got tight.

Finally, a big round of applause goes to all of the people who read various versions of this text over the past couple of years and gave me valuable feedback on how this text could be improved: Glen Matteson, Dan Panetta, Jesse Voss, Bob Kitamura, Brian Starr, Cathy Chitwood, and Terry Simons. Many, many thanks go to my former student Mark Enz for keeping me abreast of current practices in a large firm and to my colleague Will Benedict who read the final version of the book for comprehension. Thanks go to Tim White for providing a great review and for catching some major errors.

The biggest thanks of all go to my book coach, Greg Barker. He challenged every idea that was incompletely stated and made sure I clarified my fuzzy communications. After reading the first chapter, he said, "You are so damn intuitive it's driving me crazy. Having a linear thinker review your work will either bring balance or double homicide." We are both still alive and I assert that the text is more balanced and greatly improved because of our working together. As with any design project, it pays to have a very highly skilled team. I most certainly did.

Introduction

Currently, there are very few books available that address the topic of how to do architectural programming. This text is designed to provide instruction in programming processes for practicing professionals who want to improve their techniques as well as for students in schools of design. The concepts and principles illustrated here can be applied to any design discipline or problem-solving process. It is my hope that professionals and students in disciplines other than architecture will find this book of value.

Articles on programming started showing up in the architectural press in the late 1960s about the time when the failure of Pruitt Igoe became common knowledge. The housing project solved the financial and image problems of public housing, but did not respond to the behavioral and social needs of the residents and the project was demolished in 1976. This building design failure served to illustrate the necessity to understand the users of a building and to design with their needs as a compelling force for organizing the building. The 1970s saw programming become a standard part of the American Institute of Architects supplemental contract and many schools of architecture instituted programming courses. The 1980s saw those programming courses absorbed into the design studios because "everybody does programming." Now, in the 1990s, it is necessary to get back to a clear programming process that manages the vast amounts of information required to design a good building.

A well-programmed building is a functional building. The Pruitt Igoe example shows very painfully that a functional building lasts a lot longer than a building that merely looks good and is in the latest style. Good architecture is functional, meaningful and beautiful. The costliest mistakes are generally mistakes in programming — the building organization, the circulation patterns, the separation of user groups, the ease of access, and other major relationship patterns — so it pays to do a thorough job of programming. The key to good programming is asking the right questions and organizing the information so that it is readily accessible when needed. A really proficient client will have clear ideas about the desired level of excellence for the design project as well as the associated needs and functions. If the client is not so experienced, then it is up to the designer to be or to hire a committed, effective programmer who asks the right questions to uncover the information that is crucial to good design.

CLEAR STRUCTURE FOR THE PROCESS

The main goal of this book is to illustrate a clear structure for the programming process. It shows a step-by-step process for gathering and organizing programming information as well as how to create and present a program document. Chapter 1 defines programming and introduces the idea that the context for the design can be analyzed as the existing state and that programming and design proposals are descriptions of the desired future state. Chapter 2 introduces and defines design issues as categories for researching and organizing relevant design information. Chapters 3, 4, and 5 create an algorithm for producing programming goals, performance requirements, and concepts. These are the vehicles for the program to describe the desired outcome of the project in terms general enough to give the project direction without tying a designer's hands. The ideas and techniques for developing testable performance requirements are the strong points of this text.

Chapter 6 is a foundation in the basics of the scientific method. Since research is one of the most important tools for gathering information that helps shape the design, an understanding of the principles of research is vital. A grounding in the scientific method makes accurate and useful research a more realistic goal for architects not trained in the methods of sociology or psychology. An understanding of the mechanisms of research validity and the advantages or limits of different research methods helps produce results you can depend upon. Chapters 7 and 8 illustrate numerous examples of research techniques that are useful for designers — from relatively simple methods to those requiring substantial knowledge of social science research techniques.

Chapters 9, 10, 11, 12, and 13 show different applications of programming. Chapter 9 gives many examples of programming research that has already been done in the area of environment and behavior studies. Since it is the building's response to people's behavior that makes a building functional or not functional, it behooves the designer to have the greatest possible understanding of the client. Chapter 10 creates a structure for managing project information from the initial assessment of what is known to the final organization and presentation of the information. Chapter 11 outlines the structure and various page formats for producing a program document. Chapter 12 uses excerpts from two different types of program documents as case studies. Finally, Chapter 13 illustrates the use of a program document as an evaluation tool, from the initial schematic design all the way to postoccupancy evaluation.

The programming process in this book is meant to be an algorithm with a rigorous set of procedures. Once you have investigated a building type or a selected aspect of a design project, you can leave out some of the detail and shift to a shorter, more heuristic process based upon your experience. Whenever you run into an unfamiliar client group, building type or new design issue, it will serve you well to do a complete programming investigation. Doing an effective program is an opportunity to learn about an area in which you have never before designed. I know a number of people who took a lot of extra time and money to program their first building in a new type and now they are well-known experts in that building type.

FOUNDATION OF DESIGN INFORMATION

A second very important goal for this book is to create a process that produces a pragmatic foundation of design information for each design project. This means that there is a clear understanding of all the constraints for the project as well as a clear understanding of the quality of the desired solution. To build this foundation does not imply that all the sources for design inspiration are rational and methodical. Much of the inspiration for great buildings is intuitive, whimsical and based upon some rules of formalism rather than pure functionalism. Programming creates the functional basis for design.

My assertion is that whether a project is in the mode of romanticism, modernism, deconstructivism, or any newer "ism," it should also be completely workable for its inhabitants. To this end, the programming process in this text is grounded in pragmatism and empiricism with a bit of structuralism, positivism, and objectivism thrown in for good measure.

Pragmatism implies a process based upon predictive modeling that includes the following steps:

- Identify and define the problem.
- Formulate alternative actions.
- Select an action.
- Evaluate the consequences of action.
- Identify general findings.

Empiricism implies a process based upon systematic design with these steps:

- Collect and classify information into relevant categories.
- Formulate potential feasible solutions to the problem based upon information gathered.
- Judge by the use of criteria which of the feasible solutions most clearly satisfies the requirements.

Structuralism implies a process based upon pattern analysis including these steps:

- Observe the field.
- Form categories.
- Arrange typologies, hierarchies, and matrices and develop taxonomies. (Archea 1975.)

As you will notice when reading this text, I draw freely on as many theories and "isms" as I can to create a process that builds a solid foundation of design information. When it comes to formulating alternative solutions to the design problem, the sky is the limit as far as creativity is concerned.

HOW TO PROGRAM

A third goal is that this text provide clear instruction in useful methods and techniques of programming (in addition to the *structure* of the programming process) so that anyone conversant with the design process can do a decent job of programming for an unknown situation. For example, with the help of these methods and techniques, a New Englander could design housing for the coming building boom in

Eastern Europe; a Mexican American could design a community for African Americans, Anglo-Americans, or Asian Americans; an experienced housing designer could design a school or a library; and any designer could design appropriate places to accommodate the coming electronic information/media explosion. The "how to" chapters are arranged from general information to specific examples, the research chapters give step-by-step methods, and the format and information management chapters give the structure for organizing and presenting programming information. If you are a design student learning about programming for the first time, the best way to approach this book is to start at the beginning, plow through, and create practice exercises for yourself as you go to sharpen your skills. If you are an experienced designer, you may want to skim Chapters 1 and 2 and jump right into the "how to" of chapters 3, 4, and 5. Next, you may want to work with Chapter 9 to check your general knowledge of some of the major issues of environment and behavior. For the professional, the meat of this text is in the research chapters (7 and 8) as well as in the chapter on development of performance requirements (Chapter 4).

VISUALLY ACCESSIBLE

The fourth goal for the book is that it be easy to read and visually interesting. The page format was chosen for its visual appeal. To engage the visual learner, there are many diagrams illustrating the ideas in the text. Most of the chapters are of a moderate size and focus on a few main ideas. In the sidebar are statements of principles that I strongly believe to be aspects vital to good programming. The bold type within the text indicates a word that is used for the first time and is also defined in the glossary. Some words are in italics for emphasis.

It is my hope that this text will prove to be a valuable contribution to your design education or an addition to the skills you use in your practice. If you have any constructive criticism, please get in touch with me at the School of Architecture, College of Architecture and Environmental Design, California Polytechnic State University, San Luis Obispo, California 93407.

Donna P. Duerk

PART I

HOW TO PROGRAM

Chapters 1 through 5 serve to answer the questions, "What is architectural programing?" and "How do I do it?" In the simplest of terms, architectural programming is the problem definition phase of the design process. It is done by gathering and analyzing information about the context within which the design must be done and by stating the qualities that the project design must have in order to be successful. Since architecture involves so many different factors, the actual process is not as simple as the definition. This text was written to set out an orderly process for managing the mountains of information that are necessary for good programming and high quality design.

Most of the ideas presented here are not new, but are based upon the work of many other people. The main players in the development of my concepts of design programming as a well-understood, rigorous professional activity are William M. Peña, E. T. White, Michael Brill, John Zeisel, and Mickey Palmer. Others who have contributed to my understanding of the field by their work or their writings are Sandra Howell, Robert Hershberger, Wolfgang F. E. Preiser, Walter Moleski, and Jay Farbstein.

There are a couple of new ideas here. One is the idea of issue-based design, which means dividing the design problem up into smaller chunks based upon generic design issues such as circulation, image, privacy and security. These smaller chunks of the design problem can be used as categories for gathering design information, stating goals, doing research and making programming and design decisions. The second new idea is the algorithm for developing performance requirements for each issue/goal area and creating concepts for each performance requirement.

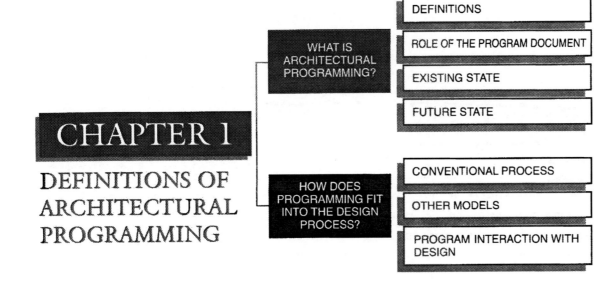

CHAPTER 1

DEFINITIONS OF ARCHITECTURAL PROGRAMMING

WHAT IS ARCHITECTURAL PROGRAMMING?
- DEFINITIONS
- ROLE OF THE PROGRAM DOCUMENT
- EXISTING STATE
- FUTURE STATE

HOW DOES PROGRAMMING FIT INTO THE DESIGN PROCESS?
- CONVENTIONAL PROCESS
- OTHER MODELS
- PROGRAM INTERACTION WITH DESIGN

DEFINITIONS OF ARCHITECTURAL PROGRAMMING

We shape our buildings; thereafter they shape us.

Winston Churchill
Address to Parliament

Definition:

Programming is a systematic method of inquiry that delineates the context within which the designing must be done as well as defines the requirements that a successful project must meet.

WHAT IS ARCHITECTURAL PROGRAMMING

This book is about designing. It is about the first part of the design process, the *problem definition and planning phase* which is the basis of good design. This first part of the design process is called **programming** — the British use the term **briefing**. This book is intended for anyone who wants to do a more thorough job of architectural programming, and thus wants to know more about asking the right questions at the right time.

Definitions

Webster's (1966) defines a program as "a plan of procedure." Architectural programming is the process of managing information so that the right kind of information is available at the right stage of the design process and the best possible decisions can be made in shaping the outcome of the building design. Programming is also the process that creates the structure for fulfilling the dreams, hopes, wishes, and desires of the building's future inhabitants. It is the orderly definition of the architectural problem and the articulation of project requirements in a manner that promotes the creation of a responsible solution for the design of the building. Peña (1987), who is for me the father of architectural programming, calls this problem definition the "problem seeking" phase — as opposed to design, which he calls the "problem solving" phase.

Until architectural firms took on the job of programming, the client was expected to provide the definition of the architectural problem and, often, the

program document as well. Now, as outlined in the standard American Institute of Architects' (**AIA**) procedure, programming is the first step in the design process. (See the sidebar on page 9 for a diagram of the AIA process.) Program documents may still be provided by a client-owner as well as by a design team or a programming consultant. Clients often produce documents that are an outline for the delivery of their services, such as an educational program for a school or a social services program for a government agency. These documents are not to be confused with architectural programs, which are the documents guiding the delivery of *architectural* services.

Problem definition and project planning are done for all projects, but formal **program documents** are usually not done for smaller jobs. More and more firms are seeing the vital need for full project information and problem definition and there are increasing numbers of people and firms who specialize in architectural programming and research. Through a survey of architectural firms, White (n.d.) has found that the inclusion of programming gives a firm a competitive edge over others that do not offer the service. He states, "Firms are realizing that when projects are carefully programmed, design can begin earlier, proceed more efficiently and suffer less slippage, false starts and client rejections. Programming saves both the firm and the client time and money." In this volume, the primary emphasis is on programming for **schematic design**. **Design development** programming is much more specific and much more detailed than most of the examples used here.

Programming is also the plan for the procedure and organization of all the resources (staff, information, budget, etc.) necessary for developing a design within a specific context and with specific requirements. Programming is the gathering, organizing, analyzing, interpreting, and presenting of the information relevant to a design project. In order to facilitate those activities, I advocate dividing programming into two main areas of concern:

1. Analysis of the **existing state**, which is the context within which the design is to be embedded and includes such things as site analysis, user profiles, codes, constraints, and climate.

2. Projection of what the **future state** should be, which is the set of criteria that the design must meet in order to be successful and includes the mission, goals, concepts, and performance requirements.

I also advocate using **design issues** as categories for searching for information or data about the existing state and as the topics for creating the **goals, performance requirements (PRs),** and **concepts** that are developed to

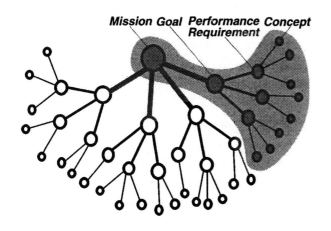

Figure 1-1 Goals, Performance Requirements, and Concepts for Each Design Issue

describe the future state (Figure 1-1). A design issue is defined as an area of concern that demands a design response. See Chapter 2 for an in-depth discussion. Goals, performance requirements, and concepts each have their own chapters as well.

What is proposed in this book is an algorithm for a rigorous programming process. When the project is highly detailed and/or the outcome of the design is very important, this algorithm should be used. When you have a lot of experience with a building type or the design will be successful with a wide variety of possible outcomes (such as a private house or a storefront), you might depend on fewer, more general concepts per issue and on serendipitous inspiration for good programming and design.

The principles of programming can be used for many other types of projects, such as landscape projects, city planning projects, developing a new business or product, and deciding what sort of job to look for upon graduating from college. This book will focus upon architectural examples with occasional references to planning and programming projects undertaken by other professions. Please keep in mind that the principles and processes described here are far more important as general guidelines than as rules for architecturally implementing the principles. Each architect or firm will adapt these ideas to suit their own needs and to serve their clients best. White (n.d., 5-6) has noted that a developed skill in programming has a number of benefits: a confidence that one can be resourceful enough to manage any situation, no matter how complex it is, by assessing and analyzing the situation, determining where to get the necessary missing information, distilling the information into a strategy for action, and knowing when to bring the project to a close.

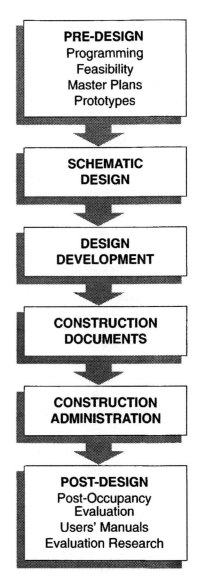

AIA Design Process

10-Step Design Process

- ACCEPT PROBLEM
- GATHER INFORMATION: Research & Analysis
- DEFINE THE PROBLEM TO BE SOLVED
- COMPLETE DATA GATHERING & ANALYSIS
- DEVELOP ALTERNATIVE DESIGNS
- EVALUATE & CHOOSE ALTERNATIVE
- DEFINE ALTERNATIVE MORE DETAILED ANALYSIS
- PRESENT SOLUTION
- IMPLEMENT SOLUTION
- EVALUATE RESULTS

10-Step Design Process

Architectural programming is not to be confused with computer programming, although the use of computers is becoming increasingly common in the process of architectural programming and the word *programming* for most people calls up images of computers. Computer programming is writing computer code to have the machine do what the computer operator wants. Architectural programming is the process of gathering information, analyzing that information and making recommendations for the performance of a building.

In practice, architectural programming has sometimes taken on Webster's (1966) first definition of "a list of the events, pieces, performers, etc., as of an entertainment or ceremony," such that the building program for many studio projects has been little more than a list of spaces and square footages with a brief statement of purpose. *This is not what an architectural program should be.* It is vitally important to know what the client wants in terms of purpose, excellence, and ambiance — beyond mere numbers — if the design is to fulfill its potential to support human activities. A good architectural programmer works with the decision makers on the client team to come up with the best possible program for the delivery of architecture.

Cyclical Design Process

The design process is often seen as a serendipitous, cyclical process covering much ground at ever-increasing levels of detail at each sweep. See Figure 1-2. Programming gives structure to the sweeps and gives the designer a greater measure of control over the information at each level of detail. It gives a pattern to the process — eliminating some unnecessary cycles — without dampening the spontaneity and

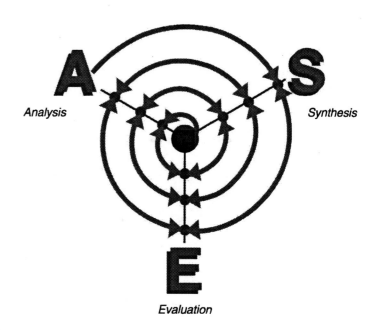

Analysis   *Synthesis*

Evaluation

Figure 1-2 Cyclical Design Process

necessary retracing. Using design issues as units of analysis and to make conceptual proposals allows the designer to set priorities for trade-offs when they are necessary and serves as an organizing tool to ensure that the right information is available at the right time.

Role of the Program Document

The program document states the **mission** (purpose) of the project and serves as the repository of all the relevant factual material pertaining to the project. It also documents all the decisions about the scope and direction of the project. It is a legal contract of agreement between the client and the architect defining the quality of outcome (goals) for the project and the context (existing conditions) within which the design work is to be done.

Design is a purposeful, goal-oriented, decision-making activity that attempts to resolve any conflicts arising so that the outcome achieves the best possible state or balance over time, therefore creating the best possible quality of life. Conflicts arise when the quality of life for all the players is not factored into the equation or when two or more requirements seem to have mutually exclusive outcomes. The act of programming gets all the facts out on the table, acknowledges all conflicting interests, and works to resolve all major conflicts before the design takes form.

Existing State

The analytical part of the programming process explores and describes the existing state of affairs or the context within which design is to be done. In programming, both the ability to synthesize and analyze skillfully are essential for outlining the future state, requirements for a project's success, and the development of goals, performance requirements, and concepts. Webster's (1966) defines analysis as "a breaking up of any whole into its parts so as to find out their nature, function, etc." and synthesis as "the putting together of parts or

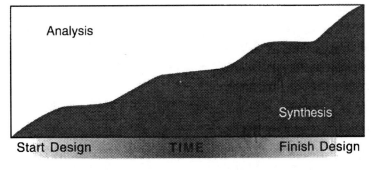

Figure 1-3 Interdependence of Analysis and Synthesis in Design

elements so as to form a whole." As the design process moves forward, the balance shifts from a greater need for analysis to a greater need for synthesis. There always seems to be a measure of synthesis in good programming and analysis is always a part of good design. (Figure 1-3.)

Gathering and analyzing data about the existing state or context for design are vital steps to successfully understanding the constraints and possibilities of a given design problem. **Facts** relating to the site, users, culture, economics, and phasing must be uncovered. The site must be thoroughly understood — data must be gathered about special site elements, views to and from the site, the site's topography, soil types, hydrology, flora, fauna, climate, available utilities, the surrounding visual context, the existing behavior patterns of the people who use the site and neighborhood, important historical events, potential future trends, and economics. Facts are not matters of opinion but are items that can be independently verified as existing or having happened. For more information on site analysis techniques see *Site Analysis* White (1983) and *Landscape Architecture* Simonds (1983).

Other sets of facts about the client/user group, such as demography, organizational structure, habits, preferences, special needs, activities, **value systems**, growth potential, and work flow, need to be considered so that the designer understands for whom she is designing. Sometimes the social,

PRINCIPLE 1

The only reason to design anything, is to create a better fit between what is and what should be; in other words, to support a better quality of life.

PRINCIPLE 2

Understand the existing state: its implications and constraints.

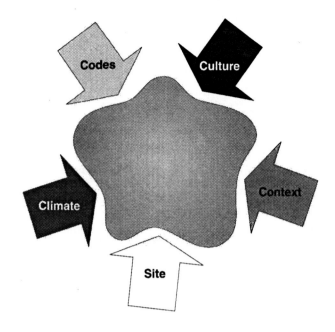

Figure 1-4   External Forces and Constraints on Design

political, intellectual, and/or spiritual contexts play very important roles in shaping the outcome of the design. See Figure 1-4.

Organizing Frameworks

Peña (1987) divides design issues into four categories: Form, Function, Economy, and Time. Palmer (1981) make's three categories for design issues: Human Factors, Physical Factors, and External Factors. White (1972) concentrates on developing check lists for facts to be uncovered about the existing context and uses the following categories: similar projects, client, financial, codes, planning by related organizations, function, site, climate and growth, and change. In Chapter 10 there are more detailed versions of these

frameworks. This text proposes the use of design issues as the categories for organizing design information with Facts, Values, Goals, Performance Requirements, and Concepts for each (Duerk's model.)

Each programmer or each project may have a different format for organizing the data required for design in such a way that is best suited to get the best results. The point is that there must be a framework for organization that allows the programmer to discover what information is missing, redundant, and useless. In my model for organizing design

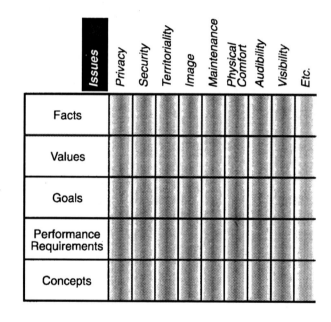

Figure 1-5   Duerk's Model

information, design issues (Figure 1-5) are basic units of analysis that can be useful within any framework. See Chapter 2 for more information about developing design issues.

Understanding does not come from a great gathering of *facts*. The facts must be grouped and analyzed so that the important issues that demand a design response are exposed for further examination and action. Analysis of site data will ascertain concerns such as whether a particular rock outcropping is an important visual feature to be included in the design or is a nuisance to be overcome and whether or not the site is suitable for the desired level of solar energy use. Analysis of client data will uncover such issues as circulation, image, safety, and privacy needs. The analysis of the social, political, economic, and spiritual contexts illuminates the value systems within which clients make their judgments. Values are the yardsticks that people use for making decisions about what is good or desirable. Values also color what issues are chosen as relevant and which facts are recorded as important. Some of these constraints on the design will also be uncovered in an analysis of local geology, zoning and building codes, material availability, and governmental or client policies. The basic structure for organizing design data should be as inclusive as possible, even though the importance of each category will vary from project to project. After a number of projects, even the basic structure may need to be updated with new technology or newly discovered information. For example, the use of certain materials is prohibited in public buildings because recently it was discovered that, even if a fire does not hurt the occupants of the building, the poisonous gases produced when the materials burn will kill or injure them.

The constraints imposed by the existing state become the *external* set of forces that shape the design. See Figure 1-4. The client's values and assumptions are the basis for determining what the desired response to the problem's constraints and the project budget will be. The designer also has a set of values and assumptions that may be in conflict with the client's set, so part of the design data needed is an awareness of both the designer's and the client's values and assumptions. When values conflict, there needs to be a negotiation and an understanding developed that serve to enhance the quality of the project for the users.

Future State

From the analysis of what already exists, one might draw certain conclusions, but the design does not spring automatically from the analysis of facts. To project future needs, the programmer must develop organizational ideas

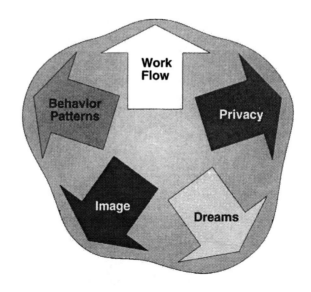

Figure 1-6   Internal Forces Influencing the Future State

(concepts) in order to determine how big the project and each of its parts must be. The proposal for the future state or completed design is the promise for achieving the level of quality of the outcome of the building itself. The client's desires for a particular quality of environment (goals) become the set of *internal* forces that shape the design. See Figure 1-6.

Hierarchy of Decisions

There are four major steps in developing a program to describe the future state: create a mission statement, develop project goals, design measurable performance requirements, and develop conceptual relationships.

Mission: In order for the promise of the design to be clearly stated, the mission of the project should be unquestionably articulated. The mission statement should answer the questions, "Why are we doing this project?" and "What is the contribution that this project will make to the world?" Webster's (1966) defines mission as "the special duty or function on which someone is sent, a special task or calling." It is the job of the mission statement to define the special purpose that the building project must perform in order to be successful. The mission statement is the conceptual foundation for the project. (See page 37.) All goals, performance requirements, and concepts must support and be congruent with the mission of the project. Figure 1-7 shows the hierarchy of decisions, from general to specific, that must be made to implement the design.

Goals: In order for the mission to be accomplished, goals must be developed that clearly express the level of quality to be reached by the final design regarding all design issues that have been uncovered in the analysis phase. A goal is a statement of an ideal quality level in which the design should have to be 100% successful. Stating goals clearly so that they focus the designer's intention in a particular direction without limiting his creative expression takes a highly developed ability to synthesize. It also takes the ability to use words rigorously so that the goal statement advocates nothing more and nothing less than is intended. (See page 43.)

Performance Requirements: In order for the design goals to be realized, the building must *function* in a way that promotes the level of excellence desired. In the programming process outlined in this book, the performance requirement is the vehicle for communicating the level of function required to implement a goal. A performance requirement is a statement of measurable function that the design must live up to in order for the goals to be reached. (See page 56.) Performance requirements are called by other names as well. Peña's (1987) "Statements of the Problem" are summary performance requirements of "design criteria." They have also been called "objectives" but I find that this word is too commonly

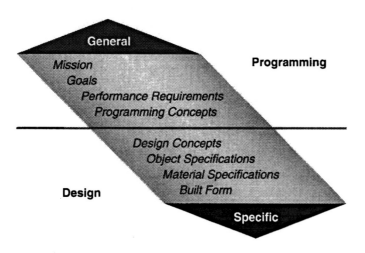

Figure 1-7 Decision Hierarchy: General to Specific

interchanged with "goals" to be of any use in creating a rigorous structure for information management. Whichever term you choose to use, be consistent and clear about its definition before starting to work with any new group.

Concepts: In order for a building to function at the desired level of performance, it must be physically organized in such a way that facilitates the appropriate level of function. Concepts are captioned diagrams that illustrate the ideal organizational relationships. A concept can be developed for every level of organization in a design, from the overall **parti** (main organizing idea) to the most minute detail of the design. In programming for schematic design, the overall organizing concept and the concepts for implementing performance requirements are relevant — all more detailed concepts (Peña calls them "design concepts" rather than programming concepts) should be a part of the design process.

When design issues are used as categories for organizing information (units of analysis), it is easy to search for facts and values related to each high priority issue and to develop a picture of the future resolution of the problems presented in terms of those issues, using goals, performance requirements, and concepts (Figure 1-8). Schematic design programming will generally need to cover ten to twelve top priority issues; design

development programming will cover all relevant issues. More detailed and specific concepts are a part of design development programming. Organizing concepts may be developed for the entire project (parti), for an issue or goal, for a performance requirement, or for one aspect of performance. This text gives examples of concepts for each aspect of a performance requirement to model an algorithm for a complete programming and design process. Some designers want less detail from programmers.

HOW DOES PROGRAMMING FIT INTO THE DESIGN PROCESS?

Conventional Process

Standard AIA documents divide the design process into the following phases: **pre-design services** (programming is included here), schematic design, design development, **construction documents, construction administration**, and post-design services (see the sidebar on page 9). Each of the stages of design in the AIA process include analysis, synthesis, and evaluation.

The program document, which is the product of this phase of the work, becomes the legal

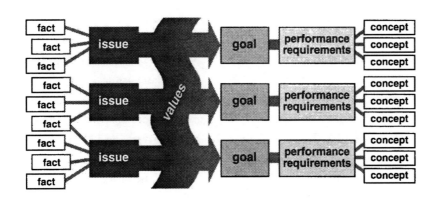

Figure 1-8 Schematic Design Programming

agreement between the architect and the client as to the scope, focus, and direction of the design project. In other words, it defines the essence of the design problem for the project at hand and is the promise the architect makes to the client regarding the quality of performance to be reached by the design.

Pre-design Services

Pre-design services may include needs assessment, feasibility studies, master and long range planning, various sorts of design research, and sometimes organizational development exercises. Programming is usually an additional service in the pre-design phase, according to AIA contract documents, and is billed when the project is large enough or complicated enough to require more than minimal research and planning.

Needs Assessment and Feasibility Studies: The pre-design phase of the design process covers many activities with which a person having programming skills might become involved. One such activity is a needs assessment study. Governmentally funded projects such as hospitals or prisons often require that the need for a proposed facility be thoroughly documented.

Another pre-design service often requiring the skills of a programmer is the development of a feasibility study for a project. This might include the development of a variety of alternative conceptual proposals for the site with various functions, sizes, concepts, and costs for the client to choose. Feasibility studies are fundamentally broad-brush programs with enough information for a banker, developer, and/or client to make the go or no-go decision.

Master Planning: Master planning, like doing feasibility studies, is programming with a broad brush and a minimum of detail. General concepts of circulation, building function, mass, and placement are developed along with a phasing plan. If the programmer can scare up a dependable crystal ball for master planning large projects, all the better. One of the most difficult tasks in the master planning game is developing accurate predictions of growth patterns and their timing. Cities do master planning with their land use elements, universities do campus master plans, and redevelopment authorities do master plans for city segments.

Building Prototypes: Programming is critical for the development of a building prototype. If a design is to be repeated in a number of situations, then the basic assumptions must be the best available. The army has commissioned many prototype studies to improve a number of building types, from religious education facilities to recreational facilities, that they construct repeatedly on bases across the country. Hotel chains have developed prototype models as have elementary school districts and restaurant chains. Probably one of the most recognizable prototype designs is the often repeated McDonald's hamburger eatery.

Programming Research: Research for programming a particular building can take many forms and will be discussed in detail in Chapters 7 and 8. There are other types of research that a programmer might wish to take on, ranging from exploring a particular issue to understanding a specific building type. Brill (1984) has done extensive work on office productivity, and Farbstein (1987) has done some interesting work on the image projected by post office lobbies. Marcus (1975) and Marcus and Sarkissian (1986) have done research in housing, and Howell (1980) has done extensive research with the elderly. The areas of gerontology, hospital design, wayfinding, prison design, and school design all have extensive research literature that an architectural programmer might use as a resource. The Environmental Design Research Association (**EDRA**) Conference Proceedings (starting from 1971) are exceptional resources for the latest research in a large number of applicable fields.

Post-design Services

Post-design services may also use the research/analysis and synthesis skills of a programmer for such tasks as preparing users' manuals for the building, fine-tuning a building after move-in, preparing a post-occupancy evaluation (**POE**), and compiling the information developed on the current project as reference material for future projects of the same building type. See Chapter 13 for more information on evaluation.

Building Users' Manuals: One of the least used outlets for the programmer's skills is the development of building users' manuals. Most often the people who are a part of the planning and implementation process for large projects are not the same people who will use the building. As a result, many of the programmer's or designer's intentions are left to interpretation — for better or for worse. A clearly written users' manual that outlines the philosophy of the design and the goals and intentions of the building will help the users be more efficient in their use of the building or will help them to know that they must adapt the building to a changing use or philosophy.

One of my favorite anecdotes is about a demonstration school that was built as a part of an education department for a major university. The classrooms were built to accommodate the special needs of each group, from kindergarten to sixth grade. When the teachers planned to move in, there were no names on the room plans, only room numbers. It came as quite a surprise to the sixth grade teacher to find that his room had a sink and was too small for all the furniture needed for the almost full-grown sixth graders. Likewise, the kindergarten teacher was unhappy to find that her kindergarten room was without a sink and was a bit too large. So the moral of this tale is that with a users' manual they would have known that all they had to do was to reverse the order of the classes down the hall and, voilá, everything worked.

Other Models

Descriptive Models: Heading for a Solution

Descriptions of the design process have evolved over the years as researchers struggle to capture the essence of what people do when they invent new and interesting ways of doing things. There are three-step, seven-step, and ten-step processes, and many other processes with various numbers and names for the steps (Koberg and Bagnall 1991, 27). All of these descriptions of the design process have three activities in common: analysis, synthesis, and evaluation. Programming consists of each of these activities at various points in the process. The process is not linear, going from analysis to synthesis to evaluation, nor is it describable in any rigorous sequence of steps. There is no *right* order that will guarantee good designs by using a single process or formula.

In very general terms, the design process can be described as a spiral, which includes analysis, then synthesis, and then evaluation in turn, with many opportunities for backtracking and jumping over the *next* step. As one continues through the process, choices are made and options are eliminated so that the design is developed at ever-increasing levels of detail to zero in on a solution. As one approaches "solution country" there is no clear stopping point that says to the designer, "*This is it! Design no more!*" (Robert Asbury 1984, personal communication). There always seems to be one more issue that can be more thoroughly explored, one more look at the fine points of composition, or one more detail to be added. Design is a process of making highly satisfactory solutions to the top-priority issues and making the most satisfactory solutions possible to the other issues. It is not a process of getting *THE right answer*.

When a solution is developed to a point where it meets the most critical criteria, the stopping point in the design process is dictated by when the designer runs out of the time, money, or energy to continue rather than reaching a point where there is nothing more to design (Donald Grant 1985, personal communication). These time, money, and energy constraints may also exist in programming and cause the designer to begin the design process with less than the desired amount of usable, relevant information. This indeterminacy means that design is an imperfect science and that good programming helps design to be a more rigorous art.

Figure 1-9 attempts to compile all the words that have been used at one time or another to describe the activities and products connected to the design process. Notice that the line between analysis and synthesis is not solid. This is to emphasize that good design ideas do not automatically follow analysis. The chart also shows the links between various activities of the design process. The products of analysis are the goals

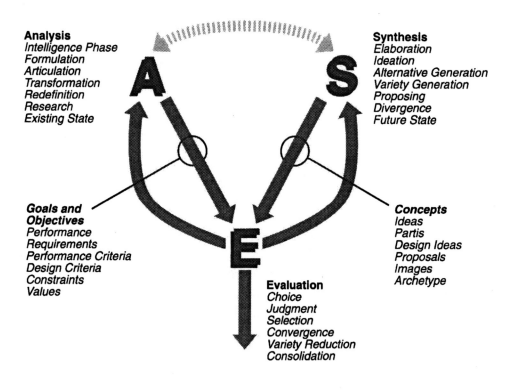

Analysis
Intelligence Phase
Formulation
Articulation
Transformation
Redefinition
Research
Existing State

Synthesis
Elaboration
Ideation
Alternative Generation
Variety Generation
Proposing
Divergence
Future State

Goals and Objectives
Performance
Requirements
Performance Criteria
Design Criteria
Constraints
Values

Concepts
Ideas
Partis
Design Ideas
Proposals
Images
Archetype

Evaluation
Choice
Judgment
Selection
Convergence
Variety Reduction
Consolidation

Figure 1-9 The Design Process: Analysis, Synthesis, and Evaluation

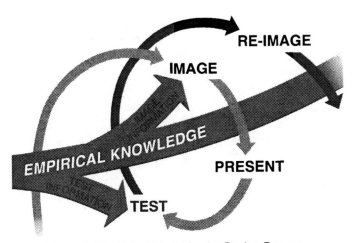

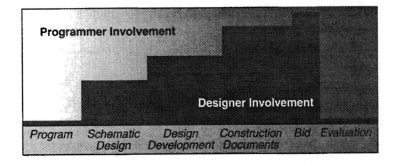

Figure 1-10   Zeisel Model for the Design Process.
Adapted from *Inquiry by Design* by John Zeisel,
1981. Used by permission of Brooks/Cole Publishing Co.

and performance requirements (criteria for making choices) that are necessary to evaluate the concepts (design ideas) that develop from the synthesis activity. Again, note that the activities are cyclical and have no set *order* that guarantees success.

Zeisel Model

John Zeisel, a sociologist concerned with environment/ behavior interaction, has conceived of the design process in somewhat different terms. He speaks of **imaging, presenting,** and **testing** to clarify the different purposes that information gathered during programming must serve. Imaging is the synthesis portion of the

process, the development of a conception of what the future state must be. Presenting is the act of making the image available to other people, whether through drawings, models, or computer videos. Testing is the evaluation portion, when the images (concepts) are determined to be appropriate or inappropriate for meeting the criteria set forth in the design program. Analysis comes in the form of gathering and using data for each of these three steps (Zeisel 1981). See Figure 1-10.

Program Interaction with Design

A programmer may develop a program document that stands alone and is handed off to the designer or that may be an integral part of the design process from start to finish with different designers engaged in different levels of programming effort. It is Canadian government policy (Harvey and Vischer 1984) and Peña's (1987) belief that, to maintain the integrity of each process, the program should be absolutely separate from the design. For designers who also do their own programming, maintaining separate program and design stages is an impossible task and, for many smaller projects, is not necessary.

An alternative model is for programming and design to be completely integrated so that it is very hard to tell when one process begins and another ends. This is probably typical of small architectural practices today where there seems

Figure 1-11   Programmer/Designer Involvement in the Design Process

to be very little acknowledgment of programming as a separate process. In this book there is a third alternative advocated, that of keeping the activities of programming clearly articulated yet distinct from those of design while still maintaining frequent, regular interaction between the programming and design processes including evaluation processes. See Figure 1-11.

As the programmer develops the program and as the parti and the major concepts are developed, contact with the designer should become increasingly frequent. It is the designer's role to articulate ideas that will work to solve the *problems* that the programmer defines, and it is the programmer's role to keep the concepts generic and abstract so that the alternatives for a concrete solution are not limited in these early phases of the project. As the design process moves forward, the programmer's role is to help the designer evaluate how well the evolving design fulfills the intent or communication. If the performance requirements are developed as measurable statements of function, then they will serve as the yardsticks for evaluating the design in both its early and final forms. When doing both programming and design, it is difficult to keep from jumping to solutions and using the program document to justify the design. An awareness of and constant vigilance for this hazard of creating "justifications" for your preliminary solutions in the programming process should be sufficient stimulus to keep you committed to developing multiple alternatives.

During the design process as the details of the building become increasingly specific, the involvement of the programmer becomes diminished until the post-occupancy or post-construction evaluation (POE, PCE) phase. Not all firms do systematic evaluations of their projects, but it is posited here as the ideal completion to the design process. During the

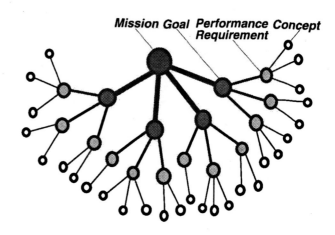

Figure 1-12 Fundamental Framework for Programming

POE, it is usually the programmer who is best suited to use the program as the tool for evaluating the building in use. POEs can serve a number of purposes: to finetune the building for the users, to complete the cycle of evaluations for the design firm in order to let them know how they are doing, to gather information for programming the next building of a similar nature, and to add to the general knowledge of that particular building type. In current practice, the most often used form of the POE is in programming a new building rather than as the end of the design cycle. See Chapter 13 for a more thorough discussion of evaluation.

SUMMARY

Design is the process of filling perceived needs and creating a better fit between what is and what should be. Programming is the problem definition and planning stage of the design process and is usually carried out as a pre-design service. It is the job of programming to uncover all the important aspects of the design problem and to specify the quality of design solution to be expected. Program documents are part of the legal agreement between the designer and the client that specifies the direction and scope of the project. For a program document to be complete, it should include an analysis of the existing state and external design forces (including facts about codes, site analysis, user profiles, and constraints) as well as a proposal for the future state and internal design forces (including mission, goals, performance requirements, and concepts). The data gathered include information about the values and assumptions of all participants as well as the implications and the constraints of all the facts. Programming paints a picture in words and diagrams of the ideal solution to the problem (the structure for fulfilling the dreams, hopes, and desires of the client) as defined by the mission statement, goals, performance requirements (PRs), and concepts. Programming is also a plan for managing the resources available to accomplish the design — from the in-house experts to the budget for the project.

This text proposes an algorithm for organizing design information by issue so that information is gathered efficiently and is available to the designer at the right time in the process. Figure 1-12 diagrams the framework of one goal plus PRs and concepts for each issue (as also seen in Figure 1-1). Using design issues as units of analysis allows the designer to set priorities and make trade-offs when they are necessary to resolve conflicts. All models of the design process contain elements of analysis, synthesis, and evaluation. This text outlines how each is used in the programming process.

Programming, as a pre-design service, will often be a major portion of feasibility studies, needs assessments, master planning, and building prototype designs. Programming often requires a brief post-occupancy evaluation study of another building or in-depth research of one particular issue that is insufficiently understood at the beginning of the project. Programming skills are useful in other post-design services, such as post-construction evaluations, systematic post-occupancy evaluations, and the development of users' manuals to guide the users in understanding the designer's intended use of the building.

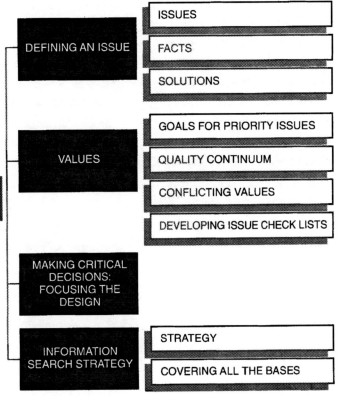

CHAPTER 2

ISSUE-BASED
PROGRAMMING:
A TOOL FOR
MANAGING THE
DESIGN PROCESS

DEFINING AN ISSUE
- ISSUES
- FACTS
- SOLUTIONS

VALUES
- GOALS FOR PRIORITY ISSUES
- QUALITY CONTINUUM
- CONFLICTING VALUES
- DEVELOPING ISSUE CHECK LISTS

MAKING CRITICAL DECISIONS: FOCUSING THE DESIGN

INFORMATION SEARCH STRATEGY
- STRATEGY
- COVERING ALL THE BASES

ISSUE-BASED PROGRAMMING: A TOOL FOR MANAGING THE DESIGN PROCESS

"Would you tell me, please, which way I ought to go from here?"
"That depends a good deal on where you want to get to," said the Cat.
"I don't much care where—" said Alice.
"Then it doesn't matter which way you go," said the Cat.

Lewis Carroll
Alice's Adventures in Wonderland

DEFINING AN ISSUE

Most architectural designers begin their projects with a broadly sweeping information search strategy that encompasses anything and everything that has to do with the building type at hand. In no time they are overwhelmed with more information than they know how to apply. By sorting information into issue-based categories, it is relatively easy to develop a strategy and research plan for uncovering missing information, for identifying the critical decisions that need to be made and, at the same time, for developing a congruent format for reporting to the client. Issue-based programming provides a tool for allowing designers to make clear distinctions between merely interesting facts and useful information in the early stages of the process. It also provides a tool for managing mountains of information in a coherent manner throughout the design process. It is a structure for sorting information into useful categories at the beginning of a project, giving the designer a strong sense of confidence in knowing that the entire process can be well managed. Issue-based programming is a technique for uncovering the unique potential for a design project by clearly identifying those design decisions that are indispensable to an individual project's success.

Issues

An issue, as used here, means any matter, concern, question, topic, proposition, or situation that demands a design response in order for a building project to be successful for its clients and users. It is a topic that makes a difference in a particular design — a concern that requires the designer to take action and make decisions. In architecture, some of the generic issues are circulation, safety, territoriality, privacy, image, energy use, flexibility, and visibility. Each of these concerns is valid for any building design, although the relative importance or priority of each issue will vary for each project. In this programming strategy, issues are general categories for sorting design information into manageable chunks to support efficient decision making. Each issue will generate a goal concerning the quality of the final design solution.

The issue check list covers most of the basic concerns in building design. It may not be complete for every building type, but all building designs will involve decisions in most of the issue areas listed. Each major issue area (all upper case in the list) will have sub-issues (upper and lower case in the list). These sub-issues are more detailed areas of concern for generating performance requirements rather than goals.

Issue Check List

AUDIBILITY	ENERGY EFFICIENCY
Behavior Settings	ENVIRONMENTAL
CIRCULATION	IMPACT
Information	FLEXIBILITY
Material	Adaptability
Parking	Choice/variety
Pedestrians	Expansion/contraction
Vehicles	Multi-use
COMFORT	IMAGE
Physical	Identity
Psychological	Message
CONVENIENCE	Ordering/proportion
DURABILITY	Status/hierarchy
ECONOMY	Symbolism
Elegant means	INTERACTION
Phasing	Group participation
Quality	Social

LEGIBILITY
  Layering
  Orientation
  Plan recognition
  Sequence
MAINTENANCE
MOOD/AMBIENCE
  Attitude
  Emotional response
  Spirit of place
OLFACTORY
PERSONALIZATION
  Group
  Individual
PRIVACY
  Group
  Individual

RESOURCE
  MANAGEMENT
SAFETY
  Accidents
  Hazards
SECURITY
  Assault
  Robbery
  Unauthorized
    access/entry
  Vandalism
TERRITORY
  Group
  Individual
VISIBILITY

Facts

Site, climate, and code requirements are *not* issues but are *facts* about the existing state or context in which the design must perform. Facts are objective, specific, and verifiable by some measurement or observation. Their existence is not subject to judgment, but their use and interpretation is based on values. Information about the constraints and the context within which the designing is done is vital to understanding the project, but the context and constraints are not usually the *major* forces in shaping a design. However, the visual qualities of the site (facts) may inspire an image (issue) response and the climate (facts) may require an energy efficiency (issue) response. For example, the facts of prevailing wind direction, number of **degree days,** and sun angles are necessary to know only if energy conservation is an important issue. If so, you must make decisions about daylighting, insulation, ventilation, and other aspects that will create solutions that are energy efficient. In this example, the facts about the climate provide constraints within which the design must operate.

Facts

SITE
CLIMATE
  Degree days
  Precipitation
  Solar exposure
  Wind speed and
    direction
CODES
  Building
  Zoning
SITE CONDITIONS
  City services/transit
  Geology
  Hydrology
  Noise
  Odors
  Site features (rocks,
    flora, fauna,
    streams, etc.)
  Soil-bearing capacity
  Topography
  Utilities
  Views to and from site
TRAFFIC LEVELS
  Bicycles
  Pedestrians
  Vehicles

PERSON/USER
ACTIVITY ANALYSIS
AGE GROUP
ANTHROPOMETRICS
DISABILITY
ENVIRONMENTAL
  HISTORY
NUMBERS OF PEOPLE/
  GROUPINGS
  Organizational
    structure
PERCEPTUAL
  ABILITIES
PERSONALITY
ROLES
RULES
VALUES

CONTEXT
CULTURAL
DEMOGRAPHIC
ECONOMIC
ETHICAL
ETHNIC
HISTORICAL
POLITICAL
SOCIAL

Solutions

Entry, roof form, lighting, room type, etc. are *not* issues either. They are concepts or potential solutions to the concerns raised by the issues. Any topic that answers the question, "What might this design or building look like?" is a candidate for a solution rather than an issue. The entry form chosen could be a result of the desire for creating a sense of arrival (image and legibility) and a roof form could be a design response to a need for natural daylighting (energy efficiency) or a requirement for an imposing image. Lighting is a choice of fixture or window opening that is made in response to the desire for particular qualities of visibility, physical comfort, and/or mood (Figure 2-1).

At the most basic level, all design solutions are physical forms that have the attributes of dimension, direction, color (hue, value, and intensity), transparency, and texture and that create size, shape, surface, location, and orientation. Myriad decisions must be made that create the final form of the building down to the last door knob. The list of solutions is an attempt to cover all the bases with very broad categories.

Solutions

COMPOSITIONAL STRATEGIES	LIGHTING
EQUIPMENT	MATERIAL
FORM	Building
Color	Interior
(hue, value, intensity)	Landscape
	Texture
Dimension	Transparency
(size, shape)	ORIENTATION
Direction	SPACE
(orientation)	DEFINITION
Location	Enclosed
	Open

Design decisions will generally be much more detailed than these general categories.

For each project the list of issues will be prioritized in an order that is different from another similar project. How each issue "should be" resolved and its priorities are a matter of a value judgment. The appropriate quality of the circulation system, degree of performance of energy conserving features, level of security required, and performance level necessary for all the top priority issues must be assigned by the architect/

client team. Different cultural groups, people from different parts of the country, and people with different educational and economic levels all have different sets of values that will

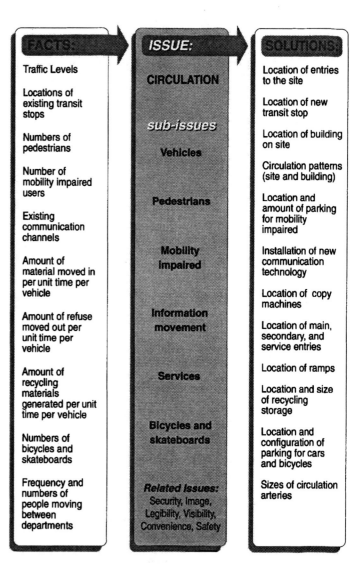

Figure 2-1 Example: Circulation: The Issue and Sub-issues with Related Facts and Solutions

influence what they think is a good outcome for a project. Different departments will have different goals and values and, therefore, they will have different priorities.

VALUES

Different building types also require different design responses to the same issues based upon the values of different users and the needs of different activities. Design issues, when processed through the filter of the values of the client, user, and designer, yield goal statements about the *qualities* the design must have to ensure success (Figure 2-2). A goal, then, is a concise statement of the designer's promise to the client about the quality of the design in relationship to a particular issue.

Goals for Priority Issues

Circulation is a high priority issue in both hospitals and botanical gardens, yet opposite outcomes result from their value-based goals. For the hospital the circulation goal might be:

> The circulation paths should be as direct and efficient as possible while separating physician/patient/visitor and clean/soiled circulation paths.

For the botanical garden the circulation goal could be:

> The circulation paths should strongly encourage all users to stop occasionally to admire the near and far views of the garden.

A small house would need a minimum amount of circulation,

whereas cross-country ski trails require a maximum amount of path length. In another example, many "yuppie" condos have sold themselves with the maximum convenience of "all electric living" that is part of the conspicuous consumption of energy, whereas many building sites in Hawaii are without water or electricity and must conserve and create energy rather than consume resources from the public utility grid. In designing housing for people from Latin America, the designer should be aware of the high value placed on a sense of community and the visual connection of individual units to a public *paseo* whereas the opposite trend toward maximum individual unit privacy seems to be prevalent in suburban North America. See Chapter 3 for a complete discussion of goals.

Quality Continuum

From these examples, each issue can be clearly viewed as a continuum of quality levels between two dichotomies. The underlying values of a particular problem determine which

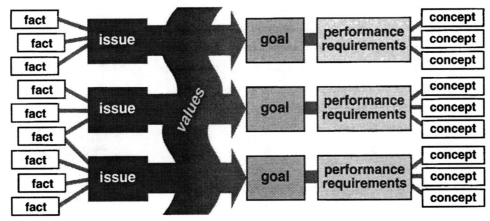

Figure 2-2 Values Influence Issues to Form Goals

PRINCIPLE 5

Different groups have different values that must be known and understood so that the designer can resolve conflicts, set priorities and make tradeoffs.

performance level is appropriate for a high quality solution. It is the job of the programmer/designer to discover the appropriate level of performance. Rooms in a Japanese house may be separated by paper walls because the cultural rules of polite behavior require that sounds from other rooms be thoroughly ignored and thus assure privacy because they are unheard. United States culture has no such prohibition, so that one of the major complaints about hotels in this country is that the rooms are not private enough because the sheet rock walls do not dampen enough sound between rooms (Figure 2-3).

Most Private   Various Levels of Privacy   Most Public

Figure 2-3   Various Levels of Privacy

When it comes to the issue of economy, a Texas oil millionaire building a house will have a very different place on the financial scale than a first time home buyer in Iowa. Fort Knox and the Pentagon have a much greater need for physical security than homes in small towns where friends are free to enter whether or not anyone is at home.

Conflicting Values

The top priority issues and the set of underlying values are very likely to be different for the client and the architect/designer as well as for the student and the professor. If these differences are clearly identified at the beginning, a successful

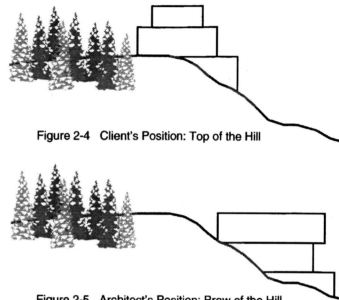

Figure 2-4   Client's Position: Top of the Hill

Figure 2-5   Architect's Position: Brow of the Hill

negotiation and understanding of these differences will be possible. For example, if the client insists upon having her home built on the top of the hill (Figure 2-4) and the designer "knows" that the best solution is a Wrightian one and insists that the home should be on the brow of the hill (Figure 2-5), there is no solution based upon these immutable opinions. If, on the other hand, they both come to understand that the client values a 360° view and an imposing

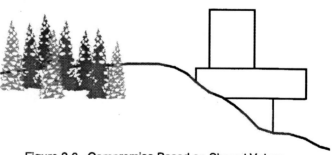

Figure 2-6   Compromise Based on Shared Values

image and the architect values building on the brow of the hill and saving the outdoor room at the top of the hill, then there is potential for a solution that conceptually captures the best of all the valued ideals (Figure 2-6). The design can have a 360° view by building a tall, rather imposing structure on the brow of the hill and can preserve the outdoor room at the top of the hill.

In another example, the City of San Luis Obispo, California, has a guideline that all structures are to be set back 20 feet from the top of the creek bank. On a difficult site with a creek slicing through at an acute angle to the street, the developer wanted to build as close to the creek as possible to get the maximum area for a building on the site. The City would consider the possibility of innovative design solutions that violated the 20 foot setback *if* the construction met the city's values in that the construction stabilized the creek bank, maintained or enhanced the riparian habitat, maintained the ecology of the creek during construction, and produced a usable building on a difficult site. To date, no such solution has been found.

Goals should reflect the values of all parties concerned and should serve to resolve any conflicts based on specific concepts or positions. It is much more likely that an appropriate solution can be devised if the values are known and appreciated than if particular solutions are pitted against each other.

Developing Issue Check Lists

Check lists of issues may be found in the books by Peña (1987), Palmer (1981) and Preiser (1985), and research topics are listed by White (1972). The topics in these check lists cover a range of concerns including issues of response to the site, cultural issues, behavioral expectations, and building messages to be delivered. Peña's matrix and White's facts list are reproduced in Chapter 10. Each of these information structures is useful for illustrating how the universe of design information can be successfully organized in many different ways. You may want to use each of them in creating your own check list.

Each of your design projects will have special issues above and beyond any "typical" issues for their particular building types. Peña's *Problem Seeking* (1987) divides issues into categories of Form, Function, Economy, and Time. Some of the issues listed are efficiency, security, identity, physical comfort, and maintenance. Palmer (1981) surveys a number of programming models and creates his own format for organizing information. He divides issues into Human Factors, Physical Factors, and External Factors. His list includes such items as organization (structure), circulation, energy use, and cost constraints. White's (1972) categories of facts are for information gathering and include many issues from mood and atmosphere to scale and image.

A prioritized issue list is vital in defining the most important pieces of information for immediate use and winnowing out the information to be used later in the design process. In sorting out the relative priorities for all the people involved in making a building happen, there are a number of useful questions to ask. Are there issues that the designer finds to be recurrent themes in many similar projects (high priority)? Are there issues that are repeatedly downplayed (low priority)? Are there generic issues by building type that could guide research and design (such as the need for sterile environments in hospitals and some laboratories)? What are the issues that the client group complains most about (potential high priority)? "What are the issues that the client group is most excited or inspired about (high priority)?

MAKING CRITICAL DECISIONS: FOCUSING THE DESIGN

Most designers are unable to handle a very large number of issues in any one project. Most architects are unable to develop a parti that fulfills the promise of *all* the relevant issues. Most clients focus on a few issues that are vital to their sense of the success of the project. The important point is to focus the design effort on the issues that make a major difference in the quality of the outcome. This process becomes the search for the essence of a design problem. It is my opinion that, for most design projects, the broader issue to focus on is the creation of a better quality of life. Even the inmates of our prisons need high quality environments that support reform.

Agreement on the top priority issues and the level of performance required gives the designer a clear direction as to where to put more energy, in reading existing research, developing new research strategies, checking precedents, or developing new design ideas. The need for agreement is especially vital when working with a client composed of many members or committees. The process of coming to an agreement on the major issues often creates a rapport between client groups that is unattainable in any other manner. Design students quickly learn to put their energies into those issues that make the most difference for their professor, their clients, and themselves.

Concentrating the programming and design effort on a few major issues assumes that the building must still respond to many other issues. For example, the building must be structurally sound and meet all the codes even if structure and codes are not the form generators. The list of major issues should be composed of issues that are of equal concern — it is unproductive to consider the issues leading to a choice of door hinges with the same intensity as the issues leading to an overall building image. After the development of the overall design concept that accounts for the major issues, the design can be fine-tuned by considering all the minor issues in order of their priority.

All major design issues usually overlap others in part. For example, measures of security influence image, privacy needs impact circulation patterns, etc. The final outcome for each issue depends upon the decisions made in other realms. Developing clear partitions between issues takes practice. Each major issue has a number of aspects (sub-issues) that contribute to understanding the whole issue. For a specific project there may be privacy concerns that relate to visual privacy, auditory privacy, individual and group privacy, gender privacy, **privacy gradients**, and so on. Some of these sub-issues may relate to other issues such as security or circulation, but if the most important aspect is privacy, then the sub-issues will become the basis for performance requirements for the goal relating to privacy.

For some building types there will be a need for more than one goal per issue. If the building is very complex, there may be different goals for different user groups or departments for the same issue. If one special issue is of singularly critical importance, such as the security of prisons or the circulation of an airport or a hospital, then there may need to be several goals to cover the issue thoroughly enough. Buildings such as international airports or border stations have potentially conflicting jurisdictions as well as numerous complex processes and multiple flows that create differences that must be resolved programmatically.

In Figure 2-7 the larger circle represents the design problem, which is the sum of all the issues. Each inset circle represents an issue such as privacy, security, image, legibility, flexibility, territory or circulation. The diagram is intended to illustrate the ideal that each major issue covers about the same amount of importance represented by area within the design problem. Even though issues overlap, they should be carefully partitioned to avoid repetition in programming.

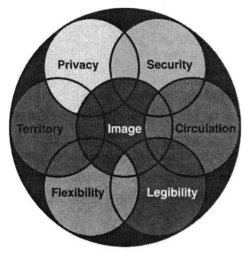

Figure 2-7   Issues of Approximately Equal Value in the Design Problem

INFORMATION SEARCH STRATEGY

Developing a focused list of issues that make a major difference in a design project allows the designer to compile a strategy for the information search, in other words, for filling in the gaps, organizing information by issue, and avoiding overload. The following model of an information search

strategy is presented in a linear sequence only because of the presentation medium. In actual practice, it is cyclical and iterative. Sometimes information about important issues will surface later in the design process because a design alternative creates unexpected possibilities. In such a case, the program document might not be updated, but priorities might have to be reordered or at least reexamined.

Whether you gather all of your client-based information in one long working session or in multiple meetings depends upon the budget, the availability of the client, and the complexity of the project. You should get client verification and feedback on your interpretation of the facts, priorities, and issues as well as on the goals, performance requirements, and concepts. Your client can also help verify that you have complete information about their concerns. Chapters 7 and 8 on research methods give more information about how to execute many of the techniques mentioned here and give references for implementing most of the others.

Strategy

Identify Issues and Underlying Values

Get to know your clients, users, and designers to understand the values that are operating for the project. Clarify the set of issues that are important to each set of people.

TECHNIQUES: meetings, interviews, focus groups, visits to the client's home base, observation of existing places in use, and review of service delivery programs and other archival data.

Organize Information and Set Priorities

Create a mental framework to allow decisions to take their priority in the information hierarchy. You may want to use one of the frameworks illustrated in Chapter 10 on information management or you may want to develop a different structure for organizing information categories for each project. Generally, young designers can handle three to five major issues as the focus for their main design idea. The requirements for minor issues can be used to fine-tune the overall concept after it is developed based upon the major issues.

TECHNIQUES: meetings, interviews, **paired comparisons**, past experience, review of existing reports and past memos, and instinct.

Categorize the Information

Look at all information on hand by issue and uncover what information is missing and what research needs to be done.

TECHNIQUES: creating a separate file for each issue, sorting cards (see Peña 1987, 56-57), checklists, program document templates, and creating an outline or draft program document.

Develop Project Goals, Performance Requirements, and Concepts

Write out the goals and performance requirements. Diagram concepts for the overall organization of the project and for each issue area. This step is the synthesis and inspirational beginning. The level of detail depends upon the designer who will be using your program. What do they need for complete information and direction and minimum constraint?

TECHNIQUES: See Chapter 3 on developing goals, Chapter 4 on performance requirements, and Chapter 5 on

developing concepts. If there is any uncertainty, check with the client and user about your assumptions.

Make a Work Schedule and Evaluate the Progress Toward the Goals

Make a task list and create a due date for each task or group of tasks. Create a check list in each issue area as you go along and change your timing or working strategy as necessary with each new level of information about how it all works together. Some information gathered will prove to be perfectly useless in making design decisions. Other discoveries may prove to be pivotal.

TECHNIQUES: past experience, detailed calendar, **PERT, CPM**.

Report to the Client

Review the program to confirm that the design is headed in the right direction. Present the information, organized by issue, to make the progress of the design clear to the client. The issues divide the information into understandable chunks for the client as well as clarify how the solution contributes to the whole.

TECHNIQUES: See Chapter 11 for more information on program document organization and page formats.

Covering All the Bases

The tree diagram (Figure 2-8) indicates a complete hierarchy of design ideas. The mission describes the overall purpose and direction of the project. Goals define the general quality of the design outcome in each issue area. Performance requirements state the level of function required and concepts

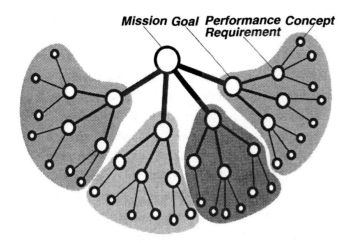

Mission Goal Performance Concept
Requirement

Figure 2-8   Tree Structure for Information Hierarchy

In the early stages of programming, there will most likely be some sense of the mission or purpose of the project, a few of the main issues and goals, and some of the concepts that are likely to be successful. It is the job of the programmer to fill in the blanks.

The question to be asked when working from the general to the specific (from mission statement, to goal, to performance requirement and then to concept) is "How?" *How* is the quality of the goal to be implemented? *How* must the building function? *How* should things be arranged if the show the physical relationship between the design's elements required to meet the performance requirements. When programming is weak, some major aspects of important issues have been left out — usually because the design is concept-driven rather than performance-driven. If you intuitively come up with a great concept, it is logical to move up the hierarchy and uncover the performance requirement behind the concept. The next step is to uncover the goal behind the performance requirement and then to find other related performance requirements and new concepts. This mental map of the issue-based information hierarchy is a plan for the inquiry into all aspects of a design. It should help the designer to become more creative and more effective in meeting *all* the client's needs because it encourages a look at a wider range of "problems" rather than encouraging an approach based upon just a few design concepts developed to the maximum. This approach gives rise to a wider range of concepts (Figure 2-8).

MISSION

HOW?   WHY?

GOAL

HOW?   WHY?

PERFORMANCE
REQUIREMENT

HOW?   WHY?

CONCEPT

Figure 2-9   The "Hows" and "Whys" of Working Through the
Information Hierarchy

building is to meet these functional requirements? When one is working from concept to PR or from PR to goal, the question to ask is, "Why?" *Why* does this arrangement work so well? *Why* is this concept functionally beneficial? *Why* is this function important and what qualities does it produce? (See Figure 2-9.) With this structure, issue-based programming is also an outline for the development of a set of questions for a post-occupancy evaluation strategy and for a building **users' manual**. One can begin planning for the next design and the next generation of designers with a well-documented design process and information management strategy.

SUMMARY

Issue-based programming divides the design problem into smaller areas of concern that demand design responses. By using design issues as categories for organizing design information and for making design decisions, the designer has more control over the design process because of the ability to make clear choices based upon priorities. Issue check lists help to make the inventory of decisions complete from major design issues, such as circulation and image, to sub-issues, such as parking and information flow or identity and status. Clients' values and architects' values are the yardsticks that measure whether an issue or sub-issue is a high priority or low priority, whether or not a particular set of facts is relevant, and whether or not a solution is appropriate. Values can be the

basis for a solution that satisfies several different images of what the ideal solution should be.

Each issue is a continuum of qualities from one extreme to the other. For one project, the appropriate level of quality might be close to one extreme, and for another project, the quality might be near the other extreme. For example, a monastery for Trappist monks would probably require a high degree of privacy for the monks' personal quarters while a summer camp cabin would require a sense of community and togetherness. Every project will have goals for high priority issues that clearly state where each issue falls on the quality continuum. The performance requirements are generated from the sub-goals.

While programming, we try to keep each issue separate so that we do not duplicate information gathering, but, in design, decisions in one issue area will affect those of another. When you are designing for both privacy and security, as in a housing project, you will have to balance the level of surveillence with the amount of unseen territory. Issue categories focus the search for information — the facts about the existing conditions and constraints within which the design must function. They also focus the search for solutions appropriate for the high priority issues. Issue-based programming encourages programmers to be thorough and insures that all important information is gathered, all the facts are in, the "hows" and "whys" are understood, and all the appropriate decisions are made. Facts are gathered to inform each issue area so that solutions to the questions posed and the decisions made might be the best possible.

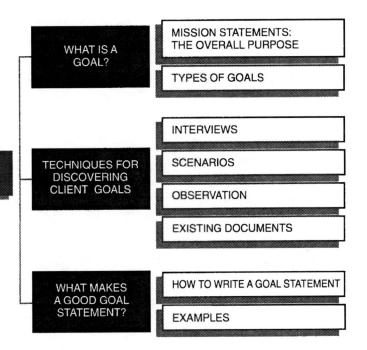

CHAPTER 3

GOALS:
THE PROMISE
FOR QUALITY

WHAT IS A GOAL?
- MISSION STATEMENTS: THE OVERALL PURPOSE
- TYPES OF GOALS

TECHNIQUES FOR DISCOVERING CLIENT GOALS
- INTERVIEWS
- SCENARIOS
- OBSERVATION
- EXISTING DOCUMENTS

WHAT MAKES A GOOD GOAL STATEMENT?
- HOW TO WRITE A GOAL STATEMENT
- EXAMPLES

GOALS:
THE PROMISE
FOR QUALITY

*When you **know** where you are going, you are half way there.*

Zig Ziglar
See You at the Top

All paths lead to the same goal: to convey to others what we are.

Pablo Neruda
Toward the Splendid City,
Upon Receiving the Nobel Prize

WHAT IS A GOAL?

A goal is a statement of intention, an end that one strives to attain or that toward which effort or play is directed. Goals are statements that move us to take action! They are vehicles for making design decisions. Dahl and Sykes (1983) state, "Human transformation [substitute "design" here] entails nothing less than clarifying values, reassessing priorities, and setting goals that foster the fulfillment of essential needs and greatest potential." Only 3% of the American people put their personal goals to paper. People don't plan to fail — they just don't plan anything (Ziglar 1974, 149). "Unless you have definite, precise, clearly set goals, you are not going to realize the maximum potential. . . . You'll never make it as a 'wandering generality.' You must be a 'meaningful specific'" (Ziglar 1974, 14). Goals allow you to "go as far as you can see and when you get there you will always be able to see farther" (Ziglar 1974, 154). A goal is a statement of what the future state should be!

Goals reflect our personal and cultural values. All of us become socialized into our culture by learning what is "good" and how things "should be." We often find ourselves saying that if we could run the world our way, it would be perfect. Everyone has a set of values and ideals about how the designed world should be put together. Sometimes these values and ideals are overt and sometimes they are unconscious, but priorities are somewhat different for different people, especially in different cultures or socio-economic groups.

A classic planning conflict, which designers are often called upon to mediate, arises from the differences in priorities between environmentalists and developers. The stereotypic environmentalist values the natural world and a stable ecosystem over the financial rewards of a specific design. The stereotypic developer values change and progress and the bottom line over the snail darter's or the western pond turtle's or the red-legged frog's habitat on a particular project.

Programmers, designers, clients, users, and project neighbors all bring to the project their own values and pictures of the perfect project outcome. To create the best solution for all the people involved, the programming and design process must uncover the basic assumptions and underlying values about what is good and worthwhile and must discover consensus, resolve any conflicts, or choose which value set has top priority for the particular project in question.

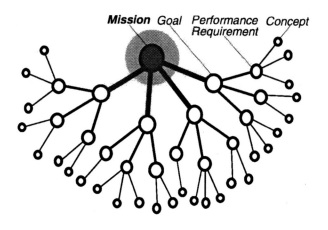

Figure 3-1 The Mission as the Foundation of the Project

Mission Statements: The Overall Purpose

The mission statement is a metagoal — a statement that concisely expresses the reason a client undertakes a project in the first place (Figure 3-1). The mission defines the special purpose that the building, landscape or planning project must fulfill to succeed. It contains or implies a set of values that were part of the impetus that generated the project. The best mission statement is a one-sentence answer to the question, "Why do we need to do this project?" Mission statements need to be clear enough for the bankers to understand them, the neighbors to understand them, and all the players on the team to know what it is they are expected to produce in the end. Often, mission statements will be reinforced with several paragraphs that set the tone and give more background about the project's purpose.

Sometimes a mission statement is a project-specific interpretation of the clients' statement of the vision they have for the ideal method of delivering their services. Other times the mission statement is created and "word-smithed" by the client and programmer together. Often it is difficult to create a one sentence statement of purpose for a very complex building, landscape, or city planning project. Nevertheless, brevity and conciseness are assets in a mission statement that must be longer than one sentence. I would suggest that a mission be distilled to one pithy sentence. If needed, have an accompanying paragraph to elaborate on the depth and breadth of the project's purpose.

Once the mission of the project has been articulated and an issue list has been generated, then goals must be developed so that priorities may be set and the design process may be aimed toward a particular set of outcomes. All goals must support the mission and be congruent with it. Rather than clarifying the mission first, the issues second, the goals third, and so on, client meetings are often used to clarify these items at various stages of the process. An initial meeting focused mainly upon composing the mission statement will probably produce issues, concepts, and factual data as well.

The programming process is described here as linear for the sake of convenience, but it usually works backwards or forwards, in leaps and bounds or in steps that slowly creep forward. It is highly likely that a good concept will spark a new area of inquiry that uncovers a goal that was missed earlier in the process.

Mission Statement Examples

For a junior high school: To create an educational facility that supports 7th, 8th, and 9th graders in making an easy transition from childhood to young adulthood.

For a new audiology office: To establish an office where listening is the most important product.

Defining "Objective"

I do not use the word "objective" as part of the structure of information in this text because it is often used to mean many different things. "Objective" has been used to mean the overall purpose (mission) to be accomplished, it has been used to be synonymous with "goal," and it has been used to mean "sub-goal" or step toward achieving a goal. It has also been used to mean a measurable part of a goal (performance requirement). Because of these multiple uses of the word "objective" and for the sake of clarity, the word will not appear as part of the hierarchy of decisions in this text.

Types of Goals

There are several kinds of goals that will influence the outcome of a project. They are separated here for clarity. These goals are *process and resource goals, educational goals, personal goals* and finally *project-specific goals*. The text is concerned with the project-specific goals for the most part and the other types of goals are enumerated here to keep from confusing them with these project goals.

Process and Resource Goals

A process/resource goal relates to the management of the process of programming and the resources marshaled to make the design complete.

Time is a resource that is often limited and influences how thoroughly the research will be conducted and the depth of the programming and design efforts for a project. The time management strategy of the design team will have a substantial influence upon the outcome of the design, and setting these goals is an important part of managing the design process.

Financial resources of the design team, the size of the fee, and whether or not the project is a competition will also influence who is on the team and how long each part of the design phase will be. Financial planning strategies are not often taught in schools of design, yet they also play a significant role in the outcome of a design process. The depth of programming research often depends upon how much time and money there is to do the job.

Critics and evaluators are not often looked upon as resources, but for any design project, keeping on track in creating the intended outcome at every phase of the project will keep the design team from having to redo schemes that are deemed inappropriate by the client and/or users. It is far less expensive to make changes during the schematic design stage than when the building is under construction. It is easy to see that major changes become increasingly expensive as the design process progresses and are less likely to be made at the end of the project. Goals and strategies about who will do the evaluation and how often it will be done impact the accuracy

and quality of the project. While evaluation techniques are not the principal issues of this book, they will be referenced throughout the text and discussed in Chapter 13.

Talents and skills of each design team member are also valuable resources that need to be managed properly to create the best possible project. Staffing strategies are most often learned on the job by experience. The goal may be to have all the members of the team contribute their best skills, or you may be more interested in cross-training so that team members will know all the jobs on the team.

Educational Goals

Every project presents to the design team an opportunity to learn something. By setting goals about the content of the inquiry and the level of skill to be developed, each project becomes a conscious educational experience. Some firms set out to learn all they can about a new building type so that they can then sell themselves as experts to their client market. With such a goal in mind, more resources than usual may be put into research and programming so that the design team learns about the new building type or develops new management or presentation techniques to increase their firm's resource advantage.

Personal Goals

A personal goal relates to what an individual or design team wants to get out of the project. A design student may have the goal of making a particular design the centerpiece of her portfolio. An architect may be working out a particular theoretical idea and may use the design under consideration to make a statement. Designers may want to get published, impress a particular group of potential clients, or one-up the competition for new contracts or for design awards. All of these personal goals are outside the project goals, although they do have an influence upon the choices made during the design process.

Project Goals

Project goals are those goals that relate only to the outcome desired for the project. They will be based upon the underlying values of the designer, the clients, and the users. These goals vary in level of detail depending upon their place in the decision hierarchy. For example, goals may concern the relationships between the project and its context, between major aspects of the project, or between various smaller subdivisions of the project, or they may concern small details of high priority.

Programming for schematic design leaves out most of the smaller details and concerns itself with the relationships of the project to the surrounding neighborhood and the interrelationships of the internal parts. Programming for design development brings in a much greater level of detail so that the next level of more specific decisions can be made. Programming for schematic design and design development together includes both levels of detail. The programmer's contract with the client should spell out what sort of programming is required, based upon the project type and the programmer's relationship to the design team. Is the programmer going to hand off the program to a separate design team? Are the programmer and designer on the same team? Is the programmer also the designer? Each of these situations results in a different level of detail and specificity for a program document.

This book focuses on programming for schematic design, although the principles are applicable to all design phases. Goals should be developed for each design issue that

has been uncovered in the analysis phase and for each issue that is subsequently uncovered as the design process unfolds (Figure 3-2).

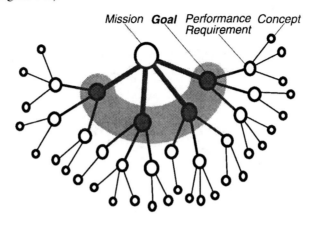

Figure 3-2   One Project Goal for Each Design Issue

It is useful for designers to begin each project by stating the mission clearly and mapping out all the known goals in each category and keeping track of their progress along the way. An awareness of personal goals on the part of the designer and the communication of those goals to the client are great vehicles for coming to an agreement about what the project should be.

Both knowing what to look for and what questions to ask are vital to good programming. One must be alert to recognize or uncover the underlying values when examples of good ideas are shared, especially those client or user values that are different from those of the programmer or designer. That big stack of clippings from *Sunset Magazine* or *Architectural Record* is far more useful as a vehicle for exploring client values, raising design issues, and searching for goals than as images to be translated directly into the finished design. Questions to the client should be based upon an outline that includes all the issues that have been uncovered to date or upon a list of issues created from the list in Chapter 2. Other useful areas of questioning include types and intensity of activities; formal flow of work, people, or information; informal information or resource flow; organization or habit structures that want to be expressed; etc.

TECHNIQUES FOR DISCOVERING CLIENT GOALS

Interviews, scenarios, and a keen eye are some of the most powerful tools that designers use to uncover client goals. Charles Rennie Macintosh and Frank Lloyd Wright often used these tools in an unusual way — they spent time in their clients' homes to understand their housing needs more clearly. Hanna and Hanna (1987, 20) wrote of Frank Lloyd Wright, "Mr. and Mrs. Wright were able to observe our children as they played with Iovanna [Wright's daughter]; to note our habits of housekeeping, family cooperation, recreation; and to learn about our research, writing, and teaching." They quote from the *Stanford Daily*, February 19, 1937 (1987, 58), "But most singular of all is the 'personality' Mr. Wright has given the construction. Not until he had lived with the Hannas several weeks did he begin designing.

"As a result, every detail in the construction is compatible with the Hannas' likes, philosophies, idiosyncrasies.

"'It takes a heap of living in a house to make a home,' says Poet Eddie Guest. But when the Hannas move into their new domicile, completely furnished by Mr. Wright, it will truly be their home, as like them as themselves!" Yet this

innovative house design was not accomplished without Wright's using his personal goals to create an experiment in geometry and construction techniques.

Interviews

A designer or programmer should do enough homework before the first meeting with a client to be able to use the initial interview as a vehicle to uncover major design issues not already considered and begin to discover what the client's priorities are. You should be alert for statements about the qualities that are to be produced as well as the kinds of things that give the client real satisfaction. At this stage, special challenges of the client's lifestyle, organization, or business should also demand close attention. The initial interview should verify issues that were assumed by the programmer before the meeting and uncover as many more as possible. (See Chapter 7 for interview techniques.) As the design process moves along, the client's reactions to proposals will also provide a great deal of information about issues and values that were not necessarily available at the first interview. Many times the reasons or values behind the clients' expressed desire for a specific feature are more important than the introduction of that exact feature.

Scenarios

If it is impossible to interview the client or users for any reason, it is a good exercise to develop scenarios about the lives of possible clients or users. This is a method of projecting oneself into the position of another person and can yield valuable design assumptions to stand in for hard and fast data. It is always wise to test these assumptions as thoroughly as possible before using them as the basis for design, but the exercise is valuable in the face of minimal real information.

A scenario takes the form of a narrative that tells the story about a portion of the clients' or users' lives. The most useful ones detail "a day in the life of. . ." or describe a particular event in great detail. The job of the scenario is to reveal the behaviors that need a design response and to raise issues that might not otherwise surface at this early stage of the design process. A good scenario is vivid and rich in details of activity and description of stage-setting ambiance without describing the physical surroundings in more than very general qualitative terms. Writing scenarios serves to raise questions about the areas of a person's or group's activity patterns or about their philosophy and values, which imply consequences for the design. It also serves to raise an awareness of what the design issues really might be.

See Appendix B for example scenarios.

Observation

The observation techniques of Frank Lloyd Wright are not always available to many of us. It is usually impossible to spend a couple of weeks observing a client for whom we are to design a home or an office or any other project. You must make the most of a limited amount of time. At the early stages of the design process, informal, casual observation is the most useful technique for uncovering values and issues. (See Chapter 7 for a full discussion of observation techniques.) This is where the watchful observer might read the existing environment for things that work or don't work, for activities and issues unmentioned in the initial interview. Later on in the design process more systematic techniques can be used to answer more specific questions.

For some building types, it may be a great idea to visit new facilities to see the state of the art. Goals may evolve to implement new technologies (resulting in a computer on every faculty member's desk), to shift to a new service delivery philosophy (open plan instead of "egg-crate" schools), or to implement improved operations (focus the design on the most efficient use of the M.D.'s time). These facility tours give the client and programmer a chance to share impressions and to come to understand the nature of the problem at hand more clearly.

As these new possibilities are introduced, the programmer works with the client to state the goals and values clearly so that multiple alternatives can be explored and evaluated.

Existing Documents

Often there will be existing client documents that are a source of goal statements. Programs for service delivery, flow charts of the standard set of processes, policy documents, and procedures manuals are good places to start.

WHAT MAKES A GOOD GOAL STATEMENT?

A good goal statement will be a statement of the level of quality or degree of excellence that the ideal solution or final product will achieve. It will resolve the question raised about the role of a particular issue in the design project. A great goal statement embodies the aspirations of the client and the users so that the designer is inspired to fulfill those dreams. A goal statement should be short and to the point, focusing on the *quality* of the environment to be achieved for the issue that the goal is delineating. The goal should *focus* the designer's

Focus Area
(Issue: To Produce Goal)

Design Problem

A Goal Focuses on One Issue

search for a solution to the problem without limiting the potential for multiple, alternative design concepts that would fulfill the goal's intention. The goal should have the quality of a **heuristic method** rather than of an **algorithm** in order to direct the inquiry of the designer in a manner more likely to produce an appropriate solution rather than a scattered, shotgun solution. The white area of the figure in the sidebar represents the focused area of the designer's search.

Each goal should be just about as influential over the outcome of the design as every other goal (Figure 3-3). That is to say, each goal should be at the same level of scope and detail. It does very little good to have some goals concerning major details such as circulation, privacy, and security of the project and other goals relating to lesser details such as electrical outlets, path material, or color. Having goals of the same scope does not assume that all goals are of equal importance. Some goals will have a much higher priority than others, such as security for prisons, circulation for hospitals,

and image for corporate headquarters. High priority goals will have more sub-issues and therefore more performance requirements and concepts than will lower priority goals.

A goal should be general, but not so vague as to give little or no direction to the designer. Because of its larger scale and massive components, a goal for a regional transit plan will seem to be more general than a goal for the circulation element of a small town and even more general than a neighborhood-specific transit plan. The scope and level of generality must be appropriate to the project at hand.

A goal should avoid words that are open to a very wide range of interpretations, such as *nice, pleasant, comfortable, appropriate,* and *homey.* Instead, you should focus on words that illustrate the intention for the outcome as clearly as possible. Examples of good descriptors can be words *or* phrases: *serene, welcomes warmly, stimulates the curiosity, soothing and restful, conforming strictly to the old customs,* and metaphorically *snug as a bug in a rug.*

Some goals will overlap others in their influence on the design. For instance, *security* and *privacy* are two issues that influence the level of visibility of the circulation routes of the project. If you want a great deal of privacy, then you wish to be on view as little as possible as you come and go. If you want to have the maximum security from unwanted intruders, then you will want to be able to see and recognize everyone who comes and goes. On this particular sub-issue, the client and designer must come to agreement about the trade-offs between being seen for security and being unseen for privacy. Sometimes these issues are in conflict — at an automated teller machine (ATM) you want your transaction to be completely private *and* you want to be able to see who else is near the ATM *and* you want the police see that you are safe as they cruise by. Each project will be different.

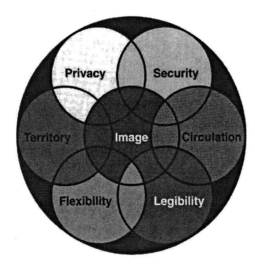

Privacy Security
Territory Image Circulation
Flexibility Legibility

Figure 3-3 Goals of Approximately Equal Value

How to Write a Goal Statement

The following six rules are guidelines for creating goal statements that are rigorous statements of the intended quality of the solution in one issue area. You may modify some of them to meet the need to communicate clearly with your client or to meet your clients' required format.

1. Goals should answer the question, "How is the *mission* for this project to be *accomplished?*"
2. A goal statement is a statement of the *quality* of the ideal solution for a design issue. It is a statement of how good your solution has to be. Therefore it should have some *adjectives and/or adverbs* in it that are as clear as you can make them, to say exactly in which direction the search for a solution should go. Try to make it *say no more and no less* than you really want it to say about what your aims are. Start with many adjectives and distill them down to the most essential ones — the quality (or qualities) that are vital to the success of the project.
3. Each goal statement should have the words *"should be"* or some close approximation in it, because a goal statement is a statement of the *future condition* that you wish to achieve.
4. A goal statement should be as *simply stated* as possible and should *allow all the relevant performance requirements* to be covered in its scope. Look for all the *sub-issues* that might affect the outcome of the project. Your goal is a good one if it encompasses all the major sub-issues and allows for the creation of performance requirements that speak to each sub-issue.
5. A goal statement should *cover a priority issue* and be about the *same scope and importance* as the rest of the other goals for the project.
6. A goal should be *positive* and proactive rather than negative. *Avoid the use of the words not, no, never,* etc., in building your goal statement. Sometimes you will want to know what the building should *not* be (institutional, imposing, showy), but those discussions should be descriptive rather than prescriptive like a goal.

A good formula for a very basic goal statement is:

The project SHOULD (*verb* of intention or "being" such as "promote," "project," "encourage" goes here) (an *adjective* or descriptive phrase goes here to define the *QUALITY* desired) (a *noun* goes here to focus on the area of concern).

Examples

Example Goal: The facility should *provide (verb)* **an** *extremely clear, simple and exciting (descriptive phrase)* **circulation** *system (noun)* **for members of the College of Architecture and Environmental Design as well as for visitors** *(noun descriptors)*.

The following mission statement and goals use examples from real projects and from architectural class work to illustrate how to develop a useful design goal. I make critiques of the first try and propose revisions that improve the goal statement and analyze the qualities that make them better goal statements. Alternative goal statements for the same project are sometimes illustrated to show different valid

> ### PRINCIPLE 9
> *The key to developing a good goal statement is to focus on the* quality *to be achieved.*

interpretations and emphases of the desired qualities for the same issue. These differences could lead to noticeably different project designs because of their varied interpretations.

Mission Statement

This mission statement is for a Massachusetts ICF-MR/A (Intermediate Care Facility for Mentally Retarded Adults who are incapable of self-preservation; Environmental Design Group 1976).

> **To create a residential environment that blends easily into a variety of New England settings, yet, at the same time, provides space and support features necessary to habitation for severely retarded/ disabled adults.**

This mission statement creates two main thrusts of the design: one for the ICF-MR/A to blend in visually with its context and the other to provide a clearly supportive environment for the clients.

The goals listed are for design development and cover each functional area rather than being for a more general schematic design. These statements are given here as illustrations only.

Example Goal #1

The meal preparation/dining areas should promote active participation by the residents and facilitate the learning of daily living skills.
(Issue: social interaction/learning)

The severely disabled need to have each part of their environment designed specifically to reinforce and to create a possibility for learning that nonretarded children and adults take for granted in their everyday environments. So,

"learning" is an issue for this design, which is not on the regular check list.

Example Goal #2

Bedrooms should promote a sense of ownership and responsibility for the residents.
(Issue: territory)

This goal could be used for dorms or for fraternity houses as well.

Example Goal #3

This goal is from a student project for a mixed-use retail building in a small downtown.

Parking should be within a five minute walk from the downtown core.
(Issue: circulation)

This goal is too specific and more like a performance requirement. It does not give the designer a sense of the desired quality of the pedestrian circulation that is the issue behind the goal.

Goal #3 Revised

The major portion of parking for the downtown core should be a short, pleasant walk from most shopping destinations.

Limiting parking specifications to a *major portion* allows for alternate, supporting solutions such as jitneys, trams, or trolleys to larger peripheral parking lots. By stating that the walk should be *short and pleasant*, a sense of the quality of the pedestrians' experience is illustrated, although *pleasant* is one of those bland and squishy words that is open to a wide variety of interpretations. If one were to qualify the word *pleasant* by adding *interesting* or *visually stimulating* or *protected*, doing so would focus the goal more specifically as to what *pleasant* is actually supposed to mean in this context. By stating that the walk is from the parking lot to shopping destinations, the designer's attention is focused on serving the specific needs of a particular part of the downtown pedestrian population.

Example Goal #4

The Science Center should reinforce the scientists' sense of creativity and productivity and promote analytical accuracy.
(Issue: mood, ambiance)

The key terms here are *creativity, productivity*, and *accuracy*, which set the mood for the work environment of the scientists.

Alternate Goal #4

The facility should provide a working environment that inspires its inhabitants to create original, quality ideas.

This goal focuses more on stimulating original and creative ideas.

Alternate Goal #4

The facility should stimulate creative thinking and promote a pleasant work atmosphere.

Here the idea of the environment contributing to creative thinking is enhanced by the addition of creating a pleasurable atmosphere in which to work.

Alternate Goal #4

The facility should provide a wide variety of possibilities to stimulate creativity and imagination.

This alternative focuses on different ways to encourage the scientists' creativity.

All the above goals speak to the need for the environment to support the creativity of the scientists and each one adds another aspect that shifts the direction of the search for an exciting, supportive solution.

SUMMARY

The mission statement of a design project is the mega goal that sets out the purpose for the project, the reason why the project is being done at all. Each project can be divided into issue areas. Each issue will have a goal statement that specifies how well that issue must be resolved in order for the project to be successful. A goal is a statement of intention for the future state of a project — what quality the project "should be." Values are the foundations for goals. They are the yardsticks that measure quality. Each project may represent a different set of values and therefore a different set of goals. Goals statements should be explicit about the level of quality that is desired in the final project and yet be general enough to be inclusive of a wide set of performance requirements and implementing concepts. If only one solution is possible, then the goal statement is too specific.

The client will have lots of ideas about the necessary quality of the project. It is the programmer's job to discover what those goals are — through conducting interviews, reviewing documents, and making observations of real clients or writing scenarios for unknown clients.

A goal statement should be brief, should focus the designer's attention on particular qualities, and should be of appropriate scope to cover the issue thoroughly. Goal statements should avoid using words such as "nice," "pleasant," or "appropriate" that are vague or open to a wide variety of interpretations.

The formula for writing a goal statement is useful for getting started. *The project SHOULD (verb of intention or* "being" such as "promote," "project," "encourage" goes here) (an *adjective* or descriptive phrase goes here to define the *QUALITY* desired) (a *noun* goes here to focus on the area of concern). This formula should be used to create the first try at a goal which will be the basis for subsequent development.

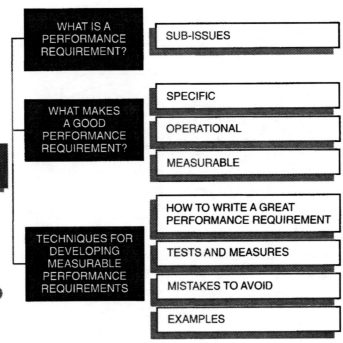

CHAPTER 4

PERFORMANCE REQUIREMENTS: TOOLS FOR EVALUATION AND MEASUREMENT

WHAT IS A PERFORMANCE REQUIREMENT?
- SUB-ISSUES

WHAT MAKES A GOOD PERFORMANCE REQUIREMENT?
- SPECIFIC
- OPERATIONAL
- MEASURABLE

TECHNIQUES FOR DEVELOPING MEASURABLE PERFORMANCE REQUIREMENTS
- HOW TO WRITE A GREAT PERFORMANCE REQUIREMENT
- TESTS AND MEASURES
- MISTAKES TO AVOID
- EXAMPLES

PERFORMANCE REQUIREMENTS: TOOLS FOR EVALUATION AND MEASUREMENT

Never promise more than you can perform.

Publius Syrus
Maxim 528

WHAT IS A PERFORMANCE REQUIREMENT?

A performance requirement (PR) is a statement about the measurable level of function that a designed object, building, or place must provide for a goal to be met. A performance requirement is also called a performance specification, standard, or criterion and is often labeled as an objective.

Figure 4-1 A Building in Action, Illustrated by the Cartoon "Home" from *The Lady on the Bookcase,* p. 417, by James Thurber, *Vintage Thurber* ,Volume 1. Collection copyright ©1963 Hamish Hamilton . Reproduced by permission of Hamish Hamilton as publishers for British Commonwealth rights and Rosemary Thurber for all others.

Whereas a goal is a statement about the *quality* to be achieved by the project, it is useful to conceptualize a performance requirement as a statement about how the environment must *behave* so that a desired environmental quality will be produced. One might imagine a building *doing* certain things to accommodate its inhabitants. In the following examples, the behaviors and qualities are in italics and the issue is in bold italics.

My house *maintains* a *warm* climate in winter and *a cool* climate in summer. Goal for ***physical comfort***: The house should maintain a *moderate* level of physical comfort.

It visually *directs* visitors to my front door. Goal for ***image***: The house should create a *welcoming* image.

It *invites* the display of many favorite objects. Goal for ***personalization***: The house should create *generous* opportunities for personalization.

It *creates* the opportunity for dinners for six. Goal for ***social interaction***: The house should support *vigorous* social interaction.

It *makes* visual access to the landscape continually available. Goal for ***psychological comfort***: The house should create the conditions for *ultimate* psychological comfort.

For James Thurber, the man/house relationship is not so comforting (Figure 4-1).

A performance requirement (PR) is more specific than a goal, since it relates to function (a doing) instead of a quality (a being). Yet, it must be general enough to allow for multiple, alternative physical solutions or concepts that enable the function and implement the goal and thereby further the purpose set out by the mission of the project. Figure 4-2 shows the position of the PR in the hierarchy of structuring specific programming information. Each goal at each level of detail will have more than one performance requirement implementing that goal and each performance requirement will have several concepts (diagrams and captions that describe physical relationships) to physically implement the function. Three performance requirements per goal is a good average for schematic design. More will often be required for design development programming or for a goal that is more important than all the others.

Sub-issues

Goals state the quality of outcome for each issue identified as critical to the success of each project. A performance requirement will state the level of function required for each sub-issue that is important to the implementation of the goal. For example, if circulation is the issue, then the Sub-issues might be vehicular circulation, pedestrian circulation, information flow, handicapped access, flow of materials and services, and bicycle traffic. If image is the issue, then the sub-issues might be identity, message, symbols, status, and order/proportion. Each issue will have a number of sub-issues — just as the mission has a variety of issues that must be handled to make the whole project work. For example, sub-issues relating to the quality of a particular circulation system might be efficiency, convenience, and visual excitement. Again, just as goals are of approximately equal weight relative to each other, so performance requirements should be of approximately the same level of importance in creating the functional components of the goal. (See the sidebar figure.)

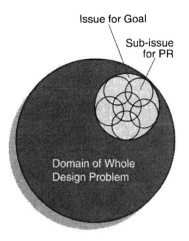

Sub-issues of Approximately
Equal Value

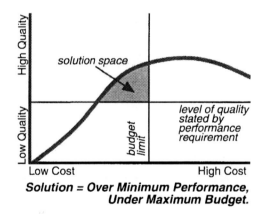

Solution = Over Minimum Performance,
Under Maximum Budget.

Figure 4-3   Relationship Between Functional Quality and Cost

Figure 4-3 is another way of showing that a performance requirement is a description of the level of performance (function) required to reach a level of quality that is acceptable. It also shows that the actual solution may perform

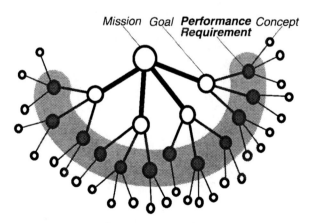

Figure 4-2   Position of Performance Requirements in the
Hierarchy of Programming

at a higher level of quality than stated by the PR, but the budget imposes another set of limits — if the level of the desired quality goes up with cost. The absolute highest quality solution may not be within the budget, but numerous appropriate solutions are within the solution space. At the upper limit of cost, the level of performance does not necessarily improve.

My favorite example of the law of diminishing returns is the mink-lined toilet seat! Surely the mink version is more expensive than the normal hardware store variety and is actually much less functional — especially when it comes to maintenance in a house full of young boys.

WHAT MAKES A GOOD PERFORMANCE REQUIREMENT?

Since a performance requirement is a statement of function, it should be *specific*, *measurable* , and *operational*. It should answer the question, "How is the goal to be implemented?" It should make clear the minimum level of acceptable function required to create the quality specified in the goal statement.

Specific

Specific means precise, definite, explicit, unambiguous, and particular. The noun definition is particularly interesting: "something *specially* suited for a given use or purpose" (Webster's 1966). The performance requirement can be seen as a mechanism for creating *how* a goal is implemented and *why* a concept works. See Figure 4-4. As with goals, performance requirements may be more or less detailed, depending upon the degree of specificity and detail required in the project. When planning for a large hospital complex or

designing the master plan for a university campus, the performance requirements will be much more general than for a particular department in the hospital or an individual building for a university department. One gets to even more detailed performance requirements when designing an operating theater or an architecture department design studio. Performance requirements will also be much more detailed and specific for design development programming than for schematic design programming.

Figure 4-4 The "Hows" and "Whys" of Performance Requirements, Relating to Goals and Concepts

Operational

Operational means applicable, usable, workable, putting into action, ready to be used. A performance requirement lets you know what you have to do, where you have to look, and the work necessary to conclude a successful search for a solution. A performance requirement is focused on a smaller part of the problem than a goal is. See the sidebar.

If the issue is circulation and the sub-issue is access by people with mobility impairments, then operational performance requirement(s) will point to a specific set of facts that need to be gathered such as regulations in the Americans with Disabilities Act Handbook (1991), local building codes comparable to California's Title 24, specific site conditions such as a steep slope, information from local advocate groups like the Centers for Independent Living, and the specific needs of people in wheelchairs or who use canes or crutches. An operational PR will also alert the designer to special areas of the building that need extra design attention: the approach, parking, entries, doors, toilet rooms and stalls, water fountains, level changes, and any place that needs to be sized for a wheelchair turning radius.

Measurable

Measurable means that there must be some means, such as set criteria, standards, rules, yardsticks, grades, benchmarks, guidelines, or limits, for *testing* whether the solution is up to the standards set by the performance requirement. A performance requirement operates as the yardstick for evaluating how well the design is doing its job. There are multiple ways of measuring design results — both in progress and as built.

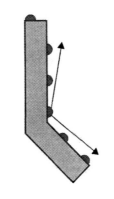

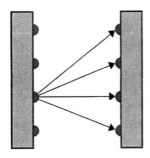

Figure 4-5 Lines of Sight in Three Apartment Layouts

Figure 4-5 shows three conceptual layouts for apartment entries. In one of them you can draw lines of sight so that four other entries are visible. In one of them, this is impossible. Assessing this is a simple binary measure: yes, you can see four entries; or no, you can't see four entries.

Measures are of Three Types: Binary, Scalar, and Judgment

As an illustration of the three types of measures, let's take a look at the issue of security for an apartment complex. A simple goal is, "The complex should discourage unwanted intruders from feeling free to enter and traverse the complex at will." Sub-issues used here to illustrate the different types of measures are "eyes on the street" (Jacobs 1961), recognizing people (strangers versus neighbors), and symbolic barriers. It is assumed that the mission and the values were already articulated.

Binary measures are either yes or no, in terms of whether or not something works or whether or not it meets the required level of performance. In Figure 4-5, the

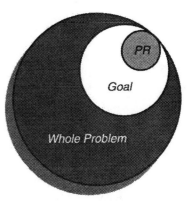

Focus of PR Concern

PRINCIPLE 10

The measurability of a performance requirement is its most important characteristic — the "make it or break it" of a good performance requirement.

performance requirement is that every person have a clear view of at least four other doorways from their door ("eyes on the street"). One look at the plans and drawing lines of sight from all doorways will tell you whether the criterion is met (yes or no).

Scalar measures are within an acceptable range of values using a physical measurement (inches, cubic feet per minute, dollars, BTUs, humidity, decibels, foot candles, degrees, etc.). Light levels, solar angles, heating/cooling calculations, minimum/maximum sizes and lengths, and direction of orientation are all entities measurable either from three-

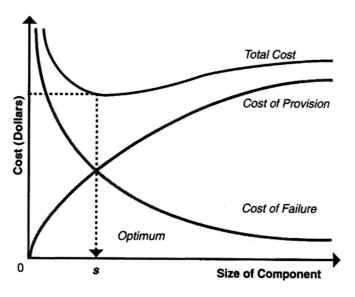

Figure 4-6   Scalar Measure: The Cost of Provision Plus the Cost of Failure Equals Total Cost

dimensional models or drawings of the design or from a mathematical model of the design. Costs are very often measures that make the major difference in design decisions.

In Figure 4-7, concepts for solving the problem of recognizing people who are 20 feet away cannot be so easily measured as successful or not. We need to know if the number of lumens or foot candles of light that fall on the side of a person's face falls within an acceptable range. We need to

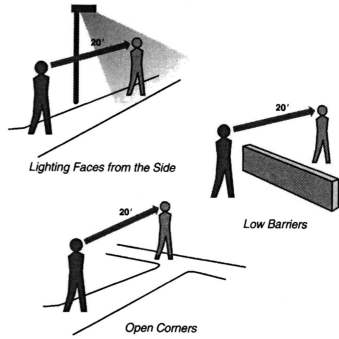

Figure 4-7   Concepts for Making People Recognizable at 20 Feet

know if any barriers are above or below an acceptable height. Also, we need to know that there are no spaces or hidden corners that are of a size range to hide a would-be assailant.

Judgment is an evaluation based upon priorities and values, in other words, a verification, ranking, estimation, approximation, surmise, prediction, guess, anticipation, or projection. Where there is no reliable scalar measure or binary decision possible, judgment must take over. Where information is intrinsically vague or is missing, the guess/judgment factor must be used. This is true for the greatest portion of the decisions that are made by designers. Judgments are most often made based upon personal values. If you know that your values are not totally relevant, you might seek experts in precedence, experts in the literature, principle investigators of relevant research projects, or experts in the client/user group. If the underlying values are clearly understood and agreed upon by all parties, then there is usually a high degree of agreement upon the evaluation and ranking of potential solutions to the problem at hand.

The performance requirement for our hypothetical apartment complex is that the entryway to it must serve as a symbolic barrier to "uninvited guests" or to "undesirables." There is little argument among most North Americans that a 6 foot brick wall with a heavy, closed, unlocked, squeaky, iron gate is a more powerful deterrent for unwanted entry than a 2 foot high boxwood hedge with an open rose trellis over the walkway. As an exercise, try ranking the following list of potential solutions in order of their ability to send out the message that only residents and invited guests are welcome here:

- A 4 foot dense hedge and arched "doorway" made with prickly bushes.
- A 1 foot level change (two steps up).
- A sign saying "Beware of the Dog."
- A change in surface from smooth concrete to concrete with 3/4 inch diameter pebbles in the surface.
- A 6 foot hedge with a closed gate made of large wire mesh and wood.
- A "doorman."
- A 3 foot white wood fence and closed gate.

Check your ranking with someone else and see what level of agreement there is. Most people within the same culture will substantially agree about the ranking for these possible solutions. Other factors may come into play to make the most powerful symbolic barrier inappropriate for this particular apartment complex.

TECHNIQUES FOR DEVELOPING MEASURABLE PERFORMANCE REQUIREMENTS

Good questions to ask as you search for performance requirements that will be useful to guide design as well as to evaluate it in various stages are: How do we read this environment? What does this part of the design need or expect in terms of people's behavior? How do we read or understand what behavior is expected of us in this environment? What clues do we have in an unfamiliar setting? Ask any question that will get to the heart of how the environment must *function* to be successful.

Make a list of all the sub-issues or components of the quality you are seeking to create. This list will give you a set of possible topics for performance requirements. If there is only one performance requirement that seems relevant, then the goal is too narrow (specific) or the PR is too broad (general). On the other hand, if it takes more than five performance requirements to cover a goal in the schematic design phase, then the PRs are probably too specific and will have only one or two concepts to implement them. Each performance requirement should have at least three concepts for schematic design programming and more than three for design development programs.

Judgments can only rank potential solutions as either more or less likely to produce the desired result — in other words, judgments only work by comparison.

How to Write a Great Performance Requirement

The following six guidelines should be applied when writing performance requirements.

1. Performance requirements should answer the question, "How is the *function* of this goal to be *implemented?*"

2. For each sub-issue, develop a performance requirement that is *specific, measurable, and operational.* The performance requirement should be clearly descriptive with *adjectives and adverbs* that indicate a level of function and are more specific than those contained in a goal. The dominant *verb* should also indicate function.

3. The performance requirement is a statement of how the *function* "should be" and what the future holds. *Should* is a major word in performance requirements as well as in goals. In most cases, a PR is a statement of ideal function, but in some cases it is imperative that the function be implemented 100 %. In this case *should* is formally replaced by *shall.*

4. A performance requirement should be as *simply stated* as possible and yet *allow for all relevant concepts* to be included. It should have the power to exclude concepts that are not appropriate or are inadequate to the task, i.e., it should be testable.

5. Each performance requirement should *cover a sub-issue* so that each major aspect of the functional needs of each goal are covered.

6. A performance requirement should be *proactive and positive* rather than negative. Telling a designer how a building should *not* function does not guarantee that it will function as desired. Other descriptions may be needed to indicate what a design should not do.

Tests and Measures

The ability of a performance requirement to test the appropriateness of any concept makes it an important tool in making design decisions and an instrument for evaluation of the design at many stages along the way. When writing performance requirements, be sure that there is some way that it can be used as an appropriate yardstick to measure the performance you are trying to implement.

Worst Case

A preliminary test for a performance requirement should be the "worst-case scenario." If the performance requirement would allow or "pass" an idea or concept that is not a good enough design idea, then the performance requirement is probably too general or broad in scope. For example, the statement, "Provide a place for design students to draw and make models," could be satisfied by *any* large empty classroom and is insufficient for the full scope of the demands of the activity of designing. The mere provision of space is *never* a performance requirement! If it were, you could provide a 10 foot by 10 foot concrete slab and say with all honesty that it provides a space for social interaction, but it does not have any *functional* characteristics that make social interaction any more likely. Measurable function is the key to performance requirements.

Tests

Each sub-issue will have its set of tests for performance. Energy conservation is one of the easiest issues to test. There are computer programs that will let you know whether or not the combination of materials, windows, shading, mass and sun exposure will give you the desired solar gain for space heating. There are calculations that will give an answer to the question

---

> ## PRINCIPLE 12
>
> *Mere "provision" of space is not performance! Performance is function and workability for the quality desired.*

of whether or not there will be enough hot water from the solar collector. There is information on the R-value for many different types of insulation and noninsulating materials. You can do calculations and angle diagrams to test whether or not the window shading is appropriate for daylighting, summer shade, and winter heat. For other issues, the tests can be harder to devise.

One interesting test is the walk away test (Gary Hack 1979, personal communication). It is a simple test for the acoustic performance of a space and the potential interference or beneficial masking of ambient noise. A person of normal hearing listens to a person walking away who is reading something as simple (like a newspaper) at a conversational volume. The distance at which the words can still be heard but not clearly understood is noted as well as the distance at which the voice becomes indistinguishable as a voice. These distances will be judged as suitable or unsuitable, depending upon the levels of performance desired for the situation being tested. Obviously, different environments have different requirements — the acoustics of a performance hall are very different from that of a subway station, although musicians play in both. Walk-away tests are appropriate for restaurants and open office environments where you want masking noise and for classrooms and amphitheaters where you don't want masking noise.

There are many stories being told, like modern myths, about the failures of some engineers to do performance tests as they go along. My favorite tale is the "chicken test" story. It may or may not be exactly true, but it makes a great example.

A large aerospace contractor was developing a new jet engine and spent some enormous sum (let's say $50 million) in the design and prototype development of the first model. As the design neared completion and the firm took it to the wind tunnels to test its efficiency, they also undertook the "chicken test." The "chicken test" consists of getting chickens from the grocery store and throwing them into the engines to test whether the flocks of chicken-sized birds that are often near airports pose any danger to the jets. In our story, the new design failed the chicken test because the jet stopped within seconds after the chickens were ingested by the engine, indicating that the plane would have crashed.

The moral of the story is: *do your chicken test first!* If there is some aspect of performance that is critical to the success of the project, make sure that your performance requirements are testable and solve that problem early. Work out the less critical details later. Do not let a performance requirement into your program that cannot be appropriately tested.

Mistakes to Avoid

A fairly frequent mistake is to write a goal that is too specific because you already have an idea of what the solution will be. It is more likely that the statement under consideration is appropriate for a performance requirement (with adjustments) and that the goal needs to be broader to allow incorporation of more ideas into the solution.

Another frequent mistake is to write performance requirements that are too general and sound as if the goal is being restated. This is where a list of sub-issues comes in handy. A performance requirement should not cover more than one functional area or sub-issue.

A third major mistake is to write a PR that calls for the provision of space or something more specific — these are candidates for concepts. If the performance requirement sounds more like a description of a physical relationship than the prescription for function, then it is more likely an idea that needs to be developed into a concept.

Examples

Example Goal #1 **The major portion of parking for the downtown core should be a short, pleasant walk from most shopping destinations.**

1.1 PERFORMANCE REQUIREMENT (PR): **Shoppers coming to downtown should have to walk less than five minutes to get from their car to 90 % of their destinations.**

The test here is to draw five minute walking circles (assume ± 200 feet/min.) around parking lots and concentrations of stores to see whether or not shoppers have to walk more than five minutes to get to 90 % of the likely destinations. It is indeed open to interpretation and assumption whether or not shoppers will park in the parking places closest to their desired destination, but this PR makes it possible — especially if the PR is linked to the expected numbers of shoppers at each destination or in each zone.

1.2 PR: **Major pedestrian corridors between parking and downtown stores should be visually interesting and substantially protected from rain and the afternoon sun.**

"Pleasant" is now defined as "visually interesting" and "substantially protected." The phrase "visually interesting for shoppers" often assumes the occurrence of some stores along the route with potential for impulse shopping, or signs showing what's showing at the movies or what the latest real estate deal might be. It could also include public art and other visually stimulating urban amenities. This one is a

judgment call as to which proposed solution is more "visually interesting" for shoppers. "Protected from the rain and afternoon sun" is measured by area/length of overhead cover, percentage of length of walk protected, sun angles, direction of storm winds in relationship to paths, and percentage of hottest hours of the day when the pedestrians would be in shade.

1.3 PR: **Major paths should create impulse shopping and window shopping opportunities.**

This PR stretches the definition of "pleasant" for the merchant's sake. It is unlikely that both PR 1.1 and 1.2 would be used together because of the overlap of concern, but they might be incorporated into one statement. Again, how much shopping opportunity there should be is a judgment call — when is enough? This PR could stand an adverb before "impulse" to indicate minimum, moderate, or maximum amounts according to the clients' desires.

1.4 PR: **Pedestrian corridors should catch the summer breezes and protect people from winter winds.**

This PR points to the plan orientation of the pedestrian corridors as a potential solution and hints at the potential for operable coverings. Measurement comes from knowing the direction of the summer breezes and the winter winds and checking flow-through of the summer breezes and stoppage of the winter ones.

1.5 PR: **Major paths should easily accommodate the full range of handicapped users, including those with minor mobility difficulties.**

This PR assumes that shoppers include the blind, frail elderly, wheelchair bound , and temporarily disabled. Often the best test is to have a wheelchair on the site and to test how it actually works. Other times mockups are useful. The design tests are to insure that maximum operable slopes are not exceeded (which could be more strict than the codes), to insure that there are resting places along a long path for elderly or crutch-bound people, and to create surfaces that are not hazardous to wheelchairs or to blind people.

Example Goal #2 **The building should encourage efficient and responsible use of energy.**

2.1 PR: **The building should use passive solar technology to the maximum extent possible for space heating.**

This PR is a bit wishy-washy on the measurability side. How do you know what the "maximum extent possible" is? Given the nature of solar technology, it would be possible to state some percentage of space heating capacity to be solar for a given climate or call attention to particular budget constraints.

2.1 Alternate PR: **Seventy-five percent of the space heating should be from the sun.**

This is just about as brief and succinct as they come.

2.2 PR: **Heat loss should be kept at an absolute minimum.**

We have learned that absolutes are not always healthy. Keeping heat loss to an absolute minimum has in the past meant a very tight building with little or no "breathing" from infiltration and has resulted in some toxins being trapped in a completely airtight space (sick buildings).

2.2 Alternate PR: **Heat loss should be no more than "x" BTU/hr/sf.**

This PR gives more measurable parameters that can produce acceptable performance levels of the heating/

cooling/ventilating systems. This could also be stated in terms of an acceptable range of BTU/hr/sf heat loss so that the various parameters can be manipulated to meet such standards as California's Title 24.

2.3 PR: **The building should take advantage of available natural daylighting techniques.**

This PR is too wimpy. It gives no sense of how much daylighting is really wanted and needed. Almost *any* daylighting will "take advantage of natural daylighting techniques!"

2.3 Alternate PR: **At least 50 % of the lighting on a cloudy day should be from the sun.**

This PR aims for a specific target and gives the technology something to shoot for. Obviously, the facts of the climate and the general type of cloud cover experienced at the site will need to be known. Also the use of the space, for reading, watching TV, or putting together small components, makes a difference here.

The following goal and PR's are listed to indicate form rather than to illustrate exact goal formulation.

Example Goal #3 **The facility (a science center) should reinforce the user's sense of creativity and ability to produce original quality ideas as well as promote analytical accuracy.**

3.1 PR: **The interior should be visually interesting and provocative without being too busy or confusing.**

3.1 Alternate PR: **The form of the building should encourage reflection and thought by being visually interesting.**

3.1 Alternate PR: **Spaces should provide adequate visual stimulation without being distracting.**

These alternatives have the same general intention with different interpretations of what the priority sub-issues are. They were done by students and could be improved by being more specific and testable.

3.2 PR: **Distracting noises should be eliminated from the work spaces and replaced by very pleasant masking sounds.**

3.3 PR: **All spaces within the building should create elements within them that appeal to all the senses.**

3.4 PR: **Work spaces should promote employee interaction while maintaining individual control of unwanted interruptions.**

3.4 Alternate PR: **The building should promote a high level of social interaction among all its users.**

3.5 PR: **Interior and exterior building forms should reveal themselves to the observer in a gradual fashion, thus promoting curiosity and a sense of excitement and exploration.**

3.6 PR: **Each work space should have access to natural light and/or view to the outside in more than one direction.**

3.7 PR: **In commonly shared spaces, frequent views of the surrounding landscape should be provided for visual relief and variety.**

3.8 PR: **Each work space should promote the easy and organized flow of the research procedures conducted within it.**

SUMMARY

A performance requirement is a statement about the expected level of function for a successful design project. When creating performance requirements it is a good idea to imagine that the building or project is doing things for its users, such as "promoting," "creating," "supporting," "inviting," or "maintaining." Several performance requirements are needed to describe the level of function required to create the qualities desired for each goal (issue area). Each sub-issue should have a performance requirement describing the level of function required for a satisfactory solution to the design problem.

Each performance requirement is specific, measurable, and operational. *Specific* means particular, unambiguous, and specifically suited to a given purpose. *Measurable* means that the PR can be used as a yardstick to evaluate how well the design creates the quality specified by the goal. Measurements are of three types, binary (yes or no), scalar (a measurable range of values), or judgment (by comparison). *Operational* means that the PR lets you know the general area where the solution might be and what to do to get to a satisfactory solution.

A good performance requirement is a simple statement of how well the design should function. It is clearly descriptive, proactive, and allows for a wide range of concepts. A good PR is a balance between the generality of a goal and the physical specificity of a particular solution or concept. The mere provision of space is not a performance requirement. If a performance requirement is too general, it will allow a bad concept to pass its test. If it is too specific, it will allow only one or two concepts as solutions to the stated function.

CHAPTER 5

CONCEPTS: TURNING IDEAS INTO REALITY

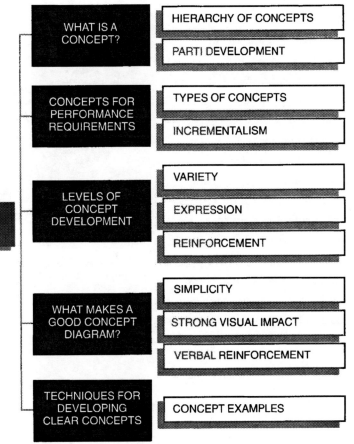

WHAT IS A CONCEPT?
- HIERARCHY OF CONCEPTS
- PARTI DEVELOPMENT

CONCEPTS FOR PERFORMANCE REQUIREMENTS
- TYPES OF CONCEPTS
- INCREMENTALISM

LEVELS OF CONCEPT DEVELOPMENT
- VARIETY
- EXPRESSION
- REINFORCEMENT

WHAT MAKES A GOOD CONCEPT DIAGRAM?
- SIMPLICITY
- STRONG VISUAL IMPACT
- VERBAL REINFORCEMENT

TECHNIQUES FOR DEVELOPING CLEAR CONCEPTS
- CONCEPT EXAMPLES

CONCEPTS: TURNING IDEAS INTO REALITY

Concept formation is an unfamiliar activity for most people, and students of architecture have as much trouble mastering it as they do other aspects of design.... Since many buildings are built without the benefit of a concept, and since most critics and many architects avoid writing about them, it is relatively easy for the beginning designer to have no ambitions for concepts and no understanding of the role they play in building design.

Tim McGinty
Introduction to Architecture

WHAT IS A CONCEPT?

A concept is a statement of an ideal set of relationships among several of the elements under an architect's control such as form (dimension, direction), material, texture, color (hue, value, intensity), and adjacency. A concept statement is made up of a simple diagram and a few words. Concepts are diagrammatic solutions or proposals that implement the requirements of the program. They can also be called patterns, design ideas, or design diagrams. A concept is an idea about the appropriate relationship between the parts of a project — the important, useful, functional, aesthetic, or noteworthy parts. A concept may encompass the entire problem (a parti) or can illustrate the ideal solution for a small part of the project. These smaller scale concepts are the elements of the design program that represent the physical relationships required to implement the performance requirements. See Figure 5-1. George W. Hartman Jr. said, "Obviously, a sound organizational diagram will not lead inevitably to a good design any more than a classic chess opening will lead to certain victory, but a sound beginning can forestall an early defeat while greatly increasing the chances of ultimate success" (Clark and Pause 1979).

At the more specific levels of detail, such as during the design development phase, concepts may include some object specifications — more detailed descriptions of materials and dimensions needed to implement the design requirements. "Concepts are ideas that integrate various elements into a whole. . . a concept suggests

a specific way that programmatic requirements, context, and beliefs can be brought together" (McGinty 1979, 208). Figure 5-2 shows an example of three different circulation concepts.

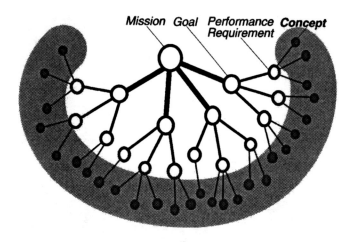

Figure 5-1   Concepts in Relationship to Goals and Performance Requirements

Through Circulation   *Radial Circulation*   *"H" Circulation*

Figure 5-2   Three Circulation Concepts

Every spider that makes a web, makes it in a certain form. It takes a human idea to make the distinction between the different *concepts* for spiderwebs, since the spiders just do what is instinctual. There are three conceptually different types of spiderwebs that show up in my yard.

1. There is the best known web in wheel form. The spokes are in tension so that the spider can feel the slightest vibration, and the spiral hangs loose in the wind to catch the hapless flying insects.

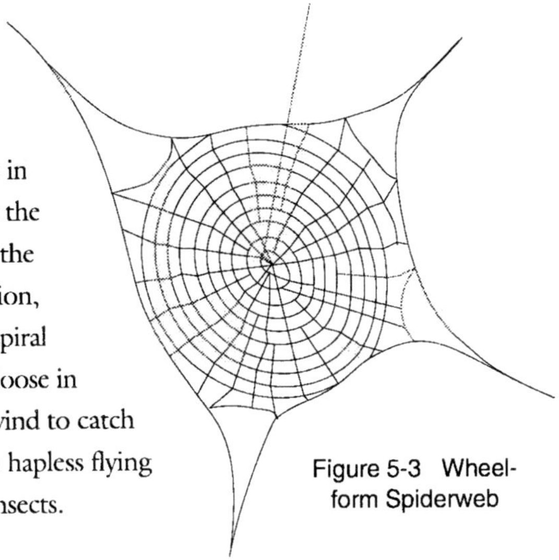

Figure 5-3 Wheel-form Spiderweb

2. There is the "fill-a-form with zigzags" type. The long tension members in this web are usually made almost parallel to some existing structure such as a leaf, a string or a window jamb. The zig-zags help create the insect traps.

Figure 5-4 Zigzag Fill-a-form Web

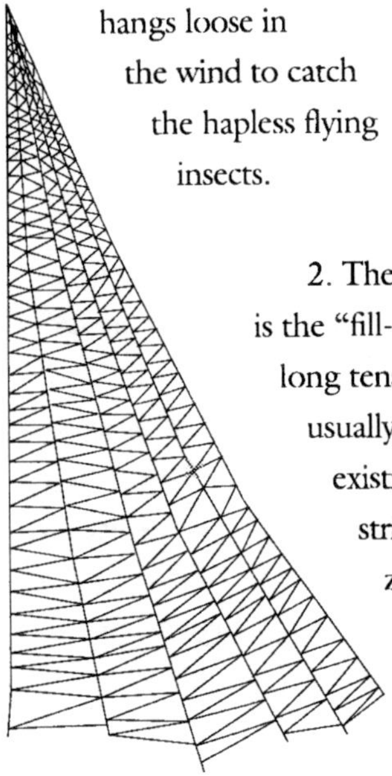

3. There is the suspended sheet type web, the network of seemingly random strands filling a cloud-like space and a web that lines a tunnel or hole. The suspended sheet type of web has several "guy wires" at the top and bottom effectively creating a suspension bridge-like structure.

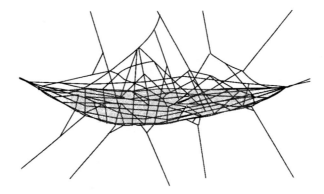

Figure 5-5 Cloud with Guy Wires Web

It is easy enough to develop a phrase and a concept diagram that explains the central idea for a variety of types of spiderwebs. Buildings are far more complex and *one* concept diagram with a few words can explain only the more general relationships and does little to explain the full complexity of the final built form. Unless it is a parti, a concept diagram usually communicates only a part of the totality of the prospective building. It takes many diagrams to convey the intention of how a building is made to fit the human use it houses.

PRINCIPLE 13

Concepts can always be diagrammed!!

Hierarchy of Concepts

Since the design process is not linear and language is by necessity a linear presentation, a few gymnastics are required to present a programming process in its full structure and then present the realistic variations of how it is really practiced.

One may develop concepts for the smaller aspects of a project and build the overall from the addition of all the parts or one may develop an overall parti or organizing concept and then develop concepts for the smaller parts in concert with the overall. If the programmer and the designer are not the same person, then the designer usually wants to be the one to develop the parti or overall concept.

Another way of looking at the design process is for you to make a design move (choosing a particular concept), such as deciding that the main circulation spine will parallel the brow of the hill, and then to make every consequent decision as a reaction to or reinforcement of the initial idea. The reality of designing is more like moving back and forth among the different scales of concern, searching for patterns and concepts that solve as many problems for as many issues as possible. The process has been diagrammed in prior chapters as a spiral. Figure 5-6 represents the hierarchy of the building as circles with concepts appropriate at each scale of building part (door, room, suite, building, campus) and the stripes represent issues of concern that cut across each scale of the building design such as circulation, security, image, etc. The domains will vary according to the scale of the project. The largest circle in Figure 5-6 could represent a region, the large interior circles

Figure 5-6 Relationship Between Building Components (Circles) and Design Issues (Stripes)

would then represent cities, the medium sized circles would represent neighborhoods, and the smallest circles would represent blocks.

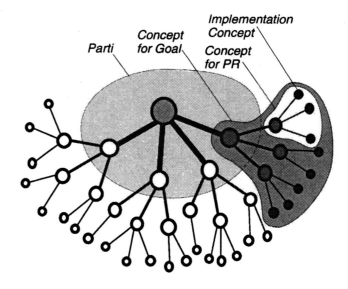

Figure 5-7 Hierarchy of Concepts from Parti to Design Concept

It is only when one is filling in the details of a design that there is a strong need to fill in the blanks in the hierarchy. The conceptualization of the total design as a tree of ideas is useful to insure that all aspects have been carefully thought out and that no issue has been left unattended. Organizing concepts that can be used at every scale of the design are very powerful and can overlap with issue concerns. Concepts may involve the whole project (as a super-organizing idea, mega-concept, theme, esquisse, or parti) or may be concerned with a portion of the design (such as the circulation patterns or the symbolic indications of entry). See Figure 5-7.

Frank Lloyd Wright used geometry as the main organizing principle for many of his Usonian houses — the

Toy Maker's (Friedman) house (Figure 5-9) used the circle and the Hanna house (Figure 5-8) used the hexagon where others used the triangle or the rectangle. Each house utilized the geometry in the overall organization, organization of each room, fenestration, furniture and artifacts that Wright designed like andirons, rugs, and china. The goal of design is to develop appropriate concepts that synthesize the discrete parts into an integrated whole.

Parti Development

Since the parti is the mega-concept for the entire design problem, it must be broad enough to include many considerations and allow for congruent solutions to design problems at every level of detail. A parti is the most abstract of all the concept levels. Design concepts are the most specific and concrete of the concept

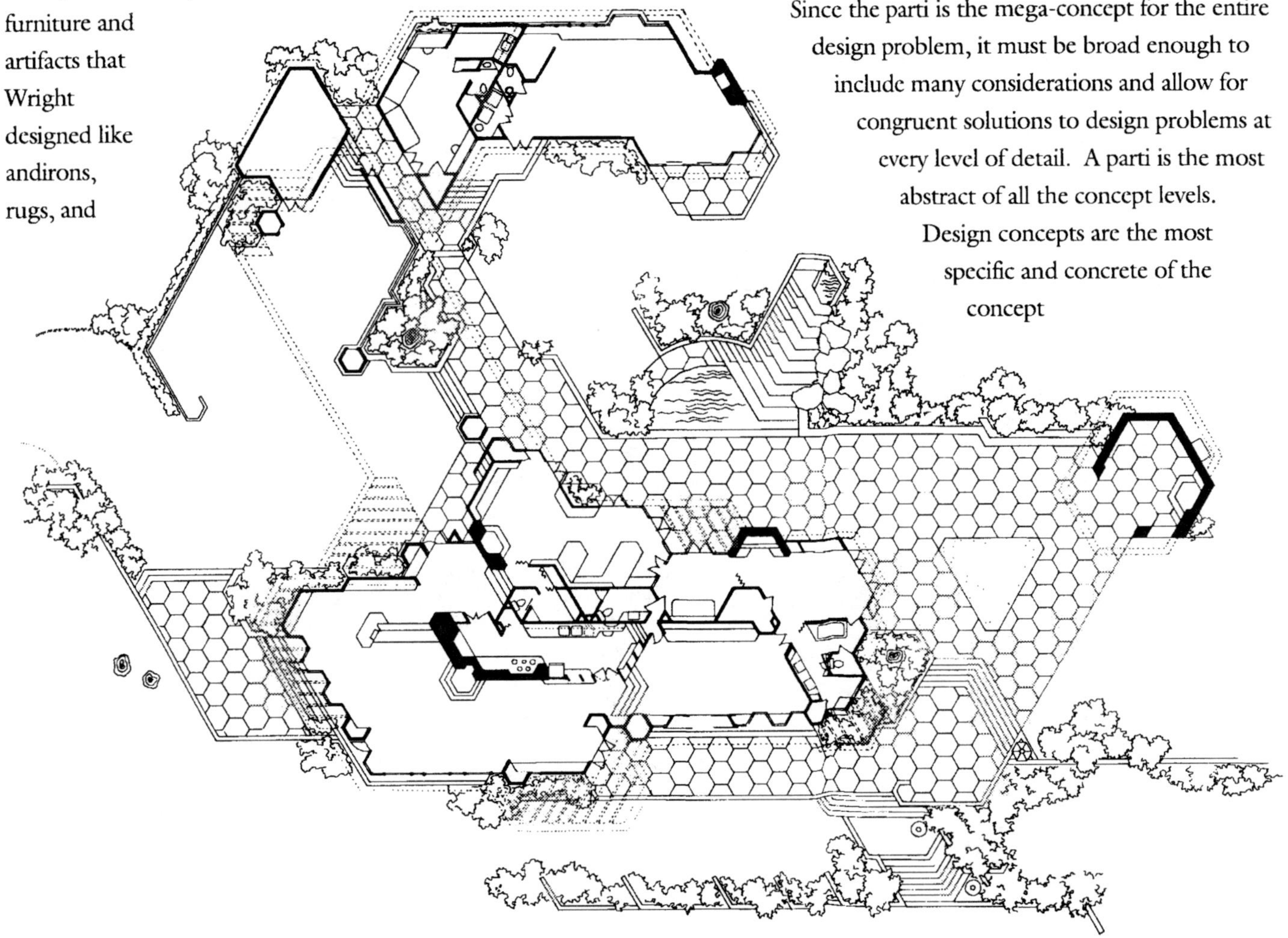

Figure 5-8   Floor Plan of the Hanna House.

From *Frank Lloyd Wright's Usonian Houses* by John Sergeant. Copyright © 1976 The Frank Lloyd Wright Foundation. Reproduced by permission of The Frank Lloyd Wright Memorial Foundation Archives and the Whitney Library of Design for Sergeant's version.

hierarchy. There are other ways to develop the overall concept besides developing a formal parti. **Analogies** and **concept scenarios** are other ways to develop the big idea.

Architects who never wrote program documents for their buildings often wrote or spoke *concept scenarios* to explain the ideas behind their designs. A concept scenario is a short essay that creates a word picture of the dominant operational concept and the major subordinate ideas that create the organization and the visual imagery of the design. The following is an excerpt from such a statement by Frank Lloyd Wright (1960, in Snyder and Catanese 1979, 217) about Unity Temple:

> "Build a beautiful *ROOM* proportioned to this purpose. Make it beautiful in this simple sense. A natural building natural for man. . . . to keep a noble *ROOM* in mind, and let the room shape the whole edifice, let the room inside be the architecture outside."

And of the Hanna house he said:

> "Here we have a preliminary study of prefabrication. . . . Another experiment because I am convinced that a cross section of a honeycomb has more fertility and

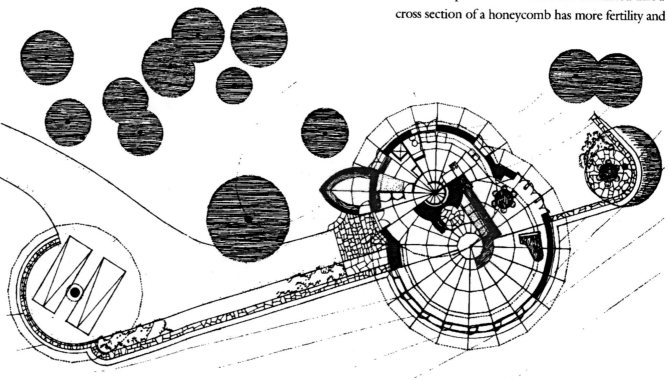

Figure 5-9 Floor Plan of the Friedman House.

From *Frank Lloyd Wright's Usonian Houses* by John Sergeant. Copyright © 1976 The Frank Lloyd Wright Foundation. Reproduced by permission of The Frank Lloyd Wright Memorial Foundation Archives and the Whitney Library of Design for Sergeant's version.

flexibility where human movement is concerned than a square. . . . That flow and movement is, in this design, a characteristic lending itself admirably to life, as life is to be lived in it. The hexagon has been conservatively treated — however, it is allowed to appear in plan only and in the furniture which literally rises from and befits the floor pattern of the concrete slab upon which the whole stands" (Wright 1938, in Hanna and Hanna 1987, 77-78).

Edward Larabee Barnes (1971, in Snyder and Catanese 1979, 219-220) had a lot to say about the Walker Art Center in Minneapolis:

"We want the visitor to remember painting in space, sculpture against sky, and a sense of continuous flow. It is flow more than form that has concerned us. The sequence of spaces must be seductive. There must be a subtle sense of going somewhere, like a river. At the same time the architecture must be relatively uneventful and anonymous.

"The generating idea behind the design is the helical plan which provides sequential flow from the lobby to the roof whether going up or down."

The combination of a concept scenario and concept diagrams to express segments or different aspects of a design is proposed here as the best operational way to communicate the intention of the designer to the client and others who need to understand the building

before it is built. Many people would even find this communication useful after the construction if it were to show up in users' manuals so that they might fully understand the intention of the design. Clear concepts are vital to clear communications with clients (Figure 5-10).

Analogies and Metaphors

Analogies are very useful for generating overall design concepts because it is fairly easy to make the necessary comparisons with known objects to generate new ideas about the object to be designed. The dictionary offers the following definitions that may guide our thinking about using analogies in design:

"analogous — adj. 2. Biol. Similar in function but not in evolutionary origin, as the gills of a fish are analogous to the lungs of a mammal."

"analogy — n. 1. Correspondence in some respects especially in *function or position*, between things otherwise dissimilar. 2. A form of *logical inference* based on the assumption that if two things are

Figure 5-10 It Pays to be Clear on the Concept.
Cartoon from *Mister Boffo: Unclear on the Concept* by Joe Martin. Copyright © 1989 by Tribune Media Services, Inc. Reproduced by permission of Little, Brown and Company.

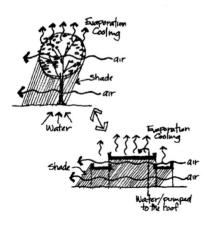

Direct Analogy: A Building
Cooled Like a Tree.
From *Graphic Thinking for
Architects and Designers* by Paul
Laseau. Copyright © 1980 Van
Nostrand Reinhold. Reproduced by
permission of the publisher.

known to be alike in some respects, then they *must be alike in other respects.*"

Direct Analogy: In design, analogies are often used to stimulate design ideas — How is a half-way house like a sleeping kitten? How is a factory like a snake biting its tail? How is an office similar to a computer? Why should a restaurant work like a factory? These comparisons are called *force-fit or direct analogies* and are useful for uncovering aspects/issues of the design problem that may not have been discovered in the initial research phases of the project. How many other force-fit analogies come to mind?

A *direct analogy* is made by comparing an object, which functions in a manner that you would like for your design to function, with your design on a point by point basis. The College of Architecture and Environmental Design is like a human body because: the administration and the student body are like the brain and the nervous system, the plumbing system of the building is like the body's circulatory system, the building circulation system is like the body's digestive system, the gallery/ auditorium is like the lungs, and so on. Each building system is compared to a system in the body to elicit new ideas about relationships between the elements and how the building might be organized into a whole.

In developing a concept diagram, the aim is to bridge the gap between the object and the building to be designed —

that elusive abstraction of function that is the key to the *organization* of the design. See sidebar and Figure 5-11.

Personal Analogy: The *personal analogy* is developed by putting yourself in the place of the object to be designed and asking some of the following questions: If you were a cabin in the Sierras how would you stay warm in the winter? Would you burrow into the side of a mountain and peek out to enjoy the view? Would you tuck into a valley and gather all the south sun possible? Or would you just build a big heating plant and let the energy bills mount up? See Figure 5-12.

Symbolic Analogy: A *symbolic analogy* is very general, i.e., an amphitheater is like a pair of cupped hands, the Sydney Opera House is like a ship sailing in the harbor, a boarding

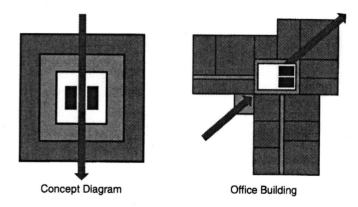

Apple   Concept Diagram   Office Building

Figure 5-11   How is an Office Building Like an Apple?

kennel is like an exotic filing cabinet for dogs and cats, etc. See Figure 5-13.

Fantasy Analogy: A *fantasy analogy* uses an ideal, exquisite condition to create an idea resource for new solutions. Much of science fiction creates this sort of solution that only needs modern technology to catch up with the ideas.

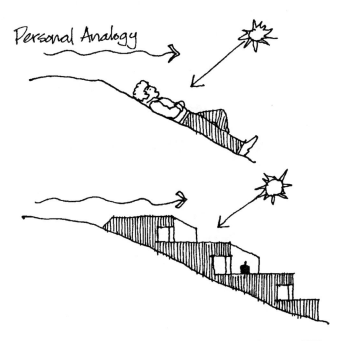

Figure 5-12   Personal Analogy: A Building Lying on a Hill*

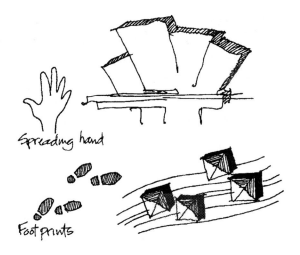

Spreading hand

Foot prints

Figure 5-13   Symbolic Analogy: A Building Like a Spreading
Hand or Pavilions Like Footprints*

Star ships have automatic, people-sensing doors; force shields for protection against intruders; transporter beams for instantaneous movement between destinations; computer data bases that map like a visual terrain; sorcerer's houses that relocate themselves; and on it goes. See Figure 5-14.

Metaphor: A metaphor is an abstract relationship, as in the dictionary definition, "a figure of speech in which one

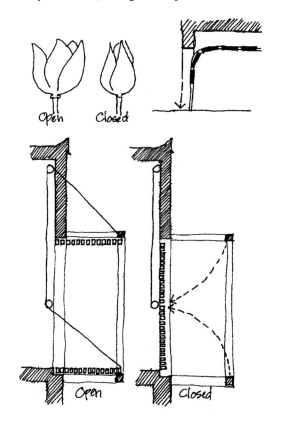

Open   Closed

Open   Closed

Figure 5-14   Fantasy Analogy: A Window that Works Like a Tulip*

*From *Graphic Thinking for Architects and Designers,* by Paul Laseau, Copyright © 1980 Van Nostrand Reinhold. Reproduced by permission of the publisher.

thing is likened to another, different thing by being spoken of as if it were that other (e.g., 'all the world's a stage')." One might design a house as if it were a "stage for the drama of life." Within this metaphor, the kitchen becomes the "Julia Child Show," the living room may be "As the World Turns," the bedroom is where "Debbie Does Dallas," and the family room is the site of "The Cosby Show." A metaphor is different from an analogy in that the analogy is a comparison between a whole object and the design problem, on a point by point basis, whereas a metaphor is taken as creating the spirit of the thing in the design problem. Corbu very clearly developed the metaphor of the house as a "machine for living" in much of his work, especially in the Marseilles Block (Boudon 1969).

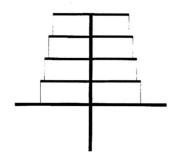

Building Structured Like a Tree

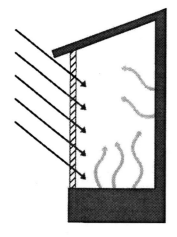

Mass and South-Facing Glass

Problem Solving

Bucky Fuller was a great one for generating design ideas from his own unique statement of the problem (Fuller 1963). When he posed the problem of creating building forms that were as efficient, with mass to strength ratio, as are boats and airplanes, he developed the idea of a geodesic dome as the solution to that problem. Charles Ames set for himself the problem of designing a house for himself based upon components that were readily available off the shelf and, as a result, created a modern house that did not look anything like its predecessors. The problem of solar space heating is often solved by south-facing glass and building mass in floor and walls. (See sidebar.)

Ideals

Ideal solutions are contained in values external to the problem — the ones the architect brings into the picture. They are the archetypal solutions that are not problem specific — rather they are issue specific. They may be based upon

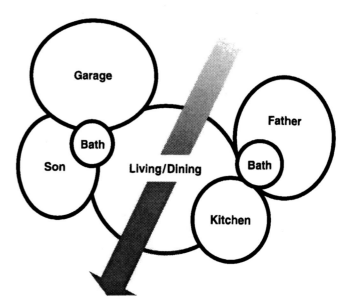

Figure 5-15 Building Organization Based upon Separation and Traffic Flow

romantic notions such as the ideal image of a cabin in the woods, or upon a philosophy such as Frank Lloyd Wright's Usonian economies, or upon practical ideals such as building a sustainable community with maximum energy conservation. The "American dream" of a one family house in the suburbs is an ideal shared by many people in the U.S. Although ideals often cannot be realized, they are useful as starting places in the search to find a solution that fills the needs of the problem at hand.

Essences

"Essences distill and concentrate aspects of more complex issues into terse, explicit statements. . . identifying the roots of an issue" (McGinty 1979, 229). Kahn used this idea in speaking of his design method. He searched for what a building wanted to be, and for what a particular material wanted to be. He is attributed with saying, "A brick wants to be an arch." An essence statement gets down to the intrinsic symbolic aspects of a design — its seed, its spirit. The search for essence is the search for a pithy concentrated inspiration. Gothic churches embody the essence of awe of a higher power. The chapels of E. Fay Jones are the essence of the forest. Robert Harris (1975) says that essence-seeking is making the intangible tangible. "The full process includes observing supportive places, learning from them what characteristics and structuring relationships are present, inspecting the potential transcendence of those characteristics as possibly common to other intangibly and profoundly satisfying places as well, and seeding the findings into the new places we may build" (Harris 1975, 30).

CONCEPTS FOR PERFORMANCE REQUIREMENTS

Types of Concepts

Concepts for performance requirements may be based upon an analogy or a metaphor (such as a structural system like a tree, see sidebar p. 68), on mechanical principles (such as

passive solar principles, see sidebar p. 68), on adjacencies (based upon flow [Figure 5-15], view, or frequency of interaction), on geometric or proportional relationships (such as a hexagonal module or the Modulor, see sidebar p.69), or on formal symbolic relationships (such as Stonehenge [Figure 5-16] or Macchu Picchu).

It is usually true that concepts developed to fulfill the criteria of the performance requirement will not be the

Figure 5-17 Bounced Light — Concept Forms Barrel Vault*

Figure 5-18 Building to Context — Building Profile as Result of Parallel Barrel Vaults*

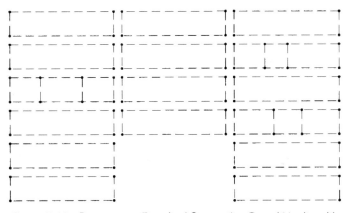

Figure 5-19 Structure — Result of Supporting Barrel Vaults with Beams and with Posts at the Ends of the Vaults*

Figure 5-16 Stonehenge: Stones Arranged for Astronomical and Symbolic Reasons

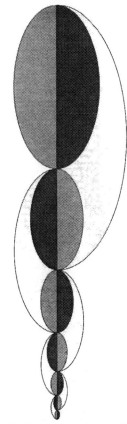

The Modulor: Based upon the Fibbonacci Series

* From *Analysis of Precedent* by Clark and Pause. Copyright © 1979 The Student Publication of the School of Design, N.C. State University at Raleigh. Reproduced by permission of the School of Design.

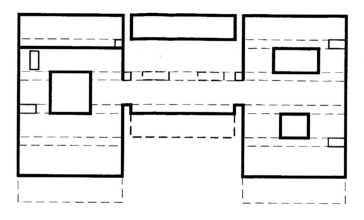

Figure 5-20   Spatial Organization — Order Develops from Implied Linear Space of Modular Vaults, Punctuated by Courtyards.
From *Analysis of Precedent* by Clark and Pause. Copyright © 1979 The Student Publication of the School of Design, N.C. State University at Raleigh. Reproduced by permission of the School of Design.

dominant ones in the hierarchy of the design, although it is possible for one fairly simple concept to dominate a design. Kahn's idea about lighting the Kimball museum did become a major influence for the whole, even though it was based on solving the problem of making the paintings visible with natural light while keeping them durable by eliminating the ultra-violet wavelengths. It can be argued that the parti was a symmetrical rectangular grid and that the vault form was the module in that grid. In Kahn's mind, who can say which came first, the module or the grid? See Figures 5-17 to 5-20.

Incrementalism

To design by developing a building scheme as the sum of concepts developed for each aspect of the building is called incrementalism. This particular strategy is best illustrated by Alexander (1964). See Figure 5-21.

Certainly one way of designing is to conceptualize the parts and build the whole from it. If one were to go strictly by the hierarchy in Figure 5-7 (which implies that each performance requirement has several concepts that support the level of function required by that performance requirement), then one could say that this text advocates such an incremental strategy. If the designer omits a parti or super-organizing concept and concepts of organization of parts larger than those supporting a particular performance requirement, that does not preclude the potential for the super-organizing ideas such as themes or metaphors. The diagrams of the information "tree" throughout this text do not imply that I advocate designing without an overall concept. The assumption made here is that young designers can learn or have learned how to develop partis or themes in their design studios and what is necessary here is to emphasize the development of incremental concepts that will help to guide the design in its parts so that they can be tested as the design progresses.

LEVELS OF CONCEPT DEVELOPMENT

Concepts are the most concrete and specific elements in the programming hierarchy. They point to the design direction and should be open and broad enough to include many different design solutions as possibilities. The process of developing variety, the most expressive alternative, and reinforcing ideas should be used at every level of the concept hierarchy. Here we focus on concepts to meet performance requirements.

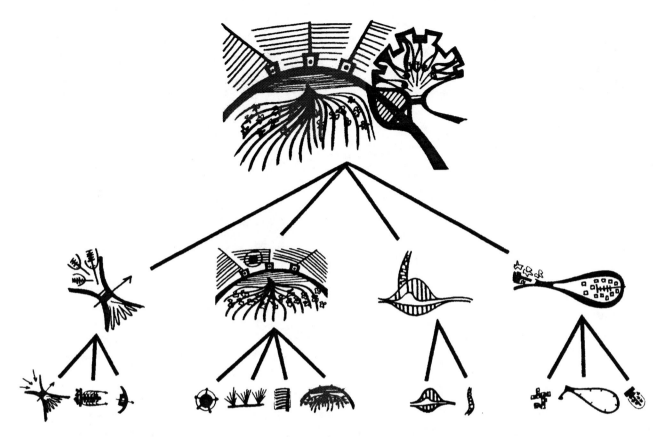

Figure 5-21 Alexander's Generation of a Village Concept from a Synthesis of Concepts for Each Major Aspect:
Cattle, Agriculture, Village Life, Private Life.
From *Notes on the Synthesis of Form* by Christopher Alexander. Copyright © 1964 Harvard University Press. Reproduced by permission of the publisher.

Variety

The purpose of concept development at the earliest stages of the design process is to make informed choices from a wide *variety* of conceptually *different* alternatives. Each conceptual alternative is evaluated for its capacity to develop the levels of function vital to fulfill the performance requirements and to embody the qualities set forth in the goals. Each geometric

Figure 5-22 Alternative Generation: Maximum Variety

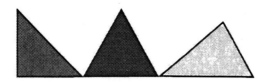

Figure 5-23   Different Ways to Express "Triangle"

figure illustrated in Figure 5-22 represents a *conceptually different* alternative — a different idea — each with its own positive and negative potentials for fulfilling a performance requirement and resolving a design outcome. The circle, square, and triangle stand for the widest possible difference between the alternatives generated in the beginning. The final program document will include only those concepts that are chosen from this process.

Expression

After the best conceptual alternative has been chosen, the designer must search for the best expression of that concept. Sometimes this part of the process leads to the combination of several initial concepts or to the development of new concepts that integrate the best features of two or more concepts. Other times a concept is chosen because it is the very best alternative and only minor adjustments are made to accommodate other concerns and to reach a satisfactory level of function as illustrated in Figure 5-23.

Reinforcement

Once the best expression is found, the next level of development is to uncover all the possible ways to reinforce and communicate that concept. See Figure 5-24. This

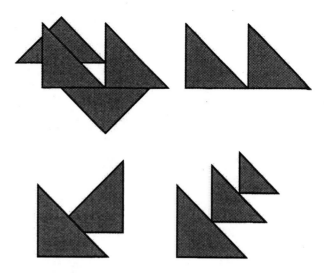

Figure 5-24   Reinforcing "Right Triangleness"

process works for all levels of the design/planning hierarchy from a parti for a city plan to the design of living room furniture. For this text we will concentrate on developing concepts that implement the performance requirements developed in previous chapters. From the tree diagram in Figure 5-7 we note that each PR will have more than one concept that meets the functional specifications. Usually, for schematic design programming, three to five PR's will be enough.

When a program is first being developed, it is a good practice to develop as many *different* conceptual *alternatives* for implementing the PR's as possible so that the designer and client will have the opportunity to make the most appropriate selection from among those ideas that will work. For the *final* program document each of the concepts for any one PR will *reinforce, complement, and strengthen* each other rather than presenting competing alternatives that demand making a choice.

WHAT MAKES A GOOD CONCEPT DIAGRAM?

The criteria for a good concept diagram are simplicity, strong visual impact, and brief verbal reinforcement.

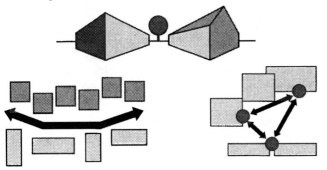

Figure 5-25   Clear, Simple Diagrams

Simplicity

The diagram is simple; it is the most elementary expression of the relationship that gives full representation of the idea. See Figure 5-25 and sidebar.

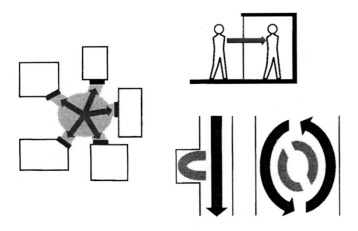

Figure 5-26   Graphically Strong Diagrams

Strong Visual Impact

The diagram has minimal detail, high contrast, strong lines, and/or arrows showing direction where necessary. See Figure 5-26.

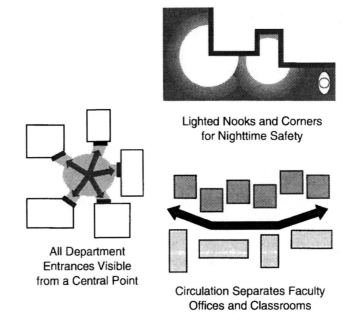

Lighted Nooks and Corners
for Nighttime Safety

All Department
Entrances Visible
from a Central Point

Circulation Separates Faculty
Offices and Classrooms

Figure 5-27   Captions Complement Concept Diagrams and
Make Them Complete

Verbal Reinforcement

Use as few words as possible to make the meaning unmistakably clear. A concept needs both words and diagrams — rarely does either part stand alone. See Figure 5-27.

Clear, Simple Diagrams for
Promoting or Preventing
Contact.
From *Life Between Buildings* by
Jan Gehl. Copyright © 1987 Van
Nostrand Reinhold. Reproduced
by permission of the publisher.

TECHNIQUES FOR DEVELOPING CLEAR CONCEPTS

The following procedures are techniques for developing clear concepts.

1. A concept answers the question, "What relationship between physical things will most likely insure the level of function required by the performance requirement?"

2. A concept can always be diagrammed simply. A sketch is *not* a concept diagram.

3. Each concept diagram should have a brief caption that, together with the simple diagram, is a whole idea.

4. The diagram should always be the most generic relationship possible to solve the functional requirement such that the designer is given a broad range of possibilities for implementing the concept.

5. There should be enough concepts for each performance requirement to cover thoroughly all aspects of performance.

Concept Examples

Example Goal #1: **The building should maximize the use of solar energy so that the operating costs of the house are minimized as much as possible in San Luis Obispo's mild climate.**

1.1 PR: **A minimum of 80 % of the winter heating power should come from the sun, maintaining a comfortable interior temperature at a minimum of 66°F.**

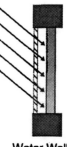

Trombe Wall: Air Space and Glass with Mass

Water Wall Behind Double Glazing

Radiant Floors Heated by Water Piped from Roof Solar Collectors

1.2 PR: **100 % of the summer cooling will be by natural means, maintaining a comfortable interior temperature with a maximum temperature of 82°F.**

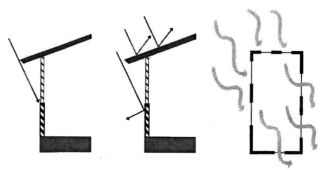

Glass Protected from Summer Sun

Insulation and Reflective Materials to Keep Out Excess Solar Radiation

Orient Operable Windows to Catch Maximum Prevailing Breezes

Example Goal #2: **The major portion of parking for the downtown core should be a short, pleasant walk from most shopping destinations.**

2.1 PR: Major pedestrian corridors between parking and downtown stores should be substantially protected from rain and the afternoon sun.

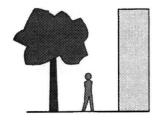

Tree-Lined Sidewalks

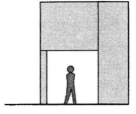

Arcades and Colonnades

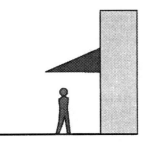

Awnings and Canopies

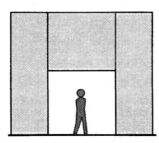

"Tunnels" or Lobbies Through Buildings

2.2 PR: Major paths should create impulse shopping and window shopping opportunities.

Line Path with a Variety of Shops

Maximum Glass in Storefront

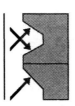

Maximize Area of Storefront Suitable for Glass

2.3 PR: Major paths should easily accommodate the full range of handicapped users, including those with minor mobility difficulties.

Level Changes with Ramps 12 % or Less

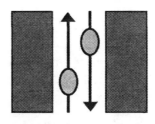

Paths Wide Enough for Groups of People to Pass Each Other Comfortably in Opposite Directions (No Obstacles)

Curb Cuts Marked with Textures

Shop Door Thresholds Less Than 1/2" High

SUMMARY

A concept is a diagrammatic statement of an ideal relationship between the elements of a design. A good concept statement is composed of a clear diagram and a concise caption that makes the meaning clear. Concepts can be developed for the whole design (parti) or for any of its component parts such as an issue or an aspect of performance. Many architects use concept scenarios to describe their ideas about the whole design. Each performance requirement will have several concepts for implementing the required function. In the algorithm presented in this text, concepts are the relationships between the architectural elements required to fulfill the level of performance stated in the performance requirements. See Figure 5-7. They are the ideas that guide the outcome of the whole project and solve the most important problems raised by each issue.

Concepts are the very beginnings of design synthesis and can be developed from many sources. A concept can be as simple as an adjacency diagram or as complex as an elaborate analogy or metaphor. Concepts can be the solution to a particular problem, the implementation of an ideal, or the manifestation of the spirit or essence of a building or building aspect. In the initial stages of concept development you should create a wide variety of different concepts in order to test which ideas are the the best, or best combination, based upon how well they meet the performance requirements. After the best ideas are chosen, the next step is to choose the most useful expression of the concept so that the idea is specific about the required relationship but general enough to allow the designer a great deal of latitude in implementation. The final stage is to develop the concepts that reinforce, complement, and strengthen the ideas that best implement the performance requirement and to choose the best possible expression of the ideas, with diagrams and captions working together for clear communication.

A good concept diagram is graphically simple and clear and illustrates a simple physical relationship. It has a strong visual impact which is usually a result of graphic contrast. In addition, a good concept diagram has a concise caption that completes the idea illustrated by the diagram.

Figure 5-28   Be Clear About Your Concepts.
Cartoon from *Mister Boffo: Unclear on the Concept* by Joe Martin. Copyright © 1989 by Tribune Media Services, Inc. Reproduced by permission of Little, Brown and Company.

A good concept diagram illustrates generic relationships and implies a wide variety of potential designs for physical implementation.

Figure 5-28 illustrates that it really pays to be clear about your concepts.

PART II

APPLICATIONS

Part II is the applications part of this book. It describes the theory, methods, and examples of programming and programming research and evaluation. The intention is not to be exhaustive, but to give you a sense of the major ideas, methods and resources available to you as a programmer/designer.

Chapter 6 introduces the scientific method as the foundation for most design research. While there are some phenomenological research methods that are useful for architects, most of the research being done is empirical. Thus it is important to understand the rules under which good research is conducted in order to be able to judge the applicability of a study to your design work. The validity of research designs and sampling techniques are also important to good research.

Chapters 7 and 8 survey a number of research methods that are useful in design research, from simple observation to experiments and model-building workshops. I suspect that video and computer technology will change the way we do our observations in the future and how we will make our presentations to clients, especially with the introduction of inexpensively produced virtual reality.

Chapter 9 introduces a framework of organizing environment/behavior information into categories of people characteristics, place characteristics, behavioral issues, method, theory, and context. Examples from each of these categories illustrate how designs can be improved by an understanding of these different aspects of the design problem.

Chapter 10 surveys a number of frameworks for organizing design information and suggests strategies for managing all the mountains of data that are generated by programming and design research.

In Chapter 11 you will find a discussion of the suggested order for presentation of the contents of a program document to your client. In addition there are examples of and critiques of different page layouts and their utility as presentation vehicles.

Two case studies are introduced in Chapter 12. One is a section of student work that follows the schematic design format modeled in this text and the other is made up of segments from a program developed for design development.

The first follows several issues through goals, performance requirements, and programming. The second illustrates how one issue is delineated in various parts of the program document.

Chapter 13 takes a look at design evaluation from initial evaluation of design concepts to formal post-occupancy and post-construction evaluations. Many of the research techniques discussed in Chapters 7 and 8 are useful for these formal evaluations. These evaluations also produce data that helps in generating information for new building programs.

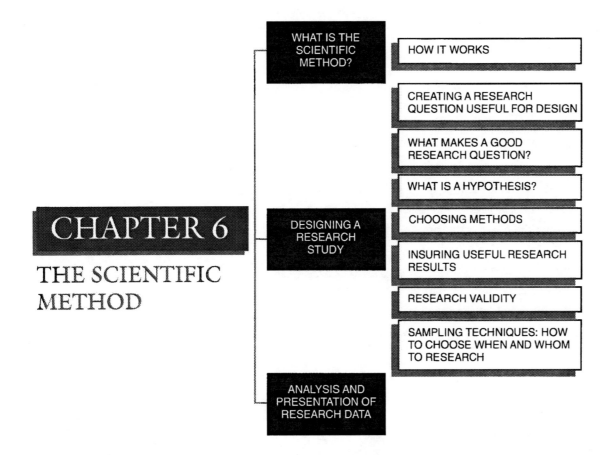

CHAPTER 6

THE SCIENTIFIC
METHOD

WHAT IS THE SCIENTIFIC METHOD?

HOW IT WORKS

DESIGNING A RESEARCH STUDY

CREATING A RESEARCH QUESTION USEFUL FOR DESIGN

WHAT MAKES A GOOD RESEARCH QUESTION?

WHAT IS A HYPOTHESIS?

CHOOSING METHODS

INSURING USEFUL RESEARCH RESULTS

RESEARCH VALIDITY

SAMPLING TECHNIQUES: HOW TO CHOOSE WHEN AND WHOM TO RESEARCH

ANALYSIS AND PRESENTATION OF RESEARCH DATA

THE SCIENTIFIC METHOD

However, if we do discover a complete theory, it should in time be understandable in broad principle by everyone, not just a few scientists.

Stephen Hawking
A Brief History of Time

WHAT IS THE SCIENTIFIC METHOD?

Knowing about the scientific method is important to programmers and designers so that we might recognize a good research study when we read one. It also helps us to be better judges of whether or not the research we read is applicable to our project. Using the scientific method in the research that we do provides a sound basis for trusting our research to fill in the gaps in our information base. Scientific methods should always be used when the outcome of the research is very important and mistakes can be very costly, such as in questions of life safety, prison security, hospital emergency room design, and public housing design.

When most of us were in junior high school science classes, we were introduced to the scientific method for research, but few of us used it in our daily lives. As a result, we are not very proficient in using this mode of thinking professionally. The purpose of the scientific method is to create exact, reproducible results so that we might "prove" that a report, a theory, or a fact is true or false. To start the ball rolling, ask a **research question** and then create **hypotheses**, or guesses, to test whether the assumptions are right or not.

In architectural or design research, we are looking for predictability and trends rather than a rigorous "proof" that the design is true or false. Too much human behavior or human response to architectural design is "caused" by things beyond the designer's control for us to be able to prove with certainty that a particular design is "right" or the "best." What we *can do* is to select parts of the problem that are difficult to know about, or difficult to understand with the information on hand, and uncover more information that will point in a design direction that is more likely to be successful than if we had not done the research. We use the principles of the scientific method so that we can be fairly certain that the results of our research are apropos to the question we asked rather than just being another set of facts that may or may not be useful. See Figure 6-1.

How It Works

Step One

The first step is to ask a *relevant research question* and create a *hypothesis* that can be tested. A good research question and good hypothesis are the most important parts of research. For designers, the best questions for testing the

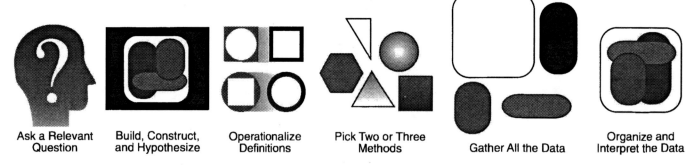

| Ask a Relevant Question | Build, Construct, and Hypothesize | Operationalize Definitions | Pick Two or Three Methods | Gather All the Data | Organize and Interpret the Data |

Figure 6-1 Diagram of the Scientific Method

value of a research question are: "What do I really *know* about my design?" "What do I know about the users that will influence the design?" and "What are the implications for the design?"

Step Two

The next thing to do is to *devise a set of methods* to test the hypothesis. This method is your research design. Testing a hypothesis means that you design the way you gather the information so that, if you have guessed wrong, your hypothesis can be proven false if it is false. One of the tenets of the scientific method is that a hypothesis cannot be precisely proven to be true. If it is not disproved and many tests fail to prove it false, then we believe that the hypothesis at hand is a good and possibly a true explanation for what we see happening. People believed for many years that the world was flat because there had been no test devised that could prove that hypothesis to be false.

Step Three

The third step in the process is to *gather the data* as accurately as possible — given the research design. Most of us do not get it right the first time so it is a great idea to run a **pilot study** (test) first to smooth out any rough parts of the process and to see if you have made any mistakes in your research design. A pilot study consists of taking a small sample and doing your research study as a trial run. Choose a place or a group of people with whom it is alright to make all your mistakes. It is also a good idea to have people in your pilot study who are willing to spend time telling you where you were unclear and what they think your mistakes were. After the pilot study, refine your research design to eliminate the problems.

Dr. Sandra Howell (1979, personal communication) reported that when she was doing a pilot study for the design of a questionnaire, one of the respondents answered that he did not have *any* friends in the elderly housing project in which he had lived for five years. This seemed to be an unreasonable answer: either the man was a grump and liked no one, or there was something wrong with the wording of the question. When a researcher went back to interview the man about why he had answered the questionnaire the way he

"Have a cup of coffee while I'm getting ready."

Figure 6-2 Operationalizing a Definition.
From *They're Gonna Settle Out of Court, Herman,* by Jim Unger. Copyright © 1989. HERMAN copyright Jim Unger. Reprinted with permission of Universal Press Syndicate. All rights reserved.

did, he said that, to him, a friend was someone he had known for over 25 years and to whom he could pour out his heart. The redesigned questionnaire *operationalized the definition* of *friend* to be: "someone whom you would ask for a cup of sugar, you would ask to water your plants or feed your cats while you were gone on vacation, or for whom you would be willing to do the same."

However language is used, there is a great deal of room for various interpretations. Be sure to ask your questions and do your observations in a manner that creates useful information for your design project. Figure 6-2 shows how the definition of *cup* might vary from our usual usage and one process for operationalizing the unusual definition.

Step Four

After gathering data, the results are consolidated and analyzed and an interpretation is made. A good question to ask is, "What are the implications for goals, performance requirements, and design concepts?" "To do a complete program, what other questions does this research raise that need answering?"

Step Five

Organizing the information and reporting the research results is the final aspect of a research study. The format, language, and graphics should be carefully targeted to your audience so that they will easily understand it.

DESIGNING A RESEARCH STUDY

The most important part of a good research study is a good research question and a good hypothesis. A good question is one for which the answer gives strong direction to a design. A

bad research question gives you useless or adverse information. For example, in her programming class at MIT, Dr. Sandra Howell gave the example of asking elderly women whether they preferred to bathe in a tub or in a shower. On the surface, it seems to be a reasonable question to decide what percentage of showers and what percentage of baths to install in a large elderly housing project. The reality of the situation is that the next person on the housing waiting list is likely to be a shower person when a bath apartment is available and vice versa. The real design solution is to create bathing options so that the elderly resident might make a choice. Researching shower or tub preference in this case is irrelevant.

Creating a Research Question Useful for Design

Preliminary thinking about creating a research question should include answering the following questions:

What is it that I know about this design when I have the answer to my research question?

Have I put the answer I am looking for into the question I am asking?

Is it applicable to the design? Does it give me a rationale for making choices that lead me in one direction rather than another? Does it allow me to uncover new thoughts or new directions that I never would have followed before?

Who needs to know the answer?

What is the worst possible outcome for my research — given the range of possible answers for the way the study is currently designed? Can I still use the results of the research under this worst case scenario, or should I redesign the study to get better quality results?

What Makes a Good Research Question?

The main criterion for a good research question is that the question should give you an answer that will *help you make programming or design decisions*. For example, in a project for a design of a student commons, you might ask a question that will give you some insight into what level of performance is necessary to promote social interaction among the students and between faculty and students. This assumes that there is a goal of wanting to create higher levels of social and intellectual interaction between faculty and students. An alternate question might be: What is the desired level of faculty and student interaction outside of class? Other questions that might also be answered include: What do students expect from faculty? What do faculty expect from students? What do they both desire? Are existing conditions different from what is expected? Are faculty and student expectations very different?

Another criterion would be the need to gather information that will help you decide between two very different concepts that both seem reasonable: i.e., Should we close this street or not? Should all copying be centralized or decentralized? Should this department be in open offices, closed offices, or a mixture of the two?

The question should focus on a fairly *narrow set of ideas* so that you can get into the question in some depth rather than cover a number of questions with shallow breadth. Again, the question should be relevant to the design problem at hand in a specific way, with some implications for similar situations. This is the idea of knowing a small part of the universe very well rather than knowing a big part of the universe superficially. One interesting research question for a juvenile services center was: What is the source of maintenance requests for the past two years — vandalism, routine maintenance, faulty design, or installation? Asking how the design works is far too broad a question and not really useful.

The question should be answered by *several complementary methods* — like "triangulation" in trigonometry. The couple sitting talking on the lawn can tell you whether they are studying, socializing, courting, arguing, gossiping, or counseling. If you depend upon only the observer's interpretation, you run the risk of seeing only what you are looking for. This would be **experimenter bias** and would invalidate the results of your study. If social interaction is part of what you are looking for, you should be able to identify it without question whenever you see it. This requires an *operational definition*, a specific measurable description(s) of the phenomena you are researching.

For a one quarter or semester of *design class*, a good research question can be answered in about *two to three weeks worth of data gathering*. In the professional world, good research questions may take a day or two or, more often, months to answer, and the *really* good ones may take a lifetime to answer.

What is a Hypothesis?

From Webster's (1966) a hypothesis is:
> ". . . an unproved theory, proposition, etc., tentatively accepted to explain certain facts or (working hypothesis) to provide a basis for further investigation, argument, study, etc."

A hypothesis is a guess about how and why things happen the way they do. In architecture, each building design is a hypothesis about how the inhabitants will behave in, use,

> ### PRINCIPLE 16
>
> *First choose the research question, and then choose the research methods most suitable for obtaining a good answer.*

react to, and maintain the building. Stephen Hawking (1988, 9) describes a scientific theory or hypothesis as follows:

> ". . . [A] theory is just a model of the universe, or a restricted part of it, and a set of rules that relate quantities in the model to observations that we make. It exists only in our minds and does not have any other reality (whatever that might mean). A theory is a good theory if it satisfies two requirements: It must accurately describe a large class of observations on the basis of a model that contains only a few arbitrary elements, and it must make definite predictions about the results of future observations."

He further explains how scientists use theories as a way of knowing and describing the phenomena under observation. These attitudes are quite useful in looking at the interactions of people and buildings. We want to predict with some degree of certainty that our buildings will serve the intended function, create the desired message, or satisfy a particular set of needs.

> "Any physical theory is always provisional, in the sense that it is only an hypothesis: you can never prove it. . . . [A] good theory is characterized by the fact that it makes a number of predictions that could in principle be disproved or falsified by observation. . . . [W]e break the problem up into bits and invent a number of partial theories. Each of these partial theories describes and predicts a certain limited class of observations, neglecting the effects of other quantities, or representing them by simple sets of numbers. It may be that this approach is entirely wrong. If everything in the universe depends upon everything else in a fundamental way, it might be

impossible to get close to a full solution by investigating parts of the problem in isolation. Nevertheless, it is certainly the way we have made progress in the past" (Hawking 1988, 10-11).

Architecture is a small part of the universe and yet it, too, is made up of interconnected parts so that everything depends upon everything else. Part of making a hypothesis testable is to outline a clear description of the rules that you think are operating in the small part of the universe you are trying to study. In the language of social science research, this part of the process is called defining your **construct** — making note of how the world works. A complete construct includes all of the rules that seem to be operating and all aspects of the situation that might make a change in the results of the research. Those aspects that alter the outcome of the research when they change are called **variables**.

Choosing Methods

The second most important part of designing a research study is to choose the appropriate methods to answer your question fully. It is not good practice to go out to do an "interview study" when you are not sure that the interview method is sufficient to answer the question. It is important to ask the good question first and then pick the methods to determine the answers you need to uncover. For most design research, a couple of complementary methods will be sufficient. Besides observing the couple on the lawn (from the previous example), one should interview them with a brief set of questions to get their point of view on their activities and not just the interpretation of the observer. The next chapter will give more details about many of the research methods that are readily available to programmers and designers.

Insuring Useful Research Results

Insuring useful research results means developing operational definitions for your **units of analysis** (Yin 1984). Units of analysis are the elements you are gathering data about to answer your research question. If you are looking at how friendship patterns develop relative to the front door/back door relationships in apartment complexes, then door relationships are your units of analysis and you do not need to observe friendly behavior at windows or gates. You must also know how to define (operationalize) *friendship* at various levels and how to recognize the significant differences between door relationships. The recognition of the differences between door relationships (operational definitions) will create a partition between categories of door relationships — so that you know in which category to count this particular door relationship.

Research Validity

Yin (1984, 40) said, "The goal of reliability is to minimize the errors and biases in the study." He describes the four basic types of validity that create high quality research as follows:

> "*Construct validity*: establishing correct operational measures for the concepts being studied;
>
> "*Internal validity* (for explanatory or causal studies only, and not for descriptive or exploratory studies): establishing a causal relationship, whereby certain conditions are shown to lead to other conditions, as distinguished from spurious relationships;
>
> "*External validity*: establishing the domain to which a study's findings can be generalized; and

> "*Reliability*: demonstrating that the operations of a study —such as the data collection procedures —can be repeated, with the same results" (Yin 1984, 36).

Construct validity is gained by creating a good set of operational definitions, using multiple sources of evidence (triangulation) and establishing a chain of evidence (logical links between the question, the research design, the data or evidence, and the conclusions).

Internal validity is gained by eliminating any contradictions and contrary definitions, by taking into account all factors that may be effective in producing the data, and by documenting all assumptions or data developed from inference. Choosing who the subjects are and the timing of the research (sampling) are two activities that contribute to internal validity as well.

External validity is gained by gathering enough data in enough circumstances to be able to say with confidence that the findings and conclusions are generalizable to your particular design or to other similar kinds of design projects.

Reliability is gained when errors and biases are eliminated and the research can be repeated with the same general results.

Sampling Techniques: How to Choose When and Whom to Research

What follows is a brief introduction to sampling techniques that can be used in short student research projects. Professionals will want to be more precise, depending upon the time allocated for the research. The concepts of sampling are important and are further explained in other references (Yin 1984, Schatzman and Strauss 1973).

PRINCIPLE 17

Gather data at the times that are most critical for the design (i.e., when the most people are there, when the most frequent behavior patterns are likely to be present, during the event that will have the maximum requirements, etc.).

PRINCIPLE 18

Choose an appropriate number of subjects to get reliable data. A number too large is better than a number too small.

Take for example a simple question: "What would be the most useful commons facilities for students between classes?" and a simple observation and interview study to discover the activities and needs of students between classes.

Time Sampling

If this is to be an observation and interview study, then when should the data be gathered? If the focus is to serve the students' needs between classes, then the weekends are certainly not a good time for gathering data. Is it important to observe during the busiest times? If so, most campuses schedule for student demand and have the greatest number of classes meeting between 10 AM and 2 PM. Is the lunch hour an important time to observe? Is there an activity hour for clubs and special events? Is the Monday/Wednesday/Friday schedule different from the Tuesday/Thursday schedule? Are classes held on Saturday? Are the needs different for midterms and finals weeks? Are the students' needs different in different seasons: fall, winter (rain or snow), spring, summer (sun and heat)? Are there any particular time-specific events or holidays that would be reflected in changed student behaviors? Ask yourself all possible questions about the differences in the times the observed spaces are used and brainstorm all the different possible use patterns that you can.

Selecting Research Subjects

If your design is to serve only students, it is not useful to gather data on faculty, staff, or visitors to campus, but if the "commons" is to be for everyone, then observations and interviews must include all the types of the users in the study. The question of how long to observe or how many people to interview will depend upon whether you are interested in a brief description of the type of place and activities, in

discovering a trend, or in statistical probabilities for long term predictions. For a simple description of the place and the range of activities that go on, one or two observation periods chosen at the busiest times would probably be sufficient. Discovering trends would be possible by selecting a few of the most critical times and observing (let's say you choose to do behavior mapping) for approximately a four hour spread over one week. To verify your conclusions, you would want to have a brief, informal interview with a minimum of 20 students of various years and majors. In addition, you would want to interview about five faculty, five staff, and five members of any other groups you wish to attract to the "commons," to verify your perceptions of their different needs and behaviors. Your observations might indicate one of the future questions you need to answer, such as, "How will it be possible to attract more faculty to a student commons?" For long term trends and statistical predictability, a much longer observation time is necessary. Whyte (1980) observed the plazas of New York for the better part of a year before making his recommendations on plaza design and standards to the NYC Planning Commission.

In selecting representative subjects for your research projects, you need to keep in mind the different factors you think will make a difference in your design. In the commons, are there different needs for students of different majors? Are the needs of the older, returning students different from the needs of the younger ones? Does gender make a difference in design preference? In your hypothesis, you will assume that certain factors make a difference for your design, and your research project should be designed to let you disprove your assumptions if they are not true. If you are looking at a wide range of differences, you need to have a greater number of subjects so that you are getting a cross section of responses, rather than a few responses with some specific bias. You need to have enough subjects in each category to be sure that you are getting the trend you are searching for or the statistically reliable data. For a study of trends and to get a feeling for the possibilities of the design problem, a minimum of five people per category is necessary to get any representation of a trend and ten people per category would be even better. For statistical probability, the size of your sample is determined by the size of your overall population: the larger the population, the larger the sample. With a big project or a very large population, it is a good idea to work with a social scientist to develop the research design and sampling techniques.

If you are doing research for a design for a small group of people, then everyone in the group should be a part of your research subject pool. If you are doing research for a very large number of people, then you need to be sure that your subject selection is random. If you ask the people in the cafeteria line for their opinions about the food, it may be that the people who would volunteer to speak to you are the ones with complaints. If you ask every fourth person, then your sample is random and will get the complaints and the compliments. Whether you want a representative sample of all the different groups or a random sample depends entirely upon your great research question and which sample will fill the bill.

ANALYSIS AND PRESENTATION OF RESEARCH DATA

The third most important part of conducting a research study is the appropriate analysis and presentation of the research results. If the data cannot be analyzed to yield useful information, then the research study is a waste of time.

Analysis is assembling the data into meaningful groups so that the results are more easily understood and interpreted. For example, comparisons between the demands for commons' activities by student major, by time of day, or by week in the semester or quarter could all yield useful information for a commons design.

For the most part, the audience for your research will not be people who are using t-tests, regression analysis, and Chi squares in their everyday life. Simple statistical techniques that lay people understand should be used. Averages, bar graphs for frequency, composite mapping of paths traveled, and activity patterns are some of the easier ways to present information and most educated people readily understand them. You must choose the method of analysis and presentation of the data aimed specifically at your audience: your audience may range from minimally educated residents of low-income housing to computer scientists or genetic research specialists. One truth of presentation is that, for any audience, the more graphic you make the presentation, the more quickly they will understand the message.

For complicated or sophisticated research designs, it is best to team up with a social or behavioral scientist to ensure appropriate research design so that the analysis will result in useful information.

SUMMARY

The scientific method was developed so that scientists could verify other people's results from their investigations. If we as designers understand the rules of scientific inquiry, then we can more easily read and understand research studies that have implications for our work. We can also design research studies of our own that we can trust to fill in the gaps in our information base. It is important for architectural researchers to understand the principles of the scientific method because it is the foundation for doing research studies with reliable results.

The first step in developing a research study consists of developing a construct (the rules and relevant variables of the study), developing research question(s), and developing hypotheses about possible answers to the question. A good research question will have an answer or set of answers that will help you to make better programming or design decisions.

The second step is to develop a research design that includes a set of methods that will give you the best possible answer to your questions. The research design should be set up in a manner that allows the hypotheses to be proven false if they are false. The methods chosen should be appropriate to the questions asked. It is not appropriate to do an "observation study" unless observation will answer the questions posed. By using several different methods you can avoid the major traps of experimenter bias. Be clear about your units of analysis before you design the study.

The third step in the scientific method is to gather the data as accurately as possible. It pays to do a pilot study first and make your mistakes upon willing volunteers who will let you know what your goofs were. Part of the job your pilot study should do is to help operationalize all your definitions so that you and your research subjects understand the terms used.

Step four is to analyze the data and to make interpretations about the important implications the results have for your design. Finally, the fifth step is to organize the information to report the results to the client and the rest of the design team.

A good research study meets the four tests for validity: construct validity, external validity, internal validity, and reliability. Careful sampling techniques support validity. Time sampling should cover the most important times for the activity under consideration, either the busiest times or the most important events. Subject sampling is also critical to validity in terms of who participates in the research study and how many people are chosen. Depending upon your research question, you might want a random sample or a representative sample, a few in depth case studies or many brief surveys, or you might need to research everyone in the client group.

Presentation of your research results must be tailored to the audience, from the terms used to the level of detail covered. One thing is certain, more people understand graphic presentations of results instead of numbers or mere words. Photographs, bar charts, traffic maps, and concept diagrams help make your presentation more understandable.

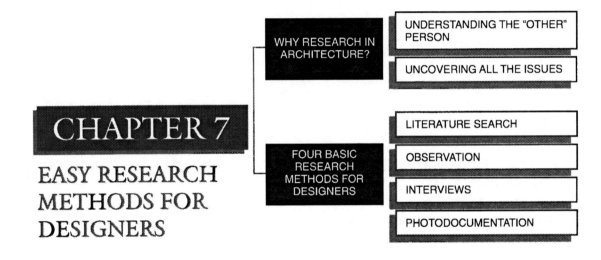

CHAPTER 7

EASY RESEARCH METHODS FOR DESIGNERS

WHY RESEARCH IN ARCHITECTURE?
- UNDERSTANDING THE "OTHER" PERSON
- UNCOVERING ALL THE ISSUES

FOUR BASIC RESEARCH METHODS FOR DESIGNERS
- LITERATURE SEARCH
- OBSERVATION
- INTERVIEWS
- PHOTODOCUMENTATION

EASY RESEARCH METHODS FOR DESIGNERS

Architects and planners may be heard to ask, "Why are people so stubborn or misguided as not to use the places and spaces we design—either not at all or not in the right way?" People may be heard to ask, "Why are architects and planners so insensitive in what they put up and expect us to live with? Why do they so often leave out just what we think is important?"

Constance Perin
With Man in Mind

WHY RESEARCH IN ARCHITECTURE?

As noted in the opening quote, there has often been a misunderstanding about how buildings are to be used — both on the part of the client, who misunderstands the intention of the architect, and on the part of the architect, who misunderstands the needs and values of the client. Programming is the major tool for communicating both the intentions of the design team and the requirements of the user. Architectural research is the tool for understanding the clients — their values, needs, and requirements — in more detail and accuracy than can be developed in a few discussions with the clients about their needs. The methods described in this chapter follow the precepts of the scientific method. Some are more rigorous and quantitative, whereas others are less rigorous and more qualitative.

At the beginning of human interactions with the environment, the fight for survival was the only fight worth fighting: if a cave or tree kept you away from predators, protected you sufficiently from the weather, and was close enough to food and drink, then you won the survival game. As humanity's needs grew, so did the ability to manipulate the environment to meet those needs — thus architecture was born. In the earliest stages, you built a structure and you lived in it: if the manipulation of the environment was insufficient to the need, you suffered — design by trial and error worked eventually. As affluence and specialization allowed some people to hire others to do the work of manipulating the environment, it was no longer the designer who suffered the unworkable consequences of the design. In today's world of specialized tasks, it is very seldom that anyone designs and builds his own house and never does anyone design and build her own hospital, school, or low-income housing. It is this

distance between the designer and the owner and/or user that mandates the need for research in architecture.

Understanding the "Other" Person

In modern times, the designer is often not a part (either physically or socially) of the same community as the users and owners of the building projects and there are many other issues to deal with above and beyond mere shelter. Therefore, it is necessary to do research to understand the real needs of people who are different from ourselves (the "other" people), whose needs for design are unexpected or unknown to us and who will have to live with the consequences of the designs we make. To assume that we as designers know how to solve other people's architectural problems without asking them to identify the problem is the height of arrogance.

In the late 1950s, the designers of Pruitt Igoe in St. Louis did a great job of designing public housing according to the ideals of the *architectural* community, but did a very poor job of understanding the housing needs of the residents. The project won architectural design awards and was demolished about ten years after it was built. Similarly, in the course of our design careers, we will design for many populations that are different from our own group: the critically ill in hospitals, the convicted felons in prisons, the six- year-old in his first year of elementary school, as well as those who are much richer or poorer than we are.

It is our job as designers and architects to *understand* the "other" people — those who are not exactly like us — in order to define the problem that really needs to be solved. The assumption that "if we like it, then they will like it" is no longer valid, if it ever was. We must discover how our client's or user's expectations are different from ours, how their values are different from ours, and how their high priority issues are not necessarily the ones we might assume.

While it is true that *everything* about a building or client cannot be completely known and *some assumptions* must be made, it is in the client's and designer's best interests to do it right the first time and do the research necessary to find all the points that make a difference in the final outcome. Programming is the most cost effective place in the design process to correct mistakes and the place where the costliest mistakes are made. The goal here is to make design choices based on knowledge and understanding rather than on assumptions and ego alone. Assumptions must be acknowledged and tested wherever possible.

Uncovering All the Issues

In order to develop a program for a building that covers all the bases, we must uncover all the issues, problems, and constraints that can be dealt with through the medium of architectural design. In Chapter 2, issues were discussed as the categories for gathering data and for making design decisions. If one of the important issues is missing, then the design will not do its job properly. It is also the job of research to discover which issues are high priority issues and which are less important. It is a classic argument that the architect concerns herself with *image* while the client's needs are for a more *functional* building. In the best of all possible worlds there is no need to forsake function for image — we should be able to have both!

With new client groups or new building types, it is especially important to document every aspect of the design

problem. What are the constraints and opportunities of the place, the people, the behavior and activity patterns, and the context? What are the stereotypic or preconceived solutions? What are the most important problems that have to be solved in order for the project to be a success?

FOUR BASIC RESEARCH METHODS FOR DESIGNERS

The discussion here is of the most basic research methods for architectural research that can be easily used. Literature search, interview techniques, observation methods, and photo documentation techniques are illustrated in detail in this chapter, whereas simulations, case studies, questionnaires, diaries, experiments, the semantic differential, and the design log method are discussed with less depth in the next chapter. Books such as Sanoff (1977, 1991), Moore (1973), and Michaelson (1975) provide the designer with still other methods for gathering a wide range of information.

Literature Search

Literature search is the gathering of data from architectural designs or research studies that have already been done. Most of us head for the subject index when we hit the library to do our book and periodical research. Many times this approach is of little value for the programming needs of a specific project because the topics required are not subjects in the Library of Congress system. Books on architectural programming can be found under "architectural design: research" (NA2750), "human factors" (NA2542), a specific building type such as "housing" (NA711), and "homesites: planning" or laboratory design (TH4652), or under some other research discipline such as environmental psychology (BF353). There needs to be a great deal of creativity in uncovering the appropriate subject headings. Programming books are sometimes listed under "architectural design: data processing" (NA2750) and post-occupancy evaluations are under "architectural design: evaluation" (NA2750).

Find an Expert

If the subject is not organized in exactly the way we want to find information, then the first stop before going to the library should be in the office of an expert on the subject you plan to research. It is most likely that she can put you on the correct path very quickly by pointing out the classic references in the area. Once you have one or two references to start with, the rest is reasonably easy.

If you do not know a local expert, be sure to check with the reference librarian. In many school libraries, there is a reference librarian assigned to be the expert in architectural and other design topics. He will also be able to assist you in developing a search strategy that suits your needs.

Book Search

Since most card catalogs are becoming electronic, you may have to ask how to find the shelf list — this is a list of all the books in the library by catalog number. Once you have the catalog number of your first reference, you can find out if there are any other titles that look promising in the same category. Next, look for other titles by the same author(s). If the references you have found have bibliographies or good footnotes, then you have a number of new leads to follow. These references may be other books with different call numbers, or they may be articles in magazines or conference

proceedings. If a particular journal or magazine shows up several times in a book's reference notes, then it may be worth your while to scan the latest several years of that periodical to see if any new articles have appeared. Be sure to note all the subject listings for your really good resource finds. Then you can go back to the subject catalog with new leads.

Each new book can be used for the following leads:

1. more books and articles by the same author (look in the author index),
2. other books with the same catalog reference number (shelf list),
3. newly discovered subject listings in the catalog (subject listing), and
4. bibliography or footnotes for other leads for new books or periodicals.

Periodical Search

There are a large number of indexes that can help you in your search for relevant articles. The *Art Index* will often have topics useful to architectural research. The *Avery Index* system has a number of different sources that you may be able to find through an interlibrary loan. Your reference librarian is an invaluable resource for what is available in your library, through a computer search, or through an interlibrary loan.

If you are working with a particular building type or a particular part of the profession, look to see if there are professional journals or magazines that will get you started. The restaurant and hotel industry has numerous periodicals that would be of use to a designer. There are also magazines for facilities managers and mall managers. If there are a sizable number of people interested in the topic, there is likely to be a magazine published in that field.

Proceedings of conferences and symposia are also good references and sometimes difficult to find. Your local expert or your reference librarian would be the best place to start looking for relevant resources. EDRA has been around for well over 20 years and its proceedings are full of information on architectural and design research as well as programming processes. The call number for the EDRA proceedings is TH6021.E65.

If none of the above procedures work or you do not come up with your first reference, then you must be very creative in developing subject key words to use in searching the catalogs or indices. Programming articles have been found under "architectural research: computers" even if the programming article has nothing to do with computers. People do make semantic mistakes in categorizing books and articles because they use only the title to make their decision of which category to file it in. Redouble your efforts to find an expert or someone who can give you the first thread into the maze of stored information.

Computer Search

After you have found all the useful topic words that seem relevant, you might want to pay for a computer search that encompasses all the libraries in the interlibrary loan system. This is not always a good idea unless your topics are narrow enough to yield a few good references rather than a flood of peripheral books and articles. This is also not a good idea if you have not gotten your key words or authors into a useful set.

With the proliferation of personal computers, many libraries have gone to completely electronic card catalogs and are available without charge, either in the library or via your own modem. Hopefully, a charge for a computer search is obsolete by now. Many university card catalog systems allow you to access the catalogs of numerous other libraries across the country.

Archival Search

Some of the best resources are in the archives of your client's files. Maintenance requests can be scrutinized to discover the relationship between design and operating costs. Committee meeting minutes might yield the thought processes that led a particular group to decide how their department should be arranged. Change order requests are a source of information about the relationship between the design and the construction processes. Be as creative as you can to utilize your client's resources to provide the maximum amount of useful information with the least amount of energy expended.

After all the literature search is done, be sure to document it carefully. Many clients want an annotated literature search delivered to them. Even if the client does not want the results of your hard labor, it is a good idea to keep your search document on file for future, similar projects. Literature search documentation should include the full reference: title, author, publisher, places of publication, call number, page numbers for quotes or diagrams used, and ISBN (International Standard Book Number) if it is useful to you. You should also include the source of the book or periodical just in case you want to find it again later. The documentation should also include any summaries or analyses that you do as well as relevant annotations.

Observation

Observation studies, in this context, are the noticing and recording of facts and events pertinent to design. For the architect, observation is one of the most powerful, readily available tools for acquiring an understanding about a design project. Observation is standard office practice on an informal basis and is usually not *called* research. Site visits are classic cases of casual observation. Visits to a client's work, social environment, or home environment are occasions for observation and are research opportunities that can be easily missed or not used to their full potential. The techniques discussed here will give designers and architects a way of maximizing the observation opportunities that they already have and suggestions for new possibilities.

The first rule of doing observational research is: *do your homework*! Know what it is that you are seeking — have questions clearly in your mind before you go to observe. Do you just want to know what the questions are? Are you searching for new issues? Do you want to know *all* the facts about the site for a thorough site analysis? Know enough about the questions you are asking to know when you have gotten enough information so that you can answer your question fully. Make a list of *known issues* that you think are important and use your observations to verify or expand the list or to eliminate certain issues that are not very important to this particular project. Make a list of assumptions that need verification and are amenable to observation techniques.

One way of classifying different types of observation studies is by level of detail. Three levels of detail for observational studies are discussed here. The first, *casual observation*, is getting the big picture. It is naturalistic observation; discovering the story of the place, group or activity; discovering questions; and gathering factual data. *Systematic observation* is counting occurrences of events, numbers of people, or other specific data sets, and then drawing conclusions. *Statistical observation* is the carefully designed research study, using the scientific method, that proves a point by making highly reliable predictions. Quasi-experimental observation studies fall into this category and include times when the observer changes particular conditions and records the observed changes.

There are other choices that you must make about the type of observation study you are going to do. Anthropologists have long done observation studies. When the observer is known to be watching the events and is participating in them — this is called participant observation. When the observer is known and is not participating — this is called being a reporter. When the observer is not known and participates in the action of the observed group — this is called being a spy. And finally, when the observer watches and is unknown and does not participate — this is called being a voyeur.

Each point of view has its uses in observational research, but you must be careful to preserve the privacy rights of those whom you observe and note in your research reports. In academia, there are committees on the rights of human subjects to protect the people who are watched, but an architectural office does not have such safeguards. General guidelines are that watching people in public places and taking their picture is acceptable as long as individuals are not recognizable in the photographs. Otherwise, you must get permission from the people being observed and photographed to use their image in your report or to observe them in more private circumstances.

<hr>

PRINCIPLE 20

Before making any observation, know what you are looking for.

Casual Observation

Casual observation consists of watching and wondering, looking for the issues, looking for the questions that the place or the situation has to pose for us, finding out the story of a place, and developing an empathy for the big picture. Casual observation identifies the important behaviors and the aspects of the environment that make a difference (the qualitative aspects), whereas systematic observation is used to quantify behaviors. Casual observation is usually done as part of site analysis, client interviews, looking for neighborhood behavior patterns, etc. When observing a place, it is useful to know what the predominant behaviors are, what the full range of behaviors might be, what the major physical characteristics are, who the different groups of users are, and what the largest numbers of people are doing.

Range of Behaviors: Any designed place will have a range of different behaviors that are most likely to happen there. Casual observation would yield a list of the variety of behaviors seen in a certain period of time. For programming purposes, you would note what's happening that should be encouraged, what should be discouraged, and what's missing that could or should happen. In a downtown plaza you might see people eating lunch, talking, napping, reading, panhandling, playing games, riding bicycles, performing or watching a performance, sunning, walking, or taking photographs. Each one of these behaviors is accomplished with the support of the place, not affected by the place, or made difficult by the place. Designers have control over those aspects of the design that will make the occurrence of some activities easier than others.

Roles and Rules: People's behavior and their needs in a particular setting are governed as much by what role they are

playing as it is by the setting itself. What range of behaviors would you participate in and what needs would you have in a park if you were a jogger, biker, thrasher (skate-boarder), picnicker, secret tryster, parent of toddlers, dog walker, or park ranger? A great test of a good design is to ask if the place measures up to the needs of all the different roles that people will enact in the setting.

With each role comes a set of stated rules and unspoken rules for behavior. What are the rules for circulation for each of the above roles in the park? What are the conflicts between different sets of rules? What are the rules for interaction among the different groups of people? Design can make the appropriate rules more explicit or minimize the potential for conflict between different rule sets, but it takes good programming to recognize the needs and the potential conflicts.

Raising Questions to Ask Using Other Research Methods: Casual observation is a good tool with which to check your general assumptions and to ask some pointed general questions that help you get to the essence of the information needed for design: What is here that should not be here? What are the users' rules, roles, expectations, and needs? What is missing, the addition of which would make this place a much better place in which to be? What are the issues that need to be covered? What are the challenges or problems of this project in this place? What are the new questions now? What other methods do I need to answer these new questions?

Systematic Observation

Systematic observation is a more focused way of looking at a setting or site. It is a way of looking for the answers to specific questions. This is where the counting begins.

Systematic observation is for drawing more than general gut-reaction conclusions; it is beginning to draw conclusions on which predictions may be based with some confidence. It answers the general questions such as, "How many?" or "What percentage?" Time sampling and careful selection of subjects becomes important here. See Chapter 6 regarding validity.

In order to do good systematic observation, you must have all your definitions operationalized. For example, you must know the different levels of behavior (such as social interaction) when you see them, know how to identify the different roles or age groups that are important to your study, and be able to distinguish the important aspects of the environment. Moos (1974, 1979) has done a great deal of work in operationalizing a number of social phenomena and his work is a good reference point for serious researchers.

Behavior mapping is an observation technique that requires the researcher to plot out the locations of specified activities and patterns of movement. There are two basic types of behavior maps: one is a traffic map that shows the paths people take through a place (Figure 7-2) and the other is an activity map that shows what people are doing when they are stationary (Figure 7-1). The traffic map(s) also shows the direction and number of people, plus any other data about the trip that the observer deems necessary to answer the question at hand. Both types of maps need to note, in a legend, the characteristics of the people that are relevant to design. Sometimes it is important to know the gender, sometimes it is important to know the role, and sometimes it is useful to know the age.

Again, it is important to do your homework before preparing to do behavior mapping. For a simple mapping exercise, the following rules apply. Choose an area to be

mapped that you can see completely from one vantage point and draw a map or plan to scale. Carefully choose the best times and days to do your mapping so that you get the best

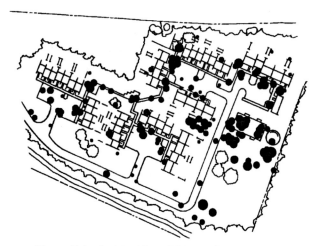

Figure 7-1   Activity Map of Places Children Play.
From *Methods of Architectural Programming* by Henry Sanoff. Copyright © 1977 Dowden, Hutchinson, and Ross, Inc. Reproduced by permission of the author.

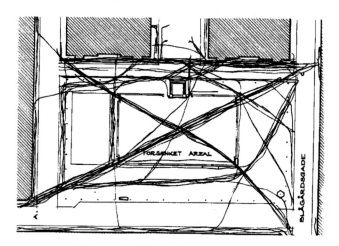

Figure 7-2   Pedestrian Traffic Map.
From *Life Between Buildings* by Jan Gehl. Copyright © 1987 Van Nostrand Reinhold. Reproduced by permission of the publisher.

research results with the least output of time and energy. Have enough copies of your map made so that you do not have to redraw it for each observation period. It is suggested that each mapping session be about five minutes long, so you will need 12 maps per hour. Alternate between traffic maps and activity maps. Composite traffic and activity maps can be made for each hour, for each day and for the total observed time. For presentation purposes, you might want to create a composite of all your observations, simplifying the graphics so that they get the point across better than a series of numbers.

Gehl (1987) has documented a number of points with maps of people's behavior: people sitting on the perimeter of spaces, paths through an open space, pedestrian traffic with different parking schemes, etc. It is this sort of research that has led Gehl to the detailed proposals he advocates for creating an architecture that encourages social activities and more active public spaces. See sidebar.

Another type of activity map is the annotated map which is good to record the activities of a room during a period of one day or week. Howell (1978) used this sort of map in her studies of elderly housing in Boston. See Chapter 11 for an example of one of these annotated activity maps.

Measuring Things: Many pieces of information needed for design answer the questions: How many? How big? How much? How far? Anthropometrics (the measures of the human body and its capabilities) are important in designing a jet cockpit, toilet facilities on a space shuttle, a kitchen for the disabled, and many other areas where cabinetwork and equipment must be chosen by designers. Angles of vision, sectors for and distances to the good views, and sizes of potential obstructions are important to placing a building so that occupants get the best views out of the building and so that visitors get the best view of the building. Examples of

things to measure are as endless as your imagination and the good questions you create to ask about your project.

A site plan is a record of everything that can be given dimension and position on or near a site. Heights of nearby buildings need to be known for shadow studies, site features such as trees and rock outcroppings need to be documented and evaluated, and existing patterns of use need to be

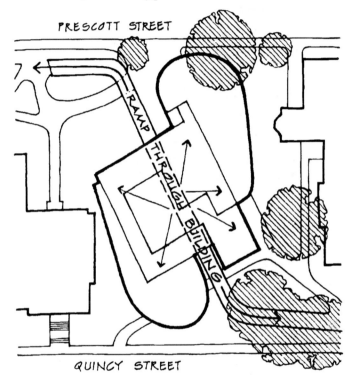

PRESCOTT STREET

QUINCY STREET

Figure 7-3 Site Plan of Carpenter Center for the Visual Arts.
From *Introduction to Architecture* by Snyder and Catanese. Copyright © 1979 McGraw-Hill. Reproduced by permission of the publisher.

surveyed and rated for potential disruption by the new project. The Carpenter Center (Figure 7-3) on the Harvard campus was designed to incorporate an already existing pedestrian path because it was determined that there were sufficient

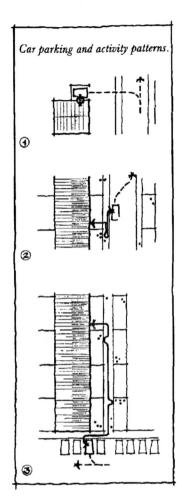

Car parking and activity patterns.

Car Parking and Activity Patterns.
From *Life Between Buildings* by Jan Gehl. Copyright © 1987 Van Nostrand Reinhold. Reproduced by permission of the publisher.

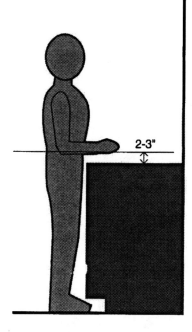

2-3"

Figure 7-4   Counter Height to
Elbow Measurement

numbers of people using the path to warrant designing the building around it.

If you are designing a kitchen for a basketball star who is 7 feet tall and is also a gourmet cook, it would be quite useful to know how long his reach is and how far his elbow is from the floor. The standard sink counter height of 36 inches is actually too low for a 5 foot 7 inch woman, and even more uncomfortable for a 7 foot tall man. Part of programming is to question the standard measures of things when appropriate (Figure 7-4).

Steinfield (1979b) has done a significant amount of research about the anthropometrics of people in wheelchairs in order to assist in developing standards for making buildings accessible. How small a circle can *you* turn in a wheelchair? How would you find out how wide the bleacher seats should be if your audience is mainly composed of elderly people? NASA has done a great deal of research on sizes of people and their ability to reach at different angles so that the space shuttles and space stations can be made to be as compact and small as possible and still be comfortable to get the job done (NASA 1989). See Figure 7-5.

Unobtrusive Measures: Webb et al. (1966) wrote a book about how to gather data without having to watch people or ask them anything. He looks for two things: accretion and abrasion. Accretion is the accumulation of something such as trash on the highways, smudge patterns on display cases or doors, dust patterns, etc. Abrasion is the sign of something wearing away such as "dog tracks" in the lawn, wear patterns of carpet, paint rubbed away, etc.

Only your imagination limits the potential for answering questions about a future design with unobtrusive measures. Much of the current data on how well we are doing as a nation at recycling comes from people gathering samples in landfills to see how the accumulation of trash has changed contents over the years.

I have long advocated that college campuses should plan their walkways by planting grass in the new landscape around a building, let the pedestrians have their way for a month or two, then fine-tune the landscaping plan based on the abraded paths in the grass. In another example, placement of trash cans in parks and zoos and junior high school campuses could be planned based upon the significant places of trash buildup.

Statistical Observation: Statistical observation is counting things in a very rigorous manner in order to prove a point or to argue for a position beyond a shadow of a doubt. It allows for a research study to be repeated with the same controls in order to get the same or very similar results. Statistical probabilities are used to create reliable predictions about the response to a design. For reliable predictions, it is necessary to use a variety of methods to verify the results or interpretation of the data gathered by another method.

Whyte (1979, 1980) chronicled one of the best published examples of what I have chosen to call statistical observation. He was making a point to the New York City

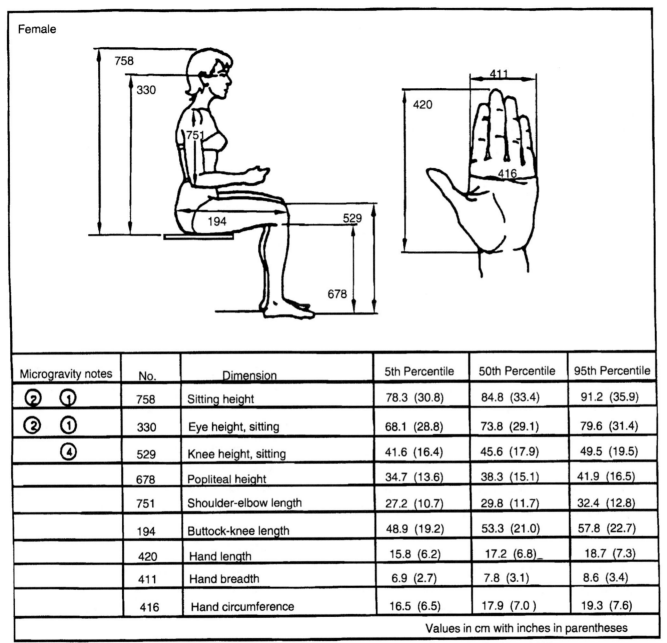

Microgravity notes	No.	Dimension	5th Percentile	50th Percentile	95th Percentile
② ①	758	Sitting height	78.3 (30.8)	84.8 (33.4)	91.2 (35.9)
② ①	330	Eye height, sitting	68.1 (28.8)	73.8 (29.1)	79.6 (31.4)
④	529	Knee height, sitting	41.6 (16.4)	45.6 (17.9)	49.5 (19.5)
	678	Popliteal height	34.7 (13.6)	38.3 (15.1)	41.9 (16.5)
	751	Shoulder-elbow length	27.2 (10.7)	29.8 (11.7)	32.4 (12.8)
	194	Buttock-knee length	48.9 (19.2)	53.3 (21.0)	57.8 (22.7)
	420	Hand length	15.8 (6.2)	17.2 (6.8)	18.7 (7.3)
	411	Hand breadth	6.9 (2.7)	7.8 (3.1)	8.6 (3.4)
	416	Hand circumference	16.5 (6.5)	17.9 (7.0)	19.3 (7.6)
				Values in cm with inches in parentheses	

Figure 7-5   NASA Chart Showing Measurements of the Average Woman in the Year 2000 A. D.
From NASA's *Man-Systems Integration Standards*, STD 3000, Vol. 1, Rev A.

Planning Commission that plazas could be made to be magnets for people with a few simple design guidelines. He needed to prove to the Commission that certain design changes would create the increase in plaza utilization that they were looking for. His research was extensive and rigorous enough to prove his points. To complete his study, he used behavior mapping, photo documentation (still photos, movies, time-lapse photos), long term observations (checking seasonal variations), and case studies of several heavily used plazas. He produced "charts in stupefying succession" in order to analyze all the data and applied statistical tests in order to determine the potential for reliability of his predictions. (Whyte 1980).

Most architects who do their own programming and design will not have the budget to do research that is this detailed, but on the larger jobs where the price of making a mistake is too high, it is a great idea to call in the research experts and design a study that works. Zeisel (1981) makes a good case for having a social scientist on the team. There are also architectural firms that specialize in programming and research that can be used as consultants.

PRINCIPLE 22

Do not plant the answer in your question.

Interviews

Interviews can range from casual, fact-finding conversations for systematically finding the answers (to specific questions) to statistically rigorous interviews of large numbers of people. I am a strong advocate of interviews and observation studies as tools for architectural research because, at the casual and systematic levels, they are fairly easy to design and conduct for gaining useful design information. When you want statistically rigorous results, call on the experts unless you are willing to hire someone with the appropriate programming and research expertise to be on your own staff.

The following rules for a focused interview are adapted from Zeisel (1981) and can be further adapted for each level of scientific rigor.

Eleven Easy Rules for a Focused Interview

1. First and foremost, *do your homework*! Know the depth and breadth of the information you wish to get from the person or group of people you plan to interview. Know the topics and issues you wish to cover and the level of detail (casual to systematic) needed for complete information. Know about how long it will take you to get the information. It is a good idea to do a dry run (like a pilot study) with a colleague if you are trying to keep it brief.

Also, inform your respondent about the nature of the interview: who you are, who commissioned the interview, why the interview or program is being done, and why his answers are valuable.

2. Maintain a comfortable level of *eye contact* with the person who is answering your questions. A team of two people can best handle an information-gathering interview, with one to ask the questions and engage the interviewee, and one to take notes on the answers given. A good tactic is to trade off on the asking and note-taking tasks.

3. Allow the interviewee to give her perspective and to raise issues you have not thought of yet. Ask general, open-ended questions first. This works for all but the survey interview, when all you are asking for is detailed information. Then, open-ended questions are usually left until the end to cover any issues that the respondent felt were left out.

4. *Do not plant the answer* you are "looking for" in the question, i.e., "Is your favorite color yellow or purple?" "That was pretty awful, wasn't it?" Instead ask, "What is your favorite color?" "What do you think of a three-way presidential race?"

5. If your respondent needs encouragement to talk, the best tactic is to *be quiet* and let him fill the silence. If you want to be more encouraging, nod and smile during the pause, murmuring "umhum" or some other positive, non-judgmental phrase. If you are not getting enough information on your topic, *gentle probes* such as the following usually work: "Could you tell me more about that?" "What else?" "That's useful information." "What about (a specific aspect or example that they have previously mentioned)?"

6. If your interviewee strays from the topic with too much detail or with irrelevant information, you will need to bring the conversation back *on topic*. The tactics that work best are:

- Be sure to let the interviewee know what you expect to accomplish during the interview at the very beginning.
- Politely thank your interviewee for the information and restate your question to direct attention to the topic you want to discuss: "Let's get back to (respondent)." "I'd really like to know about (respondent)." "What about (_____ aspect)?"

7. State your *time limit* when you make your appointment and *stick to it*! Most in-depth interviews should take between 30 minutes and 1 1/2 hours. If you are spending the whole day with a client, be sure to cover as broad a variety of topics as you will need for your programming information. Generally, the longer the interview, the more benefit your results should be to your respondent. Again, survey interviews are different. They take from 2 to 5 minutes, especially if you are stopping people on the street or in line to eat lunch or get a job done.

8. *Know when to quit*. Be sure to know when you have enough information at sufficient depth to get the job done.

Other signs that warrant a quick wrap-up are a restless respondent, repetition in the answers with no new information, or when she starts to look at her watch several times or starts to fidget.

9. When you think you have covered a topic to your satisfaction, *restate* to your interviewee a *summary* of what you think you have heard so that you are sure you understand the client's interpretation of the information. This process of verification as you go along will save numerous headaches and avoid potential misinterpretation.

10. Be sure to *acknowledge* the value of the information you have been given and thank your interviewee for his time.

11. If you find that you have not allowed enough time or that the topics are more complicated than you first thought, do not press for more than the appointed time, but set up *another appointment* for a later date.

Interviews are great formats for discovering new issues and uncovering goals, values, and preconceived solutions from your clients or building users. They are also good for getting descriptions of situations where you are unable to observe. Keep in mind that these descriptions are second hand and depend upon the selective memory of your interviewee. Interviews can also be used in the same way as casual observation — as a beginning point for your investigation to get a feel for the project at hand, to uncover the main issues, and to get the big picture. Your questions will have to be clearly focused on the type of information you are expecting to get.

Photodocumentation

The camera has long been a standard research tool for anthropologists, sociologists, and designers. More recently

PRINCIPLE 23

Summarize your interview information to confirm your interpretation and acknowledge your interviewee for the value of the information given.

video technology has become inexpensive enough to be within the reach of most researchers. Time-lapse movies are also useful photographic research tools. Developments in digitized images that can be easily fed into the computer are opening a whole new world of uses for images in design research. Photography, in all its many forms, is a great tool for architects and designers to gather and document information vital in gathering the facts and impressions that are the basis for a successful design. Visual images are also a good way to jog the memory when necessary. It is standard practice in many offices to document part of the site analysis with photos. It is not such standard practice to document the users in action on their home turf.

Wagner's (1979) case studies show different techniques for using still photos as a research tool. They clearly plot out the usefulness of photography as a tool for research. Most designers are visually trained to get the nicely composed, well-framed shot. In photodocumentation, it is the information within the image that is the primary goal of the image maker, not necessarily the beauty of the image itself. It does not hurt to have an image captured for research purposes that is also beautiful, but it is better to take the shot at the time when it has the best information in it rather than waiting to shoot until the light is right so the photo will look good.

When gathering facts for site analysis, the site itself will be the lead character. When gathering information about people's behavior, the people in that particular context become the stars of your imaging. Photographs are also good for embellishing the program document with images of the project to set the stage for design.

Other uses for photographs in the program document are to show the need for a particular facility, to show how a proposed new concept works in other places, and to show alternative ways of approaching the design problem.

A Few Brief Rules

Doing your homework is far more vital in photodocumentation than in almost any other research technique. Since a still photo is just a brief slice of time, you need to know which slice of time is most relevant to your research project. Knowing what you are looking for is a guard against having the right instant appear between frames instead of on your film. With video technology, the timing of the image taking is not quite so pressing, but the judgment about the most useful information must happen in the editing room.

For gathering behavioral data, you will want to be as unobtrusive as possible so that the people you are observing will not "perform" for the camera. In many cases you will need to have the permission of the people you are photographing. If you are photographing an institution, such as a hospital or a day care center, and people will be recognizable in your photographs, you will definitely need to get permission to use their photographs in any report or publication you produce. The need for permissions in public settings is not so much a problem if people are far enough away so as not to be recognized and their information value is in their relationship to the particular environment you are documenting. Sometimes you will need to see a scene from a different perspective and a shot from adult waist height will get just the right child's-eye view to document children's behavior.

Photographs are good for documenting conditions of crowding or maximum use, documenting a range of behaviors or roles present in a particular place, and serving as a cross-check for other research methods. I found it particularly useful in my thesis. I was about to make the statement that none of the wheelchair-bound people I was studying had included grab-bars in their tub or shower, when I looked at the photographs of all the bathrooms and discovered that I had missed a grab bar (Duerk 1980). Photodocumentation keeps a record of facts that mere researchers are likely to forget.

Photodocumentation can be used to document the full range of behaviors that a specific type of place allows, a place such as a public plaza, park, or bus stop. Photodocumentation can also be used to document the demand for a particular place or service, such as an automatic bank teller, a cash register line, or a display at a trade show. Queuing demands would probably be best documented with video or time-lapse photography. When I was working for the Facilities Planning Department at the University of Houston in the late 1970s, the landscape architect on staff did a time-lapse movie of the student traffic patterns around the site of a new building before designing the permanent sidewalks. The resultant design was far more responsive to the traffic flows than a plan-generated, geometric solution would have been.

It is very important to choose the timing of your photography very well. Missing the time your site is at maximum use is worse than missing the shot "between frames." Please refer to Chapter 6 on the scientific method for time sampling guidelines.

With the current growth in computer technology, there is a world of opportunity to integrate the use of videos, still photography, and text so that images become a much greater part of the program document than is currently the case. I can imagine a time when the program document is all electronic and, with the push of a computer button, you can see a panoramic video shot of the site or see and hear an excerpt from a critical interview or a visit to another similar building.

SUMMARY

Architectural research is used to understand clients or situations with which the designer is not familiar. It is useful for understanding people of different cultures, religions, socio-economic situations, and roles. Research is also a means for discovering the design issues and problems for a design project and for ascertaining the clients' priorities. Designers almost always use interviews and observations as part of their project initiation routine. They don't always use these techniques systematically to get the most information from their efforts. Research methods are a set of tools for understanding the constraints and the possibilities of a design problem. They allow you to test your assumptions and uncover the values, needs, priorities, and requirements of your clients. These tools are especially valuable if the client group is different from you in any significant way because their hopes, dreams, wants, expectations, and desires are likely to be a surprise. The assumption that "if I like it then you will like it" is hardly ever valid. Good programming research will insure that you uncover all the design issues that are important to the final solution.

In this chapter, four basic methods that are useful in almost all architectural offices are introduced: literature and precedent research, interviews, observation studies, and photodocumentation. If the building type or some aspect of the design problem is new to you, the first thing you should do is find an expert to point you in the direction of the most useful resources. An expert is especially important in beginning a literature search because she will be able to name for you the important books, periodicals, and other documents that will open doors to the rest of the literature. Once you have found the key literature sources, you can use them to find others by use of the bibliographies, other books with the same catalog reference number or subject listing, or books and articles by the same author. Other library resources can be uncovered with a well-structured computer search. Sometimes the client's archives will yield documents that hold valuable programming information. Clear, retrievable documentation of your literature search is important to creating good client reports and for being able to use your research again on a similar project.

Observation is probably the most powerful research tool available to you as a designer. When you do your homework and focus your inquiry by developing a good research question, observation can be very informative whether it is done on a casual, systematic, or statistically rigorous basis. Casual observation yields information about the range of important behaviors in a place, patterns of use, important physical features, and the roles and rules that are appropriate to the place. Systematic observation is a tool for measuring and counting things as a basis for predicting design implications. Here, time and subject sampling become very

important. Behavior mapping is a technique that associates activities with places and shows traffic patterns critical to understanding the circulation. Unobstrusive measures are also important techniques for systematic observation. Statistical observation is the most rigorous of the three categories and requires strict adherance to the rules of the scientific method.

Getting good results from interviews also requires that you do your homework. Know exactly what sort of information you want from your interviewee. The rules for conducting a valuable interview are fairly simple. Maintain eye contact, be quiet and listen attentively, ask open-ended questions that do not hint of the answer you are looking for, probe gently for more information and keep on the topic, summarize your findings and acknowledge your respondent, and be responsible about the time it takes to complete the interview.

The world of photodocumentation is changing from still photographs to video images, computer generated images, and movies. Soon we will be able to experience our design sites and proposals as virtual reality. Until then, visual images will be used as documentation of existing conditions with a level of fine detail that our memories cannot hold. Photos are useful for recording data and for heightening the visual impact of a program document. Good photodocumentation requires that you know what images document the facts necessary for your research and the presentation of results. Visual data often makes the project easier to understand.

CHAPTER 8

ADVANCED
RESEARCH
METHODS FOR
DESIGNERS

METHODS FOR EXPERIENCED DESIGN RESEARCHERS

- GROUP PROCESSES
- GAMING
- DIARIES AND TIME LOGS
- CASE STUDIES
- SIMULATIONS
- QUESTIONNAIRES AND SURVEYS
- EXPERIMENTS
- FULL-SCALE MOCK-UPS
- DESIGN LOG METHOD
- SEMANTIC DIFFERENTIAL

ADVANCED RESEARCH METHODS FOR DESIGNERS

But what is more important is the growing recognition "that the instruction of the architect in the development of a design solution" requires the collection of data and the development of criteria for any new environment.

Constance Perin
With Man in Mind

METHODS FOR EXPERIENCED DESIGN RESEARCHERS

The following research methods require the development of either different types of skills than those normally taught in architecture schools or they require some greater level of social science or statistical skill than the average graduate possesses. For the most part, they are relatively simple to learn and need only attention to the methods of scientific investigation to become useful tools for designers.

Group Processes

Many of the research techniques that work with individuals also work with groups of people and some techniques can only be effective with several participants. Interviews work well with individuals or groups. It just takes some skill in managing the participation process so that the topic gets covered and so that everyone gets a chance to express their own needs and opinions. Other processes are specifically designed with groups in mind.

Here are the basic rules for managing groups:

1. Introduce the problem with enough detail so that the group can do its assigned task. Pose the question for the work session.
2. Make sure that everyone is included and has a chance to have their ideas acknowledged. Introduce each person if they are not known to each other and if the group is not too large.
3. Have each person spend a few minutes preparing their own answer to the question for the day, writing, drawing or using some other notation system.
4. Call on each person to share their key ideas. Make eye contact with all of the individuals in turn and pay close attention to what they say.
5. For efficiency, each part of the process should have a time limit and one person should be appointed time-keeper.
6. Someone from the programming team should be taking notes on all the information that the process generates.

Group processes allow a large number of people to participate in the programming and design of a project. **Charette's** and **RUDAT's** are two types of group processes organized to allow a wide variety of people to have input into the design of a section of their town. These two processes typically involve design students and professionals in a design process that includes a large number of residents of the area being designed. Other participatory processes are documented in the EDRA proceedings and elsewhere. The following is a selection of techniques that have worked well for a number of firms. The list is not meant to be all-inclusive.

Squatters

Squatters is a term coined by Peña (1987) to mean taking a programming or design team to the clients' location for two to five days and working with the client group until the direction of the program or design is agreed upon. In Peña's architectural firm, CRS-Sirrine, the group interview processes are carefully managed in the "programming squatters." One person on the programming team leads the discussion by asking questions and focusing the attention of the client group on certain topics; another team member writes down the new information, and a third team member makes diagrams and brief statements on **"snow cards"** to put up on the wall in the proper categories. If the client group is patient, one person can manage leading the discussion and documenting it, but that is generally not good practice for an efficient meeting.

Snow cards are 5" x 7" blank white cards on which is written each piece of new information. In the CRS-Sirrine format, these cards are organized into categories of Form, Function, Economy, Time, and sometimes Energy with each category divided into Goals, Concepts, Facts, Needs, and Statements of the Problem. At the end of a group interview session, the new information and the categories will be reviewed to check for accuracy and missing information. Groups to be involved in a squatters session may include neighbors who are resisting the project, department staff, user groups such as students or patients, administrators, or potential investors.

The programming team then takes all the information from all the groups and develops the rest of the program, filling in the missing concepts as well as generating an accurate list of space needs and problem statements. The final stage of a squatters session is to report back to the client and get approval of the Goals, Facts, Concepts, Needs, and Statements of the Problem and for moving on to the next phase.

Squatters are a concentrated set of group interviews, presentations, and work sessions that involve the client intensely and are appropriate when you have a large client group and need to reach a consensus in a short period of time. The information generated in these sessions, combined with all the homework that the team has done, is used to develop the final ideas for the program document. Squatters do not work if used too early in the process, before most of the information is available, or if you do not include all interested client and community groups.

Focus Groups

Focus groups are similar to the group interview meeting but, as the name implies, have a very narrow focus. This technique has been developed by market researchers. Focus groups are generally made up of people outside the organization and are called together to discuss specific aspects of a project such as its image in the community, an information flow problem, the probable impact of new technology, or any of a wide variety of topics that are useful in making programming decisions. Focus groups could be called together for one meeting or for a series of meetings on a set range of topics. The results of the discussion should be useful information about the perception of the project, the community's goals, and the community's preconceived notions of what the solution should be. It is a good tool for about any topic that the programmer and client need to explore for a better understanding of the perception of the project by the community or a potential client group.

The meetings are highly structured to cover the topic very narrowly and to be sure that everyone in the group has a turn speaking. Focus groups generally start with an introduction to the problem and can include a verbal presentation, slide show, or short video. Activities of the focus group could include regular discussion, answering fantasy "What if" questions, creating collages of an ideal image, listing the best and the worst qualities of the project situation, or whatever technique seems best to get to the type and quality of information required.

In 1990 when the City of San Luis Obispo was developing a new Land Use Element (LUE) for its General Plan update, the Community Development Department used focus groups to solicit community input. There were a number of meetings held in different parts of the city and planning staff as well as members of the Planning Commission were on hand to facilitate. The people who came to the meetings were people who responded to the city's advertisements for the meetings or who had some particular interest in the LUE update. As such, it was not a random sample as might be needed for more statistical rigor in marketing research. First there was a brief introduction to the planning process and how the results of the meeting were to be used in the planning process. The participants were divided into groups of equal numbers of people (four or five groups of seven to twelve people, in this case) and each group was given a big newsprint pad and asked to write the things about the city they wanted to preserve and the things they wanted to change. Next the groups were invited to make a collage of their ideas of the ideal city using a roll of white butcher paper, crayons, markers, and pictures cut from magazines. All the collages were put up on the wall and one person from each group was then asked to present their group's image to the larger assembly. Discussion followed and all the lists, collages, and notes taken by the staff and the commissioners were collected for further analysis by the city planning staff.

Focus groups are appropriate for generating ideas from moderately large to very large groups of people. The results are qualitative instead of quantitative. People who might be included are concerned citizens, community groups, building staff, administrators, clients, etc. Focus groups do not make much sense when designing for a single department or any other small homogeneous group of people.

Quality Circles

Quality circles are another method of gathering information from a client group. A quality circle is a group of people gathered to focus on improving a set of circumstances — for example, the time it takes to produce a product, the working conditions in the secretarial pool, or the quality of a service delivered to clients. Quality circles are generally formed in house by an organization, meet on a regular basis, and typically have representatives from the groups of people most affected by the problem. The prospect of a new building or a major remodel is a marvelous time to ask the client to evaluate the existing service delivery system and to develop new ways to do things better.

The ongoing deliberations of a quality circle will be useful to programmers in understanding the issues and concerns that need to be addressed in the design. If discussions are to be project specific, it is up to the programmer to request the consideration of a distinct aspect of the design problem be considered or to extract the necessary information from the notes or minutes of the quality circles.

Model Building Workshops

Model building in groups is also a great way to get group input on the concerns about the configuration of spaces. Although the model workshop approach is seldom used with individual clients, it may sometimes be appropriate. The programmer provides a set of pieces — a kit of parts — for building a model of the proposed project or a part of the project. Groups of clients from different areas of concern (departments or services) are chosen to create a model of the spaces in question. A programmer acts as an observer in each group to note all the concerns, considerations, and points of agreement or compromise.

Each model-making group presents their finished model to the whole client group and explains what they like best about their solution, what they had the most trouble with, and what remains unresolved. A discussion follows where each group and each department (or interest area) gets to state what is most important to them to get their jobs done. One of the valuable side effects beyond getting good programming information is that the model workshop often provides an opportunity for each division to see the other's concerns and points of view in a new light. Cooperation on a model-building exercise could lead to cooperation in other ways in the future.

Model building workshops have been used to develop programs for a juvenile service center, group homes for the physically and developmentally disabled, corporate offices, design charrettes, and a wide variety of building types. Model building may also be useful in working with a client who has big ideas and a small site or any other situation where the trade-offs are made clear to the client by manipulating model pieces. Models are very concrete representations of a future building and are easily understood by people who are not designers.

Model workshops take a lot of preparation time and materials as well as a lot of time to analyze the results for programming. Because of this, model workshops are not good for quick and easy programming. They are very valuable for raising concerns with alternative configurations. They give the client group a strong sense of ownership of the design project and they allow the clients to share their ideas about how the spaces would best be arranged.

Gaming

Gaming is generally a set of "what if" scenarios in a format for people to test rules and situations. The best games are set up so that a group of people gets to play out a set of

circumstances that would affect a design's potential. Some games are designed to heighten the designer's awareness of user characteristics or the client's awareness of the design process. However they are designed, the research aspect is the discovery of design issues or areas of information that have been overlooked by other techniques.

Most planning games require a number of people to make them effective as programming tools. It is the value of different perspectives and the taking on of the objectives of the game that make gaming useful to the clients as well as to the programmers. Games can be developed for making all parties aware of the various trade-offs and the consequences of making different priority choices. This is especially true in larger developments and city planning situations. Gaming can also be used as a tool to teach the design process or the development process, or to enlighten a client group about the connections between decisions about program delivery systems and the consequences for architectural programming decisions.

When I was an undergraduate student at NCSU School of Design, a group of students (myself included) developed a game (called merely *Game*) for the Learning Institute of North Carolina that had the purpose of illustrating the connection between teaching objectives and the physical settings in which teaching and learning occur. In the first step, the teachers, principals, or superintendents would imagine a characteristic teaching situation and choose appropriate items from a stack of cards with teaching objectives written on them. The second step was to discuss these objectives with the group and choose the learning methods (another stack of cards) that seemed most appropriate for each teaching objective. The third step was to analyze the different teaching methods and to come to a decision about what physical relationships were required among the participants (students, parents, aides, teachers). Again, several cards were chosen to illustrate these relationships. The physical relationship cards were abstract diagrams representing teaching relationships such as lecture, small working groups, one-on-one discussion, etc. The final step was to work with the group to pick a drawing of a room or setting that would be most likely to support the physical relationships chosen. In subsequent years, Professor Sanoff developed the game further and called it *Role*. See Sanoff (1977) for a more thorough description of the game and its use as a device to engage clients in the design process.

Diaries and Time Logs

Sequences of events are often important to understand in order to make design decisions that enhance the flow of activities. This is true not only in assembly plants, but in many other places such as medical clinics, homes for people in wheelchairs, and offices employing a great deal of computer and business machine technology. Time logs are notations of exactly what a person is doing (in ten or fifteen minute intervals) and are useful in documenting exactly what does happen and how long it takes for certain activities or procedures. Diaries are either formal time logs or informal sequences written by the participant as a self report.

A recording format should be developed to suit the recording of relevant data and the time span of the recording. When observing for a time log, it is important to note the flow of people, things, and information; how long each interaction takes; and who has to wait. There may be other items that are important to your particular design inquiry. It is often impossible or too expensive for you to do all the observations

necessary to create a full time log. Under these circumstances, it is useful to have your research subjects do self reports on their activities, since you do not have the time to do long term observation or since the activity set may be of a private nature. You will still want the information that is critical to design and will have to depend on giving good instructions to the client on how to record the necessary information in a diary or a time log. A diary is a more informal format that focuses on specific activities and the need for notation of the time is not as critical or as exact.

With diaries and time logs you will want to have specific units of analysis so that you get directly useful information instead of peripheral, unuseful information. If, for example, you are interested in knowing the design requirements for supporting a wheelchair client in getting to work in the morning as fast as possible, you will want to instruct her that the music she listens to is not very important, but how long it takes to make the transfers from bed to chair and chair to shower seat, etc., is important. Giving an example of the important activities to note can be quite useful in instructing the diarists to give you the quality of information you need.

It is also important to be clear about how much detail is required. To have a response such as, "I got up, went to the bathroom, and got dressed," is not very useful; neither is, "I pulled myself up with my right hand on the trapeze, steadying myself with my left hand, lifting my left leg off the bed and onto the foot pedals of my chair using both hands, and shifting my weight so that I could then lift my right leg to dangle over the edge of the bed, and then leaned over and grabbed the arm of my chair with my left hand, and bearing the rest of my weight on my right hand, I pushed off the bed and onto the chair seat. . . ." The appropriate amount of information is somewhere in between these two examples — it would describe the number of transfers from bed to chair or from chair to toilet or shower seat, etc., and how long the general activity of "getting dressed" had taken (Duerk 1980).

Be sure to leave a diary or time log form as well as a good set of instructions with the clients so that they have an idea of the format you need. It is a good idea to ask the people doing a diary to observe their own behavior for a few days before writing their diary entries so that they will be more sensitive to the design issues that their behavior raises. Most of us are too busy doing our lives to be constructively critical about how we do things or how our supporting environment is arranged.

Case Studies

Case studies are in-depth investigations of a few examples of the topics under consideration. You might want to do a case study of a set of seven or eight families that will be living in a housing development you are designing or you might do case studies of several innovative schools as preparation for designing a new school. Case studies are used to take a deep, detailed look at a minimum number of situations rather than trying to find a statistical mean of predicting the outcome of a design by looking at a great number of situations or circumstances. When designing a house for a particular family, the family becomes a case study of one. Frank Lloyd Wright often did this sort of study for his clients by living with them for a couple of weeks or through extensive interviewing and observation. When designing *housing* it is not easy to know the needs of your users and case studies will yield a much richer picture of who the typical clients are than any survey could yield. Jane Jacobs (1961) used New York as one large case study.

Yin (1984, 23) has a more detailed definition of a case study:

> "A case study is an empirical inquiry that: investigates a contemporary phenomena with a real-life context; when the boundaries between phenomena and context are not clearly evident; and in which multiple sources of evidence are used."

How To Do a Case Study

First Step: Read Yin (1984). He has written a very handy and brief volume on designing case studies that will help to keep you focused and help you gather just the right amount of information instead of too much information.

Second Step: Develop a research question and define your cases. Are you going to study institutions, groups of people, or individuals? Are you going to be doing casual, systematic, or statistical research? Yin (1984) calls these three categories exploratory, descriptive, and explanatory.

Third Step: This key step is to set up units of analysis — those characteristics, issues, or situations that you will compare across cases. Are you going to compare people, places, or behaviors? If you are studying kindergartens (places) you might want to compare free play periods, meal times, art instruction, story time, and nap time in order to see what the full range of design responses might be. Or you might want to compare circulation patterns, durability of materials, energy use, and maintenance. If you are studying neighborhood groups, you might want to compare friendship patterns, hangout spots, relationships between cars and front or back doors, and children's play patterns. If you are studying doctors, you might want to compare activities such as rounds, surgery, dictation, communication with staff, and lounge behavior.

PRINCIPLE 27

*Set up units of
analysis for case
studies.*

Fourth Step: This step is to determine and clarify data collection methods. Are you going to use archival data, or interviews, observations, time logs, etc.? Case studies can use the full range of research methods discussed in Chapters 7 and 8.

Fifth Step: You must determine how the data will be analyzed in order to produce information meaningful to design. Once the case study is designed, all there is to do is carefully collect the data, analyze it, and write the report.

Almost every case study needs a pilot study to be run first. This is so that you can make all your mistakes and ask the dumb questions of someone who has volunteered for the job rather than taking the risk of offending people whose values might be different from yours. It pays to learn the basic values, major issues, vocabulary, and sensitive spots of your case study subjects before taking on the research.

Case studies can use any of the research techniques available. Since cases are in-depth studies, each question you might want answered may need a different method. You also want to triangulate your results so that you have the important discoveries verified by two or three different methods. Observation and interviewing are the two methods most often paired for doing case studies.

While the methods used in case studies can be rigorously qualitative, the major value of a few in-depth investigations is qualitative results, the answers to the "how" and "why" questions of research.

Simulations

It is too often the case that design researchers are not able to have direct contact with the actual users. In housing projects, the residents change as people move in and out and it is not usually known exactly who will be the first set of residents. In hospitals, the patients change from week to week and the doctors and nurses will change over time as well. Since it is important to understand the needs of the users in order to do the best possible design, **simulations** and samples taken from plausible user populations are the next best thing. Simulations are defined in this text as any situation or set of users that is similar to the design problem or population in enough relevant dimensions to yield useful design information. Simulation situations must be chosen carefully and data must be gathered so that it can be generalized to the design population and/or situation. Idiosyncratic data is not useful, so you must watch for trends and central tendencies instead.

Surrogates

One of the best ways to make up for not having direct access to the actual users is to find a population of people that are very similar to the group you want to study so that the research data is transferable to the new situation. If you know the general market for the housing project, then it may be a simple matter to do research with a group of people who are substantially like the pool of people who will be the eventual occupants in terms of their socio-economic status, ethnic mix, age range, family size, and preferred leisure activities. Patients currently in the existing hospital may have the same characteristics as the patients to be served by the new hospital wing you are designing. Or, women taking prenatal classes may be the target market for the new obstetrics department.

You might even put yourself in a situation that a client or user would be in. For example, try using a wheelchair downtown, on your local campus, or in your favorite restaurant. The experience will give you a very different perspective on the needs of people with mobility impairments.

The same might be done by trying out crutches on a step ramp or trying out a blindfold to see what it is like to be blind when walking across your site. College students might be queried about their dream homes to discover if there are any features that need to be developed for the future first-home-buyer market.

Scenarios

Scenarios are fictionalized accounts of what the lives of the client group might be. They need experience with the client group or a solid sense of environment and behavior issues in different groups of people. While scenarios are not actual research tools, they are good devices to get to know the client by creating a rich, simulated sense of the client's habits and needs. If you can clearly imagine and write about what it would be like to be a child coming in to the hospital for potentially life-threatening surgery, then designing for the pediatric surgery suite, emergency room, and patient room becomes a bit easier to see from the patient's point of view. If you can gather information from a number of different people on the office support staff, you should be able to build a scenario of a typical set of behaviors that raise design problems that need to be solved.

A good scenario will cover a typical day in the life of one of your users (either real or imaginary) or it will cover a specific event from the planning stages to final clean up after the event is over. It is the depth, richness, and behavioral detail of the scenario that allows the designer to use it as a tool for imagining the vital issues and the design responses required to support the people and activities in the new design. A scenario does not describe the physical surroundings to the letter because describing the imagined finished design is the role of the design team at a later time.

Scenarios can be composites of the lives of different people to illustrate a typical set of design issues encountered by a client. Time-logs and diaries could also be fruitful background material for creating a powerful image of the client group through a scenario. In school, scenarios are also used as fanciful, fictitious stories about the potential client, in order to make them come alive for student designers as genuine people.

Some people use the word *scenario* to describe the existing flow of activities in a facility or a set of procedures such as the string of events needed to admit someone to the hospital from the emergency room. I use the word *protocol* to describe an already codified procedure or chain of activities that are the written or standard operating procedures.

Role-Playing

This technique consists of stepping into the shoes of another person for long enough to discover the sets of concerns, issues, constraints, etc., that are operating in the lives of the other people. Sometimes gaming may take on aspects of role playing. Role playing can illuminate the potential roadblocks to passage of a zoning variance, the impacts of certain mitigations to a particular set of environmental impacts, or potential conflicts instigated by a particular set of design characteristics.

If I were the developer and you were a neighbor who protested, "Not in my back yard!" (**NIMBY**), what conversations would we need to have to find out how the project could be developed to satisfy both our needs? This sort of role-playing before a meeting of community groups or before a planning commission meeting could go a long way toward raising issues to be solved before they become crises or politically inflamed topics. All that is necessary for successful

PRINCIPLE 28

If you cannot do your research with the actual clients, find a group of people who are substantially similar to your client population to act as surrogates.

PRINCIPLE 29

When no surrogates are available, putting yourself in the place of the client with a scenario is the next best thing.

role-playing is a set of concerns and attitudes assigned to the players, a problem to be solved, and a willingness to play the parts to the fullest. Role-playing is a very good device to educate designers about people from different cultures as well as about the different people who play a role in the building industry — from contractors and developers to bankers and building inspectors.

PRINCIPLE 30

Raise and try to solve community issues before they become political hot potatoes.

Questionnaires and Surveys

Questionnaires and surveys are best used to discover people's preferences. Surveys cover a very large sample group, focus on very narrow topics, and are an inexpensive way to reach a wide number of people. They usually have a few questions that are very brief and to the point. Surveys may use an interview format, a brief questionnaire, a semantic differential, or any instrument that will get the desired types of responses.

Questionnaires are generally longer, have longer questions, and are looking for more detailed information than surveys. They can be delivered face-to-face just like an interview or they can be answered privately and mailed back to the researcher. Mailed-in questionnaires have a characteristically low response rate. Questionnaires are not very good for eliciting new or general ideas or for uncovering issues or doing background investigations because the instrument itself affects the response.

If you have a well-defined set of options from which to choose, then the research to discover the preferred option can be handled easily with a questionnaire or a survey. Good questionnaires and surveys are objectively very difficult to design and if the project is a big one or the results are critical, then you should get an expert on the job. There are a number of firms that specialize in design questionnaires and surveys and there are programming firms that also have the expertise.

Much of the difficulty of creating a great questionnaire is the rigor with which questions need to be asked. To ask, "Do you bring your lunch to school?" tells you very little about the total picture of the respondent's lunch-time habits that will be very critical to the design of a new campus snack bar. To ask how often students bring their lunches to school (and why) and what and where they eat when they do not bring their lunches is a much more informative approach. As with interviewing, it is also vital that the answer not be planted within the question. Many mailed political surveys use the technique of planting the answer in the question to slant the responses in the desired direction.

Each question should have potential answers that will create useful information for the designer. To know whether elderly ladies prefer showers or tubs does not direct the designer to install one or the other, or some of each, because what they really need is choice. To ask a question from your own personal set of operational definitions may not be at all useful — given that even as simple a word as *friend* can mean different things to different people. Either you must go to the trouble of standardizing your questionnaire and operationalizing all your definitions, be sure that your subject population is homogeneous in terms of definitions, or be willing to be satisfied with a set of opinions that are open to interpretation.

To operationalize definitions of *information flow* in an office (especially one specializing in research and development) you must be able to recognize all types of information: memos, reports, and other archival paper data; computer e-mail and file sharing; verbal information such as meetings, interviews, and casual conversations; and multimedia such as drawings, demonstrations, movies, videos, and photos. Operationalizing the questions will take doing a pilot study to see if you get the kinds of results you were seeking or if the questions generate unexpected answers due to the respondents' definitions.

When people agree to answer a questionnaire or a survey, they do so for their own reasons, not your reasons. Generally one of their reasons is to help and to give "good" answers. This sometimes means that people say what they think you want to hear so that you will like them or that they can feel that they are being nice or helpful. If the questions are not set up so that this potential bias is avoided, then you will not have the reliable results you worked so hard to obtain.

Questionnaires and surveys are good for finding out if people prefer Plan A to Plan B, or Site R to Site Q, especially when there is room for the respondents to give the rationale for their choices. If the choices are clear and will guide design sufficiently to be worth the energy it takes to do a good questionnaire or survey, then set it up and take enough time to do the job right.

Experiments

If it is possible to test a proposed design intervention before a project is built, it is a great idea to control the test so that the results will give a good idea whether or not the effect of the proposed intervention is as positive as envisioned. It is best to make the mistakes experimentally rather than hear about them from the client after the project is built and occupied.

Experiments can use methods of observation and interviewing and can possibly use some group processes with this addition: the test is made to determine whether the design change creates the desired change in perception or behavior. A fairly simple research design will usually suffice — the "ABA" design. The first *A* stands for the base-line or existing condition. The *B* stands for the new or experimental condition, and the final *A* stands for returning to the original conditions. The reasoning behind this design is to avoid the "Hawthorne Effect" (Adams 1979). Simply stated, the Hawthorne Effect is the effect on behavior of making any change. In some cases, no matter what the physical change is, the fact that a change was made will affect people's behavior such that, when the conditions are returned from the experimental conditions (B) to the base-line conditions (A), the change in behavior increases rather than returning to the base-line behaviors.

The story is basically this: in the Hawthorne works of Western Electric, management decided to try some experiments to see if they could change conditions to increase the productivity of the manufacturing workers. They talked to the workers to see what changes might work. The first thing to be tried was to change the light levels out on the plant floor. Production went up. After raising the light levels several more times and remarking on the increase in production levels, the experimenters tried lowering light levels to test if the light levels were at the right level and did not need to be any brighter. To their astonishment, production went up yet again. Obviously it was not the light levels that were the source of the increased production. With much interviewing, they finally discovered that the workers were so happy to be asked about their working conditions and to have a sense that management cared about them, that any change, either higher or lower light levels, produced an increase in productivity. The conclusions were that the change in productivity was an effect of workers feeling noticed and of their needs paid attention to rather than an effect of changing lighting levels.

There are a number of other simple research designs that designers might want to use if the design implications will affect enough people or if the potential for a mistake is not worth the risk of ignorance. Campbell and Stanley (1963) have written a short little handbook that explains sixteen different experimental and quasi-experimental designs that range from the one shot case study to multiple time-series designs proposed for educational settings. The basic tenets of these research designs are useful for anyone wishing to do experimental design research.

Full-Scale Mock-Ups

Often new designs for hospital patient rooms and furniture are tested at full scale before the patient wing is built because they are very expensive units and they will be repeated a large number of times. People who will be serving patients in the hospital in question will be asked to do some role playing and test the design of the room, its electronics, its furniture, and its equipment. They will try to discover any impediments to the delivery of patient care, such as surveillance, giving intravenous solutions, or giving the patient a bed bath.

Other building parts that might be subjected to full-scale mock-ups are prison cells for maximum security prisoners, laboratories demanding highly precise workstations, windows for skyscrapers, and any building part that will need to be protected from high vibrations or noise sources. Full-scale models are done only when the risk of failure is too high not to test the building room or component.

Design Log Method

The Design Log Method by Spivack (1978) is a tool to record the research efforts and the resulting decisions, not a research tool in itself. It is included here because it is a very useful way of managing the research component of a programming effort. It is also useful in keeping records of programming and design decisions with a client over a number of projects, through time, or when a new facility is designed to implement a new method of service delivery.

For the purpose of controlling, recording, and retrieving successful and unsuccessful solutions, records are kept in the following categories: observation/diagnosis, performance requirements/prescription, generic specifications/treatment (design concepts). These records are kept for each space in the building to be designed. The observations are kept in chronological order and are a record of all new information gathered as well as the changes in priorities or operation uncovered by research. The design log serves as a reminder of changes made during design that affect the programming of the spaces. It serves as a running record of decisions, so that the program doesn't have to be rewritten each time a new piece of information is uncovered or a new concept is developed. Users' manuals could be developed using the design log as a resource for the unfolding set of intentions about how the building might best be used. Design logs are useful for an ongoing building program that changes with time and technology such as a school, a clinic or hospital, a prison, an insurance company, or an architectural firm. Such a must be maintained by a knowledgeable person, with the intention of using it for regualr reference, or it becomes just one more set of files that gather dust.

Semantic Differential

Over the past couple of decades the **semantic differential** has been used for a number of perceptual studies (Osgood, Suci, and Tannenbaum 1967; Sanoff 1977; and Hershberger 1972). It is my opinion that the semantic differential is not for the novice user when applied to surveys, but that it can be an extremely valuable tool for self-communication or for communication with a client or design team with whom you have a long-standing relationship.

Basically, the semantic differential is a list of paired opposite words with a scale between them used to rate the qualities of an object or a place. There are pairs that describe the potency (strong/weak), pairs that describe the evaluation (good/bad), and pairs that describe the activity (fast/slow). Usually the scale is a five point or more odd-numbered scale, unless it is not desirable to have a neutral point in the middle of the scale (Osgood, Suci, and Tannenbaum 1967). The following is an example of some typical pairs of words:

The people rating a space will be asked to place a mark on the blank that most clearly approximates their evaluation of the space. The blanks in the first line of Figure 8-1 could be

static   __ __ __ __ __   dynamic

warm   __ __ __ __ __   cool

hard   __ __ __ __ __   soft

beautiful   __ __ __ __ __   ugly

cluttered   __ __ __ __ __   clean

Figure 8-1 Semantic Differential Scales

read as "very static," "somewhat static," "neutral," "somewhat dynamic," and "very dynamic." This is a very good tool for a discussion with a client who wants a space that is dynamic, warm, beautiful, and clean. The semantic differential could be used by the client to describe two separate spaces that he likes for different reasons and you, the designer, could discuss the qualities of each space that created the perceptions of the level of each attribute. In Figure 8-2, the box represents a response to space #1 and the circle represents a response to space #2. Such a discussion would serve to create a body of shared meanings and interpretations between you and your client about what physical qualities mean "dynamic," "warm," or "beautiful." Most novices using this instrument would have a great deal of difficulty

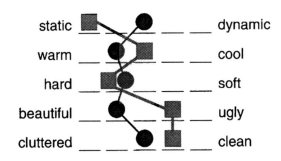

Figure 8-2 Sample Responses to a Semantic Differential

developing an interpretation useful for design from a survey using the semantic differential. This is because words in our language have so many interpretations — especially when one's aesthetic judgment comes into play. For example, should the opposite of *clean* be *cluttered* or *dirty*?

PRINCIPLE 32

Unless you are an expert, use the semantic differential only for your own evaluation of a design or to create a common vocabulary with a client.

SUMMARY

The more advanced methods in this chapter require either more preparation or more knowledge than the methods of the prior chapter. Most group processes require that the leader is skilled in making sure that everyone has the right amount of information and has the opportunity to have their ideas heard. Programming squatters are a very carefully orchestrated series of meetings with the client group(s) to insure that the maximum amount of information and maximum number of decisions are made in a minimum amount of time. Focus groups, quality circles, model-building workshops, and planning/programming games all require group management skills and a lot of preparation.

Diaries and time logs demand that you know exactly what your units of analysis are and that you develop clear, easy to follow instructions for the people you ask to do these self-reports. Since you are not there to do the looking, you must instruct them as to the best way to look and report their findings.

I think that a case study can be a very fruitful design research tool. It allows in-depth study of a few situations and can yield very rich design and programming information. Simulations are used when you cannot contact the actual clients or get them to use self-report techniques. When no surrogates are available, scenarios and role-playing techinques serve as an inquiry into the lives of the clients and to raise issues that might not be raised otherwise.

Questionnaires and surveys should be designed by someone who has experience getting good, reliable results. There are so many factors that could interfere with the outcome that it takes an expert to do an adequate job.

Experiments are useful to test the effectiveness of some design interventions. They answer the question, "Does this design change produce the desired result?" Full-scale mock-ups can be used to answer the same question. Both methods require a lot of preparation and can be expensive.

The Design Log Method is a record-keeping procedure that integrates design research and programming information management so that programmers and clients can keep track of a highly dynamic information system. Here, the results of research are tested in programming and designing in a very tight feedback loop such as an experimental psychiatric clinic that tests changes in both treatment and environmental milieus.

The semantic differential has been used by many researchers as a survey instrument. I prefer to use it as a tool to develop a vocabulary of understandable terms shared with a client or a design team. It is generally too much work to develop the paired opposites to work for your client group.

Many of the techniques discussed in this chapter would profit from the assistance of a rigorous social science researcher or from consultation with a firm that specializes in programming and design research. If the project is large enough or the consequences of making a design mistake are high enough, high quality, rigorous research is essential.

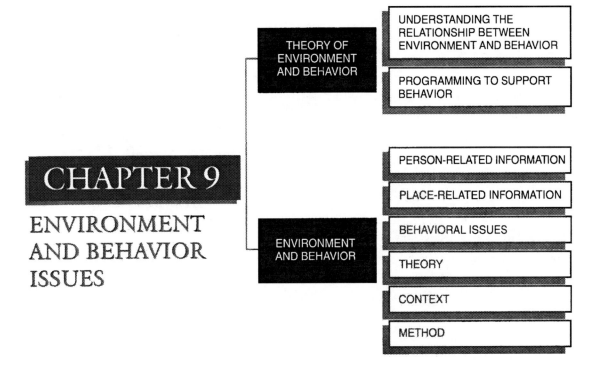

CHAPTER 9

ENVIRONMENT AND BEHAVIOR ISSUES

THEORY OF ENVIRONMENT AND BEHAVIOR
- UNDERSTANDING THE RELATIONSHIP BETWEEN ENVIRONMENT AND BEHAVIOR
- PROGRAMMING TO SUPPORT BEHAVIOR

ENVIRONMENT AND BEHAVIOR
- PERSON-RELATED INFORMATION
- PLACE-RELATED INFORMATION
- BEHAVIORAL ISSUES
- THEORY
- CONTEXT
- METHOD

ENVIRONMENT AND BEHAVIOR ISSUES

*All the world's a stage,
And all the men and
women merely players.*

William Shakespeare
As You Like It

THEORY OF ENVIRONMENT AND BEHAVIOR

Understanding the Relationship Between Environment and Behavior

Good programming demands that the programmer make available to the designer all the information about people's behavior that is useful for creating the design that best supports the clients' needs. This chapter will illustrate some of the questions that one would ask about the relationship between designed environments and human behavior and will elaborate on some of the issues raised by such an inquiry. The first part of the chapter covers environment and behavior (E/B) theory and some of its evolution. The second part covers specific environment and behavior issues and their impacts on programming and design. This discussion is but a brief look at the broad field of environment and behavior interactions and you are encouraged to use the bibliography as a resource for other sources of information to answer your further questions.

Reciprocal Relationship

A basic assumption for this chapter is that people and their behaviors are a part of a whole system that includes place and environment, such that behavior and environment cannot be empirically separated. That is to say, human behaviors always *happen in a place* and they cannot be fully evaluated without considering the environmental influence. For most people, the influence of the environment is most often subtle and may go completely unnoticed in their conscious awareness.

Likewise, place cannot and should not be evaluated as separate from human behavior. One cannot evaluate a designed environment without understanding the users for whom it was designed and the purposes and activities that the place supports. This expresses an adaptation of the ecological model of environment/behavior as described by Rapoport (1975a) and is represented in its most fundamental form by the a simple reciprocal relationship (Figure 9-1).

Figure 9-1 Reciprocal Relationship Between Environment and Behavior

The following are examples of the influence of the environment on people's behavior:

1. People going through a low space into a high-ceiling space for the first time almost always look up when they get into the larger space.
2. "People sit where there are places to sit" (Whyte 1980). Whyte (1980) illustrates a great deal of research and notes that the above statement is the most influential in the design of well-used plazas.
3. People adapt — they walk around objects and duck to go under low clearances.

Here are examples of people's behavior influencing environment:

1. At the University of Illinois, faculty were assigned top floor offices with access only through a keyed elevator. They were expected to go down to escort students to their offices. The faculty got tired of this arrangement very quickly and propped open the door to the fire stairs so that students could make their own way to the top floor. This action effectively negated the safety purpose of a totally enclosed fire stair.

2. Holding a wedding, concert, or regular service in a church sanctuary makes being in that space a completely different experience from visiting it on a weekday when it is empty. A celebration usually demands special decorations for the environment, changes in lighting, different music, and different numbers of people.

3. People take the very shortest perceived path. As a result, they create many paths through grassy areas and shrubs instead of using the sidewalk that was developed using beautiful geometry.

With just a little thought you can see that these examples are surely more complicated than just drawing an arrow representing an effect in one direction from E to B or from B to E.

Behavior Surrounded by Environments

Another way that this E/B system has been conceptualized is to look at an environment as if it were a stage for the human drama; in Goffman's terms the action happens in the middle of the environment (Rapoport 1975a, 129). Here behaviors are viewed as being embedded in an environment. See Figure 9-2. While it is true that behaviors do happen in environments, this model leaves out the interactive nature of mutual influence.

Figure 9-2   Behavior Embedded in Environment

The most basic goal for design, as a purposeful activity, is to achieve the best possible state or balance for the whole system of behavior and environment. This dramaturgical view is a useful analogy for seeing that a balance is necessary and that the set and the actors have their different roles in making the play a hit or a flop.

Behaviors and Environments as Interdependent Interactions

The richest conceptualization of the environment/ behavior field is that it is an interactive and interdependent set of systems. This conceptualization of environment/behavior interactions is further viewed as an open system exposed to the influences of outside elements and other similar E/B systems. In this manner, all behavior is a set of interacting sub-systems of E/B interaction (Figure 9-3).

Figure 9-3   Sub-systems of Behaviors Embedded in Environments

Barker (1968) has conceptualized environments as **behavior settings** (sub-systems, if you will) and he illustrates that the same people behave very differently in different places. People act in similar ways in the same place — church, post office, beach — where the agreed-upon cultural rules, the

boundaries, and the artifacts combine to signal appropriate behavior (Figure 9-4).   There is a more detailed discussion of behavior settings in the theory section of this chapter.

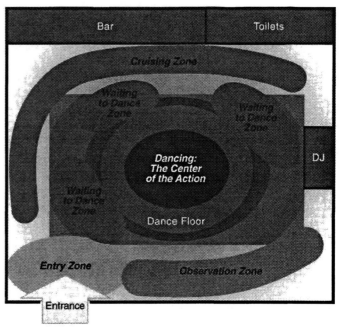

Figure 9-4   Behavior Zones in a Dance Hall

The world, as we experience it, is constituted of behaviors, perceptions, and environments that are inseparable from one another — one cannot think of a particular behavior or experience without its constitutive environment. Even in the world of our dreams we create new and phenomenal environments to go with ideal behaviors. Thus it is more reasonable to think of behavior as fused with *and dependent upon* its environment in such a manner that it takes an *activity and an environment to create an experience.*

In the same manner, any designed environment or object has behavior that is implicitly expected to accompany it. This set of expectations is a part of the culture in which the environment and the behaviors occur. When we design particular places, we are also designing the expectations for the behavior in that place. The planners of a junior high school are contemplating a set of behaviors that has to do with learning and teaching, and the students are adding another set of expectations and behaviors that has to do with seeing and being seen as social and emotional beings rather than as intellectual beings. In another example, with a chair one expects sitting, looking, and furniture rearrangement with tables or desks. One does not necessarily expect lovemaking, being balanced on a juggler's nose, or floating down a river. Yet the design of a chair does not always prohibit these unexpected activities just as the design of a junior high school does not prohibit social display. Figure 9-5 represents the intimate interaction between behavior and environment and includes the culture and social values that influence both.

Inappropriate behavior is often a response to some perceived inadequacy of the environment/behavior set (see Figure 9-6). Vandalism in the form of spray painting gang names on walls and subways shouts volumes about the unmet needs for appropriate media of expressing group identity and pride. Litter generally means that a trash receptacle is not convenient. "Dog tracks" through the shrubs or grass indicate that the shortest route is not on the sidewalk. Cars parked along the railroad right-of-way indicate that there is not enough parking near a particular destination. A target or goal painted on the side of a building speaks of unmet recreational needs.

Figure 9-5   Interdependent Environments and Behaviors in Context

Consequences / Motive	Instantaneous Damage Demanding Immediate Attention	Cumulative Damage Demanding Eventual Attention
Conscious	Malicious Vandalism	Non-malicious Property Damage
Not Purposeful	Misnamed Vandalism	Hidden Maintenance Damage

Figure 9-6   Redefinition of Vandalism.
From *Stopping School Property Damage* by John Zeisel.
Reproduced by permission of the author.

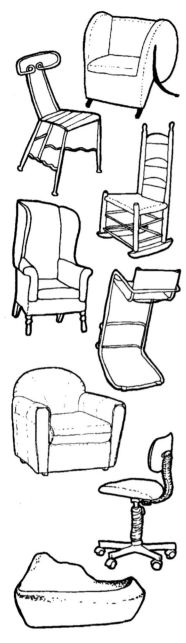

Different Chair Designs for
Different Needs

How a chair becomes exactly what it is, as a specific object, is also dependent upon the values of the people who are designing it and of the people who are going to use it. These values come from the culture at large (chairs are different in formal Japanese society than they are in the society of British commoners or North American yuppies), from religious values (compare Shaker chairs with the chairs of Gothic cathedrals) and from personal values (a chair for avant-garde pop artist Andy Warhol is different from a chair for conservative Margaret Thatcher) as well as from social rules (compare a living room chair and a kitchen chair) and from the state of the local economy (chairs in a rural African village differ from chairs designed for the castles of Germany). The sidebar shows a variety of chairs responding to different needs and values.

Programming to Support Behavior

Good questions you might ponder at this point, "What should designers do: design as if the behavior determines the environmental response, or design as if the environment determines the behavioral response? What are our priorities and values?" In any system of interacting environment and behavior there is always a balance between the power of the environment and the power of the behavior — neither *determines* the other. If the behaviors are exemplary, then environments designed to support and enhance those behaviors are ideal. If the environment is exactly as it should be, then the behaviors need to shift to keep it that way. Most of the real world is messier than that and there is a necessary interdependence of the designed environment and the ensuing behaviors.

In most human consciousness, the environment is not seen as a major definer of behavior. Yet many designers act as if their designs can make people do certain things. I do not subscribe to this attitude of architectural determinism. I believe that it is much more realistic and useful to view the influence of an environment on behavior as being supportive of the intended behavior, being neutral toward the behavior, or negating the possibility of that behavior. The environment cannot force anyone to do anything; they can only create the circumstances where the most likely tendency is to behave in a particular way. Trash cans support trash disposal behavior. Benches and ledges support sitting. Freeways support driving fast. Narrow cobblestone streets support walking or driving slowly. Store windows support looking at things to buy. Ramps support handicapped access. A path does not always support walking on it. A grassy field allows many different behaviors. A chair and a desk are the stage set for many different activities. A classroom does not necessarily insure that learning will happen or that it will not happen. A classroom will insure that a full-court basketball game does *not* happen merely by its limiting dimensions. A bank prohibits buying groceries and hardware because of the absence of those products. A strong fence with a small gate prohibits the entry of large vehicles.

The Lindeman Center in Boston is a beautiful, curvilinear, sculptural building of "corduroy" concrete. It has been reported that its unpredictable form contributes to the disorientation of the mentally ill clients who come to the Center. Their perceptions and likely behaviors were not fully considered in the programming of the building. The same oversight was true in the furnishing of the Joslin Diabetes Clinic. The big, modern, curving couches that were installed in the lobby have been uncomfortable and very difficult for older diabetes patients to get out of because of their poor circulation and frailty.

If design is the ideal shaping of an environment to support the behavior expected within it, then programming is the ascertainment and evaluation of those factors (issues and constraints) most likely to be critical to creating that fit between values, and interpreting the influence of the environment upon the desired behaviors. With the above set of assumptions, it becomes clear that complete and absolute answers about the consequences of design upon behavior and of behavior upon the designed world are not available, and any design becomes a *hypothesis* as to a final set of behaviors. Markus (1972, 10) says it another way — quantification and exact description of the human experience of an activity in an environment is nearly impossible . . . but, *designers must make decisions anyway*. It is the job of architectural programming to set out the parameters and gather the best information possible with the best research techniques (see Chapters 7 and 8), to give the designers the chance of making the best hypotheses possible, and to be able to test their progress along the way. Programming is a structure for creating an informed basis for making the best possible decisions with the incomplete information available by making assumptions and hypotheses and testing their validity.

Environment/Behavior as an Open System

For programming and design to be the most effective, they need to take into account many factors. If we look at the environment behavior interaction as an open system, then we see the wide world of influences that the programmers must

research so that the designers may have the most complete set of information. An open system is vulnerable to influences from outside the system and from other subsystems within the greater system. For example, the *idea* of democracy (a behavior) had a great influence upon the activities of the Chinese students in creating a particular sort of environment (the Statue of Liberty, the tanks) in Tienanmen Square. They have changed the meaning (behavior) of that square for many Chinese people for generations to come. An example in which behavior affects behavior which affects the environment which affects behavior.

A second example comes from Peru. El Niño warms the temperature of the ocean current close to shore and as a result, small fish do not get the food that normally comes when the cold water is churned from the bottom of the ocean to the top layers. This lack of food kills the fish, which causes the Peruvian economy to suffer, which lowers the inhabitant's standard of living, which changes both their behavior and their environment. In this example, an environmental change creates another environmental change which affects behavior which affects environment.

In a third example, the federal government decided to do away with revenue sharing, so the local officials decided not to raise taxes and to have new development fund its own infrastructure. As a result, the repairs on the old infrastructure and its expansion languish for lack of funds and the environment deteriorates. Here, behavioral changes affect behavior which in turn affects environment.

One can usually make clear distinctions between what an environment is and what a behavior is, but the influences of one upon the other are complex and not always clear or direct.

> ### PRINCIPLE 33
>
> *Environments enhance, negate, or are neutral towards behavior; they do not force or determine particular behaviors.*

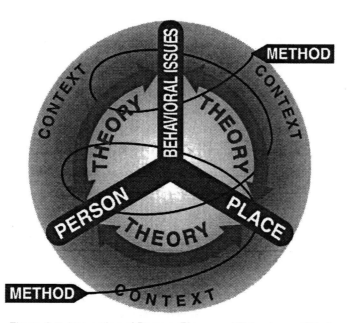

Figure 9-7 Interaction of Person, Place, and Behavior and Their Context with Method and Theory.
Adapted from *Environmental Design Research Directions* by Moore, Tuttle, and Howell, 1985.

ENVIRONMENT AND BEHAVIOR

This section introduces some of the key concepts in environment/behavior interaction and does not pretend to be totally inclusive of the field. The intention is to give you an understanding of some of the major issues and some of the research that has been done in the past and to point to a few of the resources available for further information. Each design project will have different priorities and this information will point to important considerations in some projects and to incidental issues in others. The attempt here is to share anecdotal information that will inspire you to do the research necessary to do the best possible job of programming and design.

Person-Related Information

Most person-related aspects discussed here are sets of facts that relate to the different characteristics of people that are necessary for making decisions about particular design issues. Anthropometrics (body measurements) are important to make decisions about physical comfort, about convenience, about legibility and visibility. The limits of human performance create the demands on environmental design.

Anthropometrics

NASA has developed the most complete set of anthropometric data of which I know. This extensive aggregate of data is used for sizing space suits, equipment controls, control panels, space shuttle, and sky lab compartments, etc. NASA has even projected how tall people will be 50 years from now based on the average tall male and the average short female (NASA 1989, 3-1 to 3-75). The standard for the tallest male is the 95th percentile of North American men and for the shortest woman, the 5th percentile of Japanese women, assuming each to be 40 years old. It is projected that the average North American male will grow by 0.4 inches (1.0 cm) per decade and that the average Japanese woman will grow by 1.0 inches (2.6 cm) per decade. NASA periodically updates these projective assumptions with real data.

Environmental History

Meaning, Values, and Symbols: We carry the meanings we give to environments into the future from our past. The things we loved or appreciated as children are the basis for our preferences and choices in adult life, as well as the basis for what we avoid. Starting with our early experiences we build a

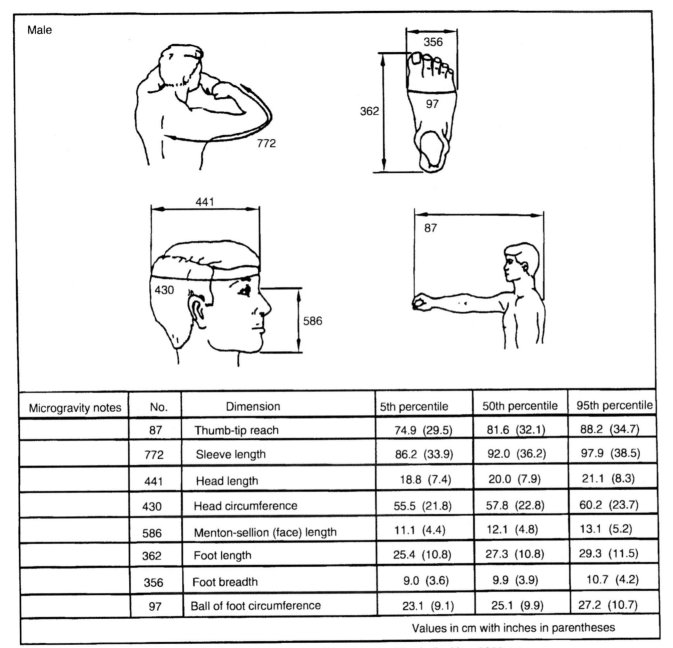

Microgravity notes	No.	Dimension	5th percentile	50th percentile	95th percentile
	87	Thumb-tip reach	74.9 (29.5)	81.6 (32.1)	88.2 (34.7)
	772	Sleeve length	86.2 (33.9)	92.0 (36.2)	97.9 (38.5)
	441	Head length	18.8 (7.4)	20.0 (7.9)	21.1 (8.3)
	430	Head circumference	55.5 (21.8)	57.8 (22.8)	60.2 (23.7)
	586	Menton-sellion (face) length	11.1 (4.4)	12.1 (4.8)	13.1 (5.2)
	362	Foot length	25.4 (10.8)	27.3 (10.8)	29.3 (11.5)
	356	Foot breadth	9.0 (3.6)	9.9 (3.9)	10.7 (4.2)
	97	Ball of foot circumference	23.1 (9.1)	25.1 (9.9)	27.2 (10.7)
			Values in cm with inches in parentheses		

Figure 9-8   NASA Measurements of the Average Man in the Year 2000 A.D.
From NASA's *Man-Systems Integration Standards,* STD 3000, Vol. 1, Rev. A.

repertoire of experiences that become the foundation for our values: cultural, aesthetic, sociological, and behavioral. Our value system is the basis for making judgments about what is good, bad, or neutral, about what the ideal situation might be. In the United States, the symbols of home (a pitched roof), church (a tall, white steeple), government (some modification of the Greek temple), and business (the urban tower) become a part of our identity that is absorbed from our culture.

Expectations: Designers' and clients' values and expectations vary depending on their past experiences with a different set of environments. It is the job of programmers and designers to understand how their values and expectations are different from those of their clients so that the project does not impose a clashing set of values and expectations. One reason why it is so important for architects to travel and actually experience as much of the world as possible is that it is critical to have an understanding of your own values and be able to determine the differences between your own system and your clients' system of values. With a broad understanding of different values, conflicts can be recognized and resolved rather than assumed not to exist. Knowing an assumption when you see one is a very valuable tool.

Perceptions of Environment

Noticeable Differences: **JND** is a term in the study of psychology that stands for "*just noticeable difference.*" It means the change required in a stimulus (such as sound, color, light, pressure, etc.) that is just barely noticeable. Degradation of our environment usually happens so gradually (below the JND) that it has to get to be very bad before it is truly noticeable. It is important for programmers to be able to specify the performance of an environment in terms that lead to an optimal environmental design rather than one that is a

slight misfit and with wear and tear will become a worse fit. Where differences are supposed to be noted, it is important not to make them too subtle, like changes in color might be. Many people are color blind and need a great contrast in color if noting color differences is an important communication. One step in a walkway is generally forbidden and considered bad design because the level change is too small for many people to see and they often trip over the single step.

Information from Five (or Six) Senses: Most of us who are design professionals, such as programmers, architects, landscape architects, or graphic designers, are visual people. That means that our preferred mode for deriving most of our information from the environment is through our eyes. It also means that we do not always take into account the design potential of information gathered through the other senses. Blind people need an environment that is tactile and acoustically tuned so that they might navigate more easily. Tom Grondona designed Claudia's (a cinnamon roll store) so that the odors from the bakery were wafted out into the corridors of Horton Plaza, thus ensuring that all hungry passers-by were tempted to stop. The sense of taste is very difficult to design into an architectural artifact and I do not advocate lick and taste buildings.

The sixth sense is the sense of time: to plant a redwood sapling is to envision a magnificent tree of 40 or 50 feet in height in a mere 30 years. To design rental housing is to create the stage set for a number of different domestic lives. To build a nursing unit is to predict how patient care will be managed for years to come.

Visual Illusions: The illusions of perspective were manipulated by the Romans and Greeks to great effect. The Parthenon is a monument to this type of visual enhancement of a visual phenomenon. Luckeish (1965) describes the

<hr>

PRINCIPLE 34

Discover and test assumptions about client meanings, values, and expectations.

Muller-Lyer illusion, which creates the perception that lines of equal size are of unequal length (Figure 9-9). Gregory (1966) argues that this illusion is not perceived by people who live in round houses, but only by those of us who are used to the inside corner of a room being closer than the outside corner of a building of the same height.

Another experiment that shows the potential distortions of our visual perception is the Ames room. Since we judge distance from the cues of relative size, overlap, convergence of parallel lines, regression of surface details and textures, and changes in light and shade to indicate depth, it is possible to create a mock-up of a room that is dimensionally distorted but looks real enough to make the viewer think that a person grows or shrinks when walking across the far side of the room (Architectural Psychology Research Unit 1974). See the sidebar diagrams.

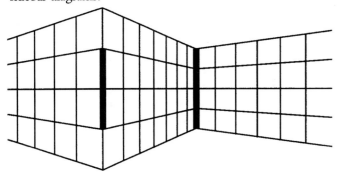

Figure 9-9 Muller-Lyer Illusion

Interaction of Material Data and Perceptual Data:
Much of the data that designers use, such as information about building materials, is unrelated to the potential human behavioral responses to different variables. For one telling example, Sweets Catalogs give us information about the STC (sound transmission class) and other properties of building materials. Anatomy books give us much information in great detail about how the human ear works. Yet we design as if we really know very little about the interaction of these two sets of information. We do not have a standard set of design guidelines or strategies for making great acoustic environments. See Figure 9-10.

Many poorly designed acoustic environments occur in our schools and colleges. The "cafetorinasium" of elementary schools with a tight budget generally does not work acoustically for the auditorium or cafeteria functions. More examples are the gallery that is turned into a lecture hall because of the lack of an appropriate space; the office building that bounces sound off a hard, reflective underfloor through an air space above the well-insulated wall; the classroom building built of concrete for aesthetic or budget reasons; and the chemistry or design lab turned into a lecture hall or a place to view videos. Each of these designs do not work because the placement or use of a particular material did not meet an ideal combination of the human need for privacy and noise separation, building form and material, and the anatomy of the human ear.

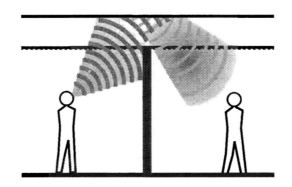

Figure 9-10 Partitions That Are Below the Structure Allow Sound to Bounce Between Rooms

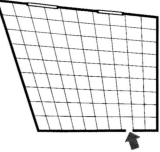

Plan with View Hole

Actual Rear Wall

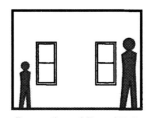

Perception of Rear Wall

Ames Room Illusion

People Types

Different groups of people have different requirements, needs, and desires that require design responses. There are two types of characteristics that need a programmer's attention. One is a set of fixed characteristics, and the other is a set of ascribed characteristics. Body, age, and ethnicity are characteristics that are unavoidable and can't be changed. These immutable characteristics make up the fixed set. Roles, jobs, and socio-economic characteristics are a shifting set of attributes that we can change, depending upon the setting and upon our choices. These malleable characteristics make up the ascribed set of characteristics to which designers need to respond.

Age Characteristics: The elderly are a community of people designers paid a great deal of attention to in the 1970s and 1980s because of the abundance of funding for elderly housing. As people get older and more frail, they have a tendency to loose their agility, their sight, hearing, and sensitivity to touch that they had in their youth. Aging is a progression of physical degeneration that is sometimes accompanied by mental degeneration as well. Under these conditions, the physical environment needs to be especially supportive in order for many elderly people to live independently as long as possible.

Middle-aged people are not specifically thought of as a special-needs category. They are customarily thought of as part of the normative population for whom we are designing. If they are full-sized, fully functioning adults, then they are the usual client, rather than the unusual client.

Yuppies — young urban professionals — are the idealized norm in North American society. These are the young, healthy, beautiful people with money to buy the architect-designed house with a professionally landscaped lawn in a planned community. These are the owners of the houses that show up in architectural magazines: the people we all wish we could be, the realization of the American dream. Yet, for the most part, they are not the ones who live in all the housing, work in all the buildings, or inhabit the inner city or farms. Designers need to be aware of the clientele for whom they are really designing and realize that their clients are not merely a reflection of themselves.

Teenagers are probably the one age group that lacks representation in the normative design of places. When teenagers are not in school and not working, they need places to be social and to play. They need places for sports, for just belonging with their friends, for seeing and being seen, for practicing adult responsibilities, for being away from the adults, and for making a contribution to their world. The design of cities cannot do all the above, but with an awareness of the specific needs of teenagers, city design can be improved to support more of their needs.

Preteens need to be able to explore and to expand their known world in safety. They, too, need places to play, trails and bike paths, places to gather, places to practice sports skills, and places to discover new things. This is the group for whom many parks and playgrounds have been designed.

Toddlers are just beginning to explore their world. They need protected places to play, make messes, and be close to their parent or responsible caregiver. In some instances, such as day care centers and kindergartens, they need special design supports because of their size. Such things as windows, furniture, and cabinets at standard adult heights do not serve toddlers' needs. Marcus and Sarkissian (1986) go to great detail about the kinds of places that work for medium density housing and emphasize landscaping for toddlers and preteens.

This is a superlative book for understanding how site planning and design make a considerable difference in people's use of and satisfaction with their housing situation.

Physical Ability: In recent years the advances in medical technology have allowed people confined to wheelchairs to live longer and to be more vital in their participation in the stream of life. As a result, the old ways of making buildings without accommodations for travel by wheelchair are no longer appropriate. ANSI standard #111.7, the ADA, and California Title 24 give a very complete set of guidelines for making buildings accessible to the handicapped. They cover not only accessibility by the mobility impaired, but also people who are blind or have hearing impairments. One of the best tricks I have heard is of a contractor who had a wheelchair on site and used it to test the building as it went along — especially if there were any uncertainties about the exact dimensions to be built.

Creating an environment that allows people in wheelchairs free access to all places also creates an environment that is "user friendly" for people pushing strollers or shopping carts; for people on bikes, tricycles, or skateboards; and for people making deliveries of heavy objects on dollies. People on crutches are often hindered by some of the design accommodations that facilitate wheeled travel. Ramps are much more difficult to negotiate than stairs. The ideal is to have both options close to each other so that a choice can be made.

Blind people are minimally accommodated by having Braille labels on elevator buttons and in other places likely to cause confusion. Their world can be greatly enhanced by textures and acoustics that contribute to their ability to orient themselves by touch and sound. Drinking fountains that are clear underneath so that people in wheelchairs can use them easily are a potential hazard to blind people using canes, unless they are properly recessed and do not protrude into the line of travel. Curb cuts can also be a hazard unless they are textured sufficiently to warn a blind person that a change is coming up (Steinfeld 1979c).

People who are mentally retarded often have physical disabilities as well. Special design considerations for group homes and schools must take into account the need for getting out quickly and easily in the case of an emergency and must accommodate specific teaching strategies. Often, making signs in larger letters and symbols will be useful for these individuals (Environmental Design Group 1976).

People who are emotionally unstable need places that are easy to navigate and exceptionally clear to understand. The physical environment need not add any additional pressures of potential confusion and difficult way-finding.

Gender: Designing for the differences between men and women has as much to do with the cultural roles that each assume as it does with the anthropometric differences. Who are the executives? Who is the main caregiver for the children? These questions and many others have traditional stereotypic answers that are coming into question as most North American families have to have two incomes and men and women must share the roles of producing income, maintaining the home, and raising the children. Design and programming must support the choices that people are making to uphold or to break away from the stereotype. Single parents are most likely to be women and, as such, need supportive living environments (Franck and Ahrentzen 1989). The elderly are more likely to be women than men. Men sometimes need diaper changing areas in airport restrooms.

Where are men supposed to lie down when they are feeling sick if they are not afforded a "fainting lady's" room? Programming and design need to consider all the possibilities and plan for what is needed. To avoid long lines, plumbing codes should change to reflect the numbers of fixtures needed in public restrooms for women in correlation with the numbers of women who attend public events and the length of time it takes to use the restroom.

Women are, on average, physically smaller and not as strong as their male counterparts and, as such, are susceptible to purse snatchers or rapists if the environment creates rather than minimizes the potentials for surprise attacks. Lighting on college campuses has become a big issue because women demand to be able to work late hours on campus without fearing for their safety. Escort services work and the environment should be designed to do its part as well. An environment that accidentally creates hiding places for would-be assailants is inappropriate. The ideal is to create environments safe for both sexes. For a much fuller discussion of gender issues, see Prussin (1984).

Roles: Much of our behavior and the subsequent demands made on our environments are governed by the roles we choose for ourselves in terms of our employment, our desire to learn new things, our expressions of religion or political participation, our choices about play and recreation, our modes of travel, our choice of how to pay for our housing (renter, condo association member, owner, landlord) or whether or not we own a pet. Each of these roles is associated with a certain set of places and we change roles as we move from place to place in our lives.

Designed places need to take into account all those roles that require a design response to be appropriately supported. For example, park design needs to plan for the ball players, the picnickers, the dog walkers, the bike riders, the joggers, and the people watching their children play. Each of us could play many of these roles at different times.

Personality: To help students understand themselves a little better in relationship to their design processes, I had them take the Kiersey Scale (Kiersey and Bates 1984), a personality "test" based on the Myers-Briggs Type Inventory (**MBTI**). I discovered that there were very definite differences in the way the introverts and extroverts designed public spaces. The introverts tended to prefer to be in and to design secluded spaces where they could watch the action without being seen. They wanted to have prospect, refuge, and a big choice about whether or not they joined in the ongoing action. Extroverts, on the other hand, had very large, very open public spaces and *assumed* that everyone wanted to be a part of the action. The most valuable lessons learned here were that public spaces need to be designed with choices appropriate to both extroverts and introverts and that there needs to be some places of prospect, of refuge, and that invite the participation of all. The primary directive is to provide a choice so that a wide variety of people might find a place within the larger place to be comfortable and to participate whether as a player in the drama or as a viewer.

Place-Related Information

Many of the concerns about place are reactions to specific sets of facts about a particular place. The climate is a set of facts readily available to anyone with access to weather station data. However, the real *issues* that require design decisions, such as level of energy usage, levels of physiological comfort, building durability, etc., need decisions based upon the facts about the climate in a particular place.

Scale of Concerns

Many design issues are valid at several different scales: circulation is important in a country, a region, a city, a neighborhood, a building or a room. Convenience and durability are issues for designing doorknobs, doors, corridors, buildings, and freeways. Every design problem, no matter what its scale, is a problem of making the best fit between the intended behavior and the designed environment. Each project has a different set of facts and a set of issues that are the highest priority for its design. Careful consideration of all the relevant issues at each scale creates the potential for better solutions.

Geographic Features

Regionalism is an image response to an area's geographic and cultural features. In architecture, this means a repetition of similar features that give a distinct character to the regional context. In the U.S. there are many stylistic regions, such as the Southwest, New England, and the deep South.

Specific sites have big rocks or large trees or other geographic features that are special because of their visual qualities or because of the meaning that the local population has given to them. To the American Indian, the land is a spiritual resource and many places have particular significance to their rituals. In Peru, the mountains are given names and personalities based upon the mythology of the origins of the gods and protective spirits. The point here is to remind us of a wide variety of historical responses to geography and the meanings associated with them so that, as programmers, we might be on the lookout for information in these areas that we might use or borrow for inspiration.

Urban Versus Rural Areas

Building in the city is very different from building in the suburbs or in rural areas. Different considerations about density, about circulation, and about different land uses and their potential conflicts arise in each zone. In San Luis Obispo, California, the ideal image is one of a small city surrounded by a green belt. The difficulty arises when the best soils for growing crops occur near the edge of city development. The dust, pesticide spraying, and smoke often produced by agricultural practices, combined with the wind blowing in the "wrong" direction creates a condition to which the residents and retail managers of nearby city development protest. It becomes a very difficult balance to maintain open agricultural land that is producing income and to resist the increasing pressures to develop the farm land that is "too close" to urban development.

The high density of building development required by land costs in large cities brings with it large numbers of people, increasing traffic congestion, a high crime rate, and a high concentration of the poor and homeless, as well as a high proportion of wealthy people. It is quite a challenge to consider all the issues that can make the designs of our cities more pleasant and safer places to be. While programming and design cannot insure pleasure and safety, they can create a better fit between behavior and environment.

Building Height and Density: The "American dream" has long been the single family house on its own lot. Garden cities like Reston, Virginia, became the abode of the almost wealthy, or the upper middle class, because of economics rather than the dream of the designers for a mixed population. In the cities, the solution to low-income housing has been to create great tall apartment blocks. Much has been said in the

1970s and 1980s about high density living and the difficulties of making it work for low income people. While not statistically perfect, Newman's (1972) studies point to the issues of territory and a sense of ownership that are not often fostered by the physical design of high-rise apartment buildings.

The failure of Pruitt Igoe in St. Louis in the 1960s was pivotal in creating an investigation of what went wrong with the process of design that predicted great success yet failed its users so miserably. I maintain that it was much more a sociological and management failure than a design failure, but the major design error was that the buildings did not take into account the sociological needs of the specific population that lived there. If the buildings had been inhabited by middle to upper income people with door guards, the buildings would never have been torn down.

Newman's (1972) studies point out that mid-rise buildings are safer than high-rises because having a small number of people sharing an entry leads to a shared sense of ownership through knowing other residents, being able to recognize strangers, being neighborly, and maintaining the public space adjacent to the apartment entry.

Environmental Controls

Climate demands a response in terms of protection — whether from the cold, the rain, or the heat. It also can be an element utilized for energy conservation from natural daylighting to hot water heating to passive space heating or cooling. Climate response has shaped many vernacular buildings from the courtyard house of hot climates to the steeply pitched roofs of the snow country. Programming should set the criteria for the level of climate response and energy conservation.

Health and safety concerns redesigned New York's building codes for tenements so that light and air could reach most of the rooms (McHarg 1971). The recently understood Seasonal Affective Disorder, or SAD, is caused by an insufficient exposure to light. It seems that we need daily exposure to at least twenty minutes of full-spectrum light per day. The people in Barrow, Alaska, who have six weeks of no sunlight must depend on artificial light.

Often the perception of the state of environmental control systems is more important than the facts. Bob Neuman (of the firm Bolt, Baranek, and Neuman) told many anecdotes about people who thought that the room was too cold or too hot because they could not hear the fan for the HVAC (heating, ventilating, and air conditioning) system. All he had to do was to put a pencil in the vent with a small piece of paper attached that would flutter enough to make the right amount of noise.

Noise can be the comforting *white noise* of a waterfall in an urban park or it can be a profound disturbance if it is intrusive, unexpected, and contains information that demands our attention. Existing research concludes that a large segment of our population suffers harmful effects, both physiologically and psychologically, from prolonged exposure to high intensity noise. With all other factors being equal, living over a subway affects children's abilities in reading and learning. This is probably due to the masking of communication between parent and child as well as the disturbance/distraction factor. Psychological factors that influence whether a noise is deleterious or not are predictability, controllability, and the meaning associated with the noise (Cohen and Weinstein 1982).

Train noise can be mitigated by wall insulation and triple glazed windows. In a San Luis Obispo condominium project next to the railroad tracks, the developer proposed to mitigate the noise problem by fixed glass in the windows on the railroad side. The Planning Commission required that the triple glazed windows be operable so that the residents could have control over the ventilation and the noise.

Some people adjust to regularized loud noises, such as the daily 4 AM train passing nearby, and waken if the noise does not occur. Rock musicians, construction workers, and some factory workers tend to go deaf early because of the physical effects of working regularly in very intense noise without adequate protection. Have you ever tried to do some serious work with the wrong kind of music turned up just a little too loud?

Behavioral Issues

The issues discussed here are only a portion of the issues listed in Chapter 2 and are mentioned in more detail because I believe that these issues easily illustrate how the programmers' or designers' understanding of the issue impacts the design. The priority of each issue will change from project to project and, most likely, will also change over time and with different sets of users.

Territoriality

Territoriality is the natural tendency to claim territory as one's own special space, or to lay claim to a group's particular set of places. Students have a tendency to sit in the same seats in the same classes. There is "Dad's chair" in the TV room. Books and papers left at a table in the library reserve your seat for a very long time. We all share a need to identify a part of the environment as being ours and being off limits to certain others.

Territory is marked by international borders customs officials, state lines, fences, locked doors, and other barriers to the passage of people and vehicles. People feel accountable for their own territory and maintain it in proportion to their sense of ownership and responsibility. There are not too many people who will pick up trash on a busy city street — it just isn't part of the territory for which they feel they must be accountable. The quality of the boundary markers is the most obvious contribution that design makes to territoriality. For a more thorough discussion of the research on territoriality, see Altman (1975, 126-45).

Home Range and Life Space

Home Range is a person's usually inhabited territory. Life space, an idea generated by Lewin (1935) is the set of places one knows and can revisit mentally as known home ground. As a baby grows from an infant to a fully functioning adult, her home range and **life space** likewise expand. The infant is confined to a bed and a parent's arms until she gains the mobility to crawl. At that point, parents usually set up barriers to the young child's exploration so that she is protected from household items that might contain a threat. As the young child learns to walk and to ride wheeled vehicles, her home territory expands to the neighborhood and friends' houses. Going to school, riding the bus, and riding a big bicycle often mean an exponential expansion of a formerly limited home range. In the U.S. going to high school and getting a driver's license would give another boost to the size of a child's home range. Then she's off to college, work, or marriage for another expansion of places she can call home territory.

Middle age is the time of the largest life space and home range; a time of maximum travel and visiting other places.

Changing Home Range Over a
Lifespan

When she becomes elderly and frail, her home range begins to shrink physically because of shrinking physical ability, weakness, or fear of danger or accidents. Travel decreases, driving may be limited to daylight hours, and home seems like just the place to be the most comfortable. Later she may move to congregate housing and give up her car entirely. Toward the end of her life, she may be confined to a wheelchair or to a bed in a nursing home. As the physical body declines in strength and agility, the home range narrows physically, but is kept alive in her mind as a life space in memory. This mental image of past places is usually kept alive by mementos or photographs of people and places that are or were a part of the home range that is now no longer physically accessible. See the sidebar figure.

Environments that we design are part of people's home ranges, from small children who need safe play to older people who need safety from accidents or assault and the ability to display their favorite memories — whether in congregate housing, a nursing home, or a long-term care hospital. The movie *Fried Green Tomatoes* showed very poignantly how the main character in the story memorialized her roses and attempted to contain her larger past life space within the smaller current one by putting rose pictures cut from catalogs up on the wall along with photos of friends and family from her girlhood. The environments we design need to accommodate each life phase and allow for expansion and contraction of the home range while maintaining a rich, full life space.

Personal Space

The concept of personal space is defined by Sommer (1969, 26) as "an area with invisible boundaries surrounding a person's body into which intruders may not come." The idea of an ideal distance between people for various types of interactions has a profound influence on the design of architectural spaces. E. T. Hall and Robert Sommer are the two researchers who have written the seminal works on this subject.

Edward T. Hall (1959, 1969) wrote two books that expand on the concept of personal space: *The Silent Language* and *The Hidden Dimension*. Hall uses Humphrey Osmond's terms to describe the spaces that establish the conditions that support people being together and communicating (sociopetal space) or the conditions for separation and isolation (sociofugal space; Hall 1969, 108). Arranging people around a conference table facilitates communication among the participants, whereas theater-style seating inhibits it. L-shaped seating arrangements facilitate conversation (across a corner); airport linear arrangements (facing straight ahead) make it more difficult. See Figure 9-11. These examples are for the U.S. and what is sociofugal in our culture may be sociopetal in another culture.

Hall further describes his anthropological model of space with fixed-feature space, semifixed-feature space, and informal space. Fixed-feature space is the codification of territorial and behavior setting boundaries: city planning, buildings, rooms, walls, and equipment are all elements of fixed-feature space. "Fortunately, there are a few architects who take the time to discover the internalized fixed-feature needs of their clients" (Hall 1969). Semifixed-feature space has elements of furniture that can be moved to suit the needs of the occasion. For some of us the furniture arrangement becomes fixed-feature space by habit and ownership of "my chair." For others the semi-annual or annual cleaning and rearranging of the furniture becomes a welcome ritual of renewal. Informal space is the spaces between us that we create in different social

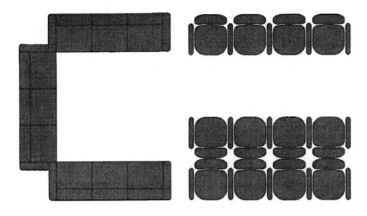

Figure 9-11   L-Shaped Sociopetal Seating for a Lounge and Parallel Sociofugal Seating for Airports

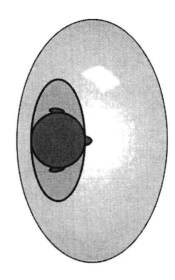

Personal Space Bubble – More Space Needed Face to Face Than Side to Side or at a Person's Back

circumstances that translate into intimate, personal, social, and public distances (Hall 1969, 115). The sizes of these zones vary with culture. In the U.S. intimate distances (either for affection or anger) are 6 to 18 inches; personal distance ranges from 18 to 30 inches to conversational distances of 2.5 to 4 feet; social distance for impersonal conversations is 4 to 7 feet and for more formal interactions is 7 to 12 feet; and finally, public distance for small lectures or presentations is 12 to 25 feet and formal "important person" distance is over 25 feet. (Hall 1969, 116-25). Beyond 30 feet the features of the face are not readily distinguishable and the voice is not clearly heard unamplified so that the main communication is by hand or body gesture or speaking loudly rather than facial expression or normal speech.

Robert Sommer: Sommer's book, *Personal Space* (1969), is a study of the distances that people keep between themselves in different circumstances. He investigated different circumstances that illustrated the idea that we create a zone of space around our bodies that is a space of no entry for other people except under certain circumstances. This comfort zone is characterized as a "bubble" of personal space — a boundary to our body's own territory, a zone of body privacy. For face to face conversation we will allow people to come within a few feet of us; a person approaching our side can come closer than that. A person standing near our back can be even closer. Remember standing in a crowded elevator or in a long line? Almost no one stood face to face unless they were intimate friends. The personal space bubble changes size depending upon the relationship of the people involved, the body orientation, and the activity being performed. See the sidebar figure.

This concept has changed the way airport seating is designed. It assumes that strangers will sit closer together if there are arms on the chairs to fill in as a boundary for one's personal space and if the seats are facing in the same direction so that face to face contact is not required or is far enough away not to be threatening. In older railroad stations with its benches with no arms, strangers will tend to sit far enough away from each other so that there is an empty space between them even when the terminal is crowded.

Sommer takes a close look at behavior in terms of personal space and its relationship to privacy, small group interactions, hospital wards for the elderly, classrooms, dormitories, and bars. He makes it very clear that the interaction of the designed environment and behavior is so powerful that it should be impossible to teach design without the consideration of user behavior.

Personalization

Personalization is the ability to mark your own territory by decorating it with objects that are meaningful to you and that are an expression of your own interests, activities and accomplishments. This creates a space or set of spaces that are adapted to you and your needs for expression. Many designers of the past were not attuned to this human need for personalization. Mies van der Rohe was said to have been miffed when a client changed the color of the drapes in a home he designed and Frank Lloyd Wright was upset when clients "ruined" his house designs by adding their own furniture.

Dorm Example: Altman (1975) did a study of freshmen who lived in dorms and discovered that when the level of personalization was correlated with a student's persistence in school, the students who were at the highest end of the personalization scale tended to stay in school and those at the lowest end of the scale tended to fail, drop out, or transfer. The scale that he designed took into account the amount of material that was used to decorate the room and the degree to which the decoration was personal or impersonal. A ski poster was relatively impersonal, whereas a project or award that resulted from the student's work was very personal.

The lesson here is that the people who participate in making their new college living space their own by personalizing it are more likely to identify the school as part of their world and stay to finish the year. Programmers need to plan for fulfilling this need for personalization in dorms and in other settings.

Hertsberger's Office Building: Herman Hertzberger designed an office building in Apeldoorn, the Netherlands, that had a very plain concrete finish on the interior. His stated intention was to make it so bland that it was a background that invited the office workers to personalize their spaces — both individual and group spaces. Duct caps became eyes, walls were covered with posters and office-related messages,

and the whole experiment was a great success. Some of the negative comments were that the building was so ugly inside that it had to be brightened by the people working there.

Corbu's Pessac: In 1926, a journalist for the French magazine *Mon chez moi* wrote of the newly built, low-cost housing project (Quartiers Modernes Frugés), "There I was able to observe a new style, a completely new, and in my opinion, successful conception of what a modern house ought to be: a 'machine to live in' . . ." (Boudon 1969, 1). Four years later, the residents, instead of living in this machine passively and adapting their lives to the architecture, took on an active role in making their homes work for their life styles and personalized them to fit their needs and the image they held of what a home should look like. Instead of each flat looking exactly like its neighbor as it was designed, each unit is now differentiated from its neighbor in many ways. Some residents have enclosed all the areas that were once open to expand their living space, some residents have made the windows smaller and others added pitched roofs or added decorative elements to doors and windows. Corbu's response was, "You know, it is always life that is right and the architect who is wrong . . ." (Boudon 1969, 1). Boudon concludes differently; he believes that the architecture that Corbu produced was one that invited, almost demanded, personalization and allowed it to the point that each owner was able to modify the building to meet the specifications of a particular family.

Crowding/Density

Density is defined for planning purposes as the number of people per unit area. The density of a room would be the number of people per square foot, and the density of a land use zone is the number of people per acre. This measure is physical and finite, but people perceive density as a function of the relationships between things (people/people, people/object, object/object; (Rapoport 1975b, 133). These relationships are a function of distance, height, spacing, boundaries, and/or juxtaposition. The actual density may be very different from the perceived density or different from the desired density.

Although density affects the perceptions of crowding, it is not the same thing. Much has been written about the negative effects of high density living, but not much has been offered about the potential negative effects of low density living. There is a potential for isolation and sensory deprivation (Rapoport 1975b, 154).

Crowding is an experience or perception rather than an objective measure of people per unit area. A classroom is crowded when there are more people than there are seats, regardless of how many square feet there are per person. When is an elevator crowded? The research shows that perceptions of crowding relate to social conflict and psychological stress (Loo and Ong 1984, 82). People who grew up in a crowded environment have a higher tolerance for crowding than do people who grew up in uncrowded areas, but there is no evidence that cultural differences make some people prefer highly crowded environments. In fact the reverse is true, extended exposure to crowded conditions creates an aversion to living in such conditions (Loo and Ong 1984, 84).

Sometimes the culture can be a mitigating circumstance to one's ability to tolerate crowding. People in Tokyo have behavioral patterns that allow them to cope with higher density than people in the U.S. can handle. Japanese rules for polite behavior mitigate the potential for social conflict in crowded living and neighborhood conditions. In the rural

areas of the U.S. there are still people who say, "It gets too crowded around here when the next neighbor is less than three miles away." There are also socio-economic differences in perceptions of crowding in housing conditions. Understanding these differences in the perceptions of crowding can lead to maximum workable densities such as the possibility of creating a ceiling of 15 dwelling units per acre for HUD subsidized housing.

Orientation and Wayfinding

Getting lost is a very frustrating experience, especially if you are trying to be on time to an appointment in unfamiliar territory. Part of being lost is knowing where you are and which direction is which (orientation). There have been a number of studies that have looked into what makes orientation and wayfinding easy or difficult. The methods used range from post-occupancy evaluations of old and new buildings to experiments and wayfinding "games."

Some important architectural features that contribute to the ease of finding one's way in a large building are the familiarity the user has with the building, the placement and legibility of signs, the comprehensibility of the building plan and whether it is memorable, the differentiation of building zones by color and by form, the number of doors, and the degree of difficulty in finding stairs (Garling and Lindberg 1984). Many of these elements can also be useful to the understanding of town plans, subways, neighborhoods, and smaller buildings so that it is easy to orient yourself and find your way.

Panic Behavior: Wayfinding becomes critical in fires and smoky conditions. Gerald Weisman (1985) has pointed out that the fire codes were based on physical science models such as fluids flowing through a gravity system instead of on behavioral processes such as orientation and wayfinding. The assumptions of these physical models are that people will go to the nearest exit and will do so in fairly evenly divided numbers. The way people actually behave is to go toward the exit they know (the one they came in) or that they can see, regardless of where the other exits may be. Weisman goes on to state that, in an emergency, people will go where they know or have been and will possibly not even notice emergency exit signs. Building landmarks help visitors to know where they are and to be able to find their way back to the way they came in, not to find new exit paths. Finally, he states that building plan configuration will help people find their way out if it is simple and easily imaged mentally. He argues for a cognitive model of orientation and wayfinding rather than the mechanistic models used by the codes (Weisman 1985, 167-71).

Jake Pauls (1985) has done similar work in Canada and proposed that changes in codes should include a wider tread and lower riser for stairs (maximum 7 inches rise and minimum 11 inches tread), a handrail height of 36 to 38 inches above tread nosing and be no more than 60 inches apart on wide stairs, an effective-width model for calculating exit corridor and door size, and an egress time of 3 ½ minutes maximum. Pauls comments that, ". . . professionals involved with building design must become more sensitive to the ways that people actually use buildings" (Pauls 1985, 235-40).

Another group of Canadian researchers looked at the legibility of exit signs under the smoky conditions of a simulated fire. They discovered that in smoke, emergency exit signs should be bright (changing from incandescent to fluorescent), they should be protected from light scattered from other sources (far enough away from other lights, especially down lights), and that green signs with clear cutouts

for letters read better than red backgrounds or translucent letters (Rea 1985, 295-297). These examples are but a few of the many available through the American Institute of Architects or through the Environmental Design Research Association.

Accidents

NBS, the National Bureau of Standards, works to develop standards for safe use of materials and projects. Much of their work is based upon what is known about human anthropometrics and behavioral tendencies. Some of their major research in the recent past has been to look at causes of stair accidents, causes of accidents with glass (windows, doors, and sidelights), fire retardant requirements for auditorium seating, etc. With the economics and politics of the 1980s, the scope of work and the numbers of people working in the NBS has recently been dramatically reduced.

Stair safety: One million people per year have stair accidents, thousands are killed, and over 10,000 people are disabled. Stair accidents cost 10 billion dollars per year. The leading cause of death among people over 65 years of age is falling down (Chadwick 1992). A programmer's knowledge of the potentials for accidents should lead to much safer design of stairs.

Treads and Risers: Part of the difficulty in maneuvering stairs is the ratio of the tread to riser. If the tread is too small for a big foot to find steady purchase, then one careless placement of the foot leads to a slip and possible injury. When the tread is too large, as in outdoor stairs, then the awkwardness of the spacing (like a tread 1 ½ strides wide) can also lead to a misstep. Safety experts say that changing the residential tread/riser proportion from an 8 inch rise with a 9 inch tread to a 7 inch rise and an 11 inch tread will be far safer. Liz McLaughlin from the San Francisco Injury Center (part of the Center for Disease Control) says that the benefits to children and older people are significant (Chadwick 1992).

Misperceptions: If you are walking down the stairs and you are unable to discern the edge of the stair tread, then it is easy to put your foot too close to the edge and take a tumble. On the upward journey, if you cannot judge where the next rise ends, it is easy to trip over the nose of the tread as well. Visual conditions that contribute to this sort of misperception of the size of the tread or the riser are visual patterns that continue evenly over the entire surface of the stair and obscure the edge of the tread or riser (such as a painted tile or patterned carpet), undifferentiated color over the entire stair, glare or low lighting conditions, and no shadow when there is low contrast at the edge of the tread (Archea 1979).

For safety's sake, we must go beyond the "just noticeable difference" between treads and between risers to create the best possible distinction. Other factors that will help overcome some of these problems with stair design are better lighting and more grippable railings.

Distractions: Sometimes the cause of a fall on a stair is just not paying attention to where you put your feet. The design of some department store stairs contributes to this phenomenon. As you come down from the upper floor, the displays are designed to catch your eye so you are much more interested in looking at the newest merchandise than in where you are putting your feet. Merchants are not intentionally creating the distractions to make you fall, but are creating them for their own merchandising purposes. If programmers specified the viewing angles for displays near stairs, built-in distractions could be avoided.

Windows and Glass: Window or door glass in the wrong position can invite serious accidents. Glass doors and sidelights at the foot of stairs are potentially dangerous if kids crash through as they run down the stairs and cannot stop. Glass doors that are so clean and unmarked that they seem to be a clear passage that invites people to walk through them. Sofas in front of windows invite preteen girls to do handstands into them and kick the glass out with their feet. Programmers need to be aware of the full range of possible behaviors and the potential misperceptions created by the locations of glass.

Stressors

There are physical stressors such as noise, pollutants, and either too hot or too cold a temperature. There are psychological stressors such as crowding, lack of privacy and poor quality environments. Most of the stressors from the built environment fall into the category called "daily hassles" by Lazarus and Cohen (1977). Much of this stress stems from either actual or perceived lack of control over the situation: the stressor is neither predictable nor modifiable by a change in behavior. Other types of stressors include having your personal space invaded; boring redundancy; fear of a potential event such as an earthquake, mud slide, flood, or a nuclear accident; extreme climates; and air pollution.

A person's ability to cope with stress is mediated by a number of variables. Prior experience may create a source of predictability or some other resource for coping. The cultural value and meaning of some stressors serve as mediators. Personal disposition to resist or to succumb to stress may be higher in some people than in others, and the same is true of development of skills or social support to cope with stress (Baum, Singer, and Baum 1982).

Many conditions in the environment are stressful and can be mediated by good programming and design. Gary

Evans (1982) has edited a book containing a number of papers dealing with the research topics ranging from thermal stress to stress in the office environment to the public policy implications of environmental stress. It is a good place to start in developing your understanding of the relationship between the built environment and chronic stress. It is more difficult to use design to mediate the psychological effects of acute stress, such as that from a natural disaster, but we can design buildings to withstand the effects of earthquakes, hurricane force winds, and flood waters. The following is a brief discussion of some aspects of stress that programmers should know about that can be ameliorated by design.

Pollutants: A recent hot topic in the local press is the effects of "sick buildings." Sick buildings are defined as buildings that have substances in them that cause people to have symptoms of illness ranging from mild allergy-type reactions to serious conditions of nerve damage and cancer. The culprits are radon (a radio active gas that decays from granite), finishes on materials such as the formaldehyde used as sizing in some carpets, glues in plywood and other adhesives, asbestos from old insulation, lead from old paint, bacteria growing in ventilation ducts (Legionnaires' Disease), and a long list of carcinogens, allergens, irritants, and poisons used in the construction process. Many new materials, such as Drivit, have been found to produce noxious gasses when they are burned and are not allowed in hospitals where people may take longer evacuating a building in case of fire. Programmers need to know something about the sensitivity of the population planning to use the building as well as know counter measures such as the appropriate level of ventilation. The best antidote is to specify safe materials so that the problem does not start.

Choice: One's sense of control is enhanced by having different choices. This is true in many areas of our lives: noise control, temperature control, having the choice of a different path, or choosing between a bath or a shower.

Tektite (Nowlis 1972) was an underwater simulation of closed-system living conditions conducted by NASA in the late 1960s. Information on both sociological and human factors from such research was used to design the space shuttle and the planned space stations. One of the most telling discoveries was that the participants much preferred to have a *choice* in creating their own meals (even if it meant choosing a peanut butter sandwich) rather than having no choice about great meals planned by other people.

Theory

Theory creates a structure for linking the facts about people to the characteristics of a place or for predicting the behavior of people in a particular place. At present there are very few comprehensive theories that thoroughly correlate the interactions of people, place, and behavior. Much of the sociological and psychological research has been developed for very small parts of these interactions and is sometimes minimally useful to programmers in creating guides for design. Theories need to answer Rapoport's (1975a) questions: (1) What characteristics of people as individuals and groups are important in shaping the environment? (2) How and to what extent does environment affect people? (3) What are the mechanisms that link people and the environment? Theories start with descriptions, move to explanations of relationships, and eventually move toward a predictive model. Most current theories of environment and behavior interactions are descriptive rather than explanatory or predictive.

Behavior Settings

Barker (1968) spent the better part of his life working out his theory of environment/behavior interaction that he called behavior settings. Using behavior settings is a very good way to understand the units of behavior that need a design response. Simply stated, a behavior setting has these characteristics:

1. The activity is *bounded by time* — it has a starting point and an ending point.

2. The activity has *physical boundaries* — the party happens at your house, the basketball game happens on the court, the sales event happens in a particular store.

3. The activity has *particular equipment or props required* to produce the desired activity — music, food, and drink for the party; bleachers, balls, and goals for the game; or shelves, merchandise, and money for the sale (Barker 1968).

The objects and the activities are compatible with each other, that is to say they have a **synomorphic** relationship. This compatibility between the sets of activities and the human and object components is responsible for the comprehensibility of the setting as a whole unit (Wicker 1979, 10). For example, the homecoming football game is a behavior setting made up of: (1) the stadium as its physical boundary; (2) all the fans, players, coaches, and officials as participants; (3) the bleachers, line markers, balls, uniforms, and goal posts as the props; and (4) the time boundary from 2:00 PM till 4:00 PM Saturday. These elements create the namable behavior setting called "the homecoming game."

When searching for the minimum number of rooms that have to be created in order for a design to work, it is necessary to look at the number of behavior settings and the requirements of each setting to allow the designer to ascertain the number of different types of spaces required. A number of settings can share the same space at different scheduled times if they have similar requirements. The minimum number of spaces is equal to the minimum number of categories of behavior settings that can fulfill all the required functions. Each category consists of all the behavior settings that can share a space because of similar needs in terms of size and equipment and different needs in terms of schedule or time.

My favorite example of the use of behavior settings in programming is the design of a small church with a correspondingly small budget. If a church is small, that does not mean that it does not have all the functions and behavior settings of a much larger congregation. Behavior setting theory in programming for this small church is used to discover how many different settings can share the same facilities by scheduling them at different times. I know of a couple of congregations that share the same building — one is Jewish and one is Christian. They share office machines but not office or file space. They manage to schedule all of their activities (behavior settings) so that they do not conflict.

Wicker (1979) has the simplest definition of behavior settings I have found: ". . . the social/physical situations in which human behavior occurs." Behavior settings are the units for describing, analyzing, and understanding the interdependence of activity and setting. To my mind, it is one of the best theoretical tools available to programmers and designers for comprehending a building project. See Figure 9-4 for a diagram of a dance hall behavior setting.

Environmental Competence Versus Environmental Press

In a world where there are increasing numbers of elderly and handicapped people living independently and able to participate in public activities more than ever in our history, it is useful to look at Lawton and Nahemow's (1973) transaction model for environment/behavior interactions. This model proposes that the competence of an individual interacts with the difficulty or press of an environment to create adaptive behaviors. Competence includes cognitive ability, psychological adjustment, physical health, and strength. Environmental press is the sum of environmental forces that demand a response to such forces as high temperatures, heavy doors, stairs, a potential employer who misunderstands, or high shelves. Adaptive behaviors may be to avoid the pressing situation, to buy a device to assist in overcoming the difficulty, to write angry letters to the legislature for passage of a particular bill, or to remodel the physical environment to be less pressing and more supportive. Adaptation may also be emotional or attitudinal: becoming resigned to the way it is, explaining whenever necessary, complaining, or ignoring the problem. See Figure 9-12.

In the transaction model, the adaptation level is the point at which the press of the environment and the competence of the individual are a good fit or are balanced. Maximum performance and positive adaptation are demanded of an individual when the press is just a bit more than the adaptation level but is not beyond one's ability to manage. Negative adaptation occurs when the environmental press is overwhelming. Many old people get very sick or die when they are moved from one rest home to another or when the temperature gets too high for sustained periods. Negative adaptation also occurs when the level of competence far outstrips the environmental press (learned helplessness occurs when institutions overprotect their clients).

Sense of Place

Much of architectural design education is aimed at teaching the skills of creating a sense of place. Yet the burden of creating a memorable experience in a particular place is not totally upon the environment. We bring to each place our own expectations, intentions, experiences, mood and perception. It is the interaction of each individual's interpretation of a place with the features and events of the place that create the experience of a sense of place, or a sense of meaning, if you will. Fritz Steele's (1981) model is as follows: physical surroundings + social context = the setting, which adds to a person's psychological factors and leads to a sense of place.

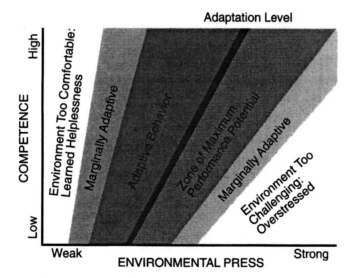

9-12 The Transaction Model.
Developed from Lawton and Nahemow 1973.

Steele (1981) also characterizes people as "place people," "people people," and "things people." Place people find their satisfaction from the way they relate to their physical surroundings — where they go is generally of more interest than with whom they go or what they do when they get there. People people are primarily interested in relationships and whom they are with rather than where they go or what they do. Things people are most interested in their work or other things they do rather than whom they are with or where they are (Steele 1981, 43-51). Obviously this is an oversimplification, but it serves to make programmers and designers aware that the form of a place is perceived differently by different types of people. Programming can identify the issues and the audience that contribute to the sense of place.

Obviously the physical characteristics of certain places are so powerful that its sense of place can be readily predicted. San Marcos square and its cathedral in Venice, the Eiffel Tower in Paris, and Big Sur on the California coast tend to have a strong sense of place for everyone who visits them. Not much empirical research has been done regarding sense of place. It is very "squishy" and unrigorous at this point in time, yet it is an important consideration in programming.

Other Theories

Rapoport (1975a) is one of the few people who have attempted to construct an overview of the environment/ behavior theories. He points out that each set of theories is based upon a model of how the world works and that, in general, we see what we are looking for. That is to say, if we take a metal detector to the beach, we are likely to find only metal, not plastic or beautiful shells.

Rapoport offers a series of models within which theories might be developed.

1. *Perception-Based*: These models are based upon the idea that perception is the essential link between people and their environments. Cultural biases and theories about other perceptual mechanisms belong here.

2. *Cognitive and Image-Based*: These models recognize the importance of perception, but stress the mental processes — the cognitive maps and images of the environment — as the overriding mediator between people and environments. The learning-based models fit into this category.

3. *Behavior Setting Models* are discussed on page 143.

4. *Environment as Communication, Symbolism:* These models work on the premise that the environment provides cues for our behavior. Hall's notions of fixed feature, semi-fixed feature, and informal or non-fixed feature space fall into this category. See page 136.

5. *Competence and Adaptation:* models are discussed on page 144.

6. *Information Flow Models.* These models cast the environment as either a facilitator or inhibitor of communication between people. Studies of density and privacy using the environment to control unwanted interruptions/communications are of this category.

7. *Ecological Models:* This model is more of a general perspective that looks at people in environments rather than as just interacting with one. Behavior settings are a subset of the ecological model. Field studies and anthropological methods are used as opposed to laboratory studies.

8. *Ethological Models.* These models are based upon the idea of studying people in very different settings — both in the field and in the laboratory. In this group are models of behavioral sinks (such as Calhoun's rat studies), personal space, and crowding.

9. *Evolutionary Models:* These models gain insights about people's attributes, predispositions, and limits by examining the physical and social environments in which they evolved. The developmental model (which assumes that people in the same life phase are more similar in their needs than they are similar to people in other life phases) is a part of this group.

10. *Socio-Cultural Models:* These models assume that the most important thing to design for is the ways certain groups of people define and solve problems. Culture is an important mediating variable for developing values, images, choices, and preferences.

11. *Preference in Environmental Quality:* This model assumes that environmental quality is the main criterion by which people make choices, however they perceive and define it. This model is implicit in some others.

12. *Performance-Based Models:* These models tend to be more empirically oriented and based upon the physical science methods rather than anthropological approaches. They measure behavior under various conditions of noise, environmental press, etc.

None of these models are mutually exclusive. Many of them tend to overlap and most understanding of environment/behavior interactions uses more than one model. If you look closely at this text, you will be able to find many of these models as the foundation for the ideas expressed here.

Context

We are born into a set of circumstances that included our finances and economic situations, the economy of the world, the politics of our time, the social rules, and the culture of our neighborhood and country. These contextual forces create a set of rules and values for how to operate in the world that are most often in the background of our awareness, unless they are extremely constraining (such as a deep recession) or unless they present new possibilities (such as the democratization of Eastern Europe). The influences of these different aspects of context are not easily separated as distinct cause and effect scenarios. The influences of culture, sociology, politics, and economy are intertwined and so interrelated that the distinctions that are presented here are pointing to areas of concern rather than making a case for sole influence. The following are only a very few of the many possible examples of the influences of culture, sociology, economics, and politics.

Culture

House Form and Culture: In 1969 Amos Rapoport wrote a wonderfully broad-ranging monograph titled *House Form and Culture* in which he examined vernacular house-building in order to discover the major factors that determined house form. This work is a superb study, in the anthropological tradition, of many different kinds of houses and the multiple influences upon their forms. He argues clearly that socio-cultural factors are the most important shapers of house form and that the forces of the climate, economy, site, construction technology, and materials available are only constraints or modifiers of house form. I believe that the same argument can be made for most other types of buildings as well.

The cultural factors can be summed up as the image of the ideal form for fulfilling the idea or symbol of what a house should be, which includes the religious ideal and the ideal for social and status relationships called for by the culture.

Houses reflect ceremonial (ritual) and religious beliefs, needs for prestige and status, social relationships between men and women (marriage and family customs), relationships between family and stranger (defense), and gregariousness or a need for privacy. They also reflect the family or clan structure, customs, taboos, traditions, the need to store animals, food or possessions, and the idea of a house as a social control mechanism — a tool for teaching the young about social relationships and attitudes expected from them.

Rapoport argues that the site, the technology, the climate, and the available building materials make certain building forms possible — not inevitable. The most important idea here is that the house is an expression of a particular world view. It is the wealth of possible combinations of all these socio-cultural and physical factors that gives us the multiplicity of different house types that have been developed around the world.

"House as Symbol of the Self": Marcus (1976) wrote a "think piece" about one's house being a disclosure about the inner nature of one's self. It is an interesting article about how we give our homes our personalities and/or the image of our desires — how we want the world to know us. The self-made business person chooses the ostentatious columned mansionette, the people in helping professions tend toward inward-looking "well-designed" homes, and the individualists choose the unique and different house. Marcus admonishes us to be aware of a person's conception of self when designing custom homes as well as looking at what sort of images we might unconsciously create in apartments.

Navajo Example: I relate the following story as an example of what's possible, rather than relating accurate details. Here is the *sense* of the story, not the exact details. A teenage Navajo boy was very seriously, but not fatally, injured in an automobile accident and taken to the nearest hospital rather than to his home. It was a single room rather than a ward or a double room and was painted a clean, hospital white. Although his injuries were not seriously life threatening, he became convinced that he was going to die.

When he woke up, he was aware that he was hurt badly, he was alone, and the room was white. Those three things were all he needed to "know" to deduce he was going to die, so he turned his head to the wall and proceeded to do so. It took visits from many members of his family and other people he trusted to overcome his cultural perception of his situation. He had to be convinced that, in his case, his being alone had nothing to do with the standard Navajo practice for the terminally ill. The hospital personnel were doing their best to keep him alive, not to let him die in peace. He also had to be convinced that the room was white for cleanliness reasons, not because the color of death for the Navajo nation is white.

Designers and programmers usually become so immersed in their own culture that they see their own criteria for what works as the only criteria rather than as a set of possible values. This is true for most of us because our cultural structure is transparent. "It is difficult for a fish to discover water." We are not always aware of our most basic assumptions about how and why the world works for us the way it does. This is because we grew up in a culture that taught us what was true without offering any other possible alternatives. Good programming assumes nothing — unless the information is completely missing and then we must test our assumptions to the best of our abilities.

Politics

Shifts in the political wind are often shifts in the value system — what's acceptable, what's best, what's awful, and what's unacceptable. In the U.S., people's values have become much more conservative in the 1990s than in the free-wheeling 1960s. For twelve years Republican politicians in the U.S. White House effectively put a stop to a substantial portion of the design research funds. The National Bureau of Standards has had its program drastically reduced. NASA is struggling to keep its space exploration budget at a level sufficient to do the tasks on its agenda.

Locally, politicians duke it out over growth and no growth decisions that have a lot to do with how much building goes on in an area and how much housing costs. In California, the political decisions often have to do with the water supply and how much water at what price goes where. In many people's minds the decisions about water are also decisions about growth rates and therefore about what gets built. These decisions tend to create an atmosphere of doing the known and safe designs so that programming and design innovation are not given support. Every project will have its political climate and political decisions that influence the outcome of the project, either directly or as part of the background set of rules for creating the project.

Economics

Economics and politics go hand in hand. Whether the world or local economy is good or bad often has as much to do with politics as with economics. Who is able to build a building in a particular place has as much to do with the economics of the situation as the political zoning, etc. does. When land prices are high, there is very little low-income or moderate-income housing. When land prices are very, very high, we get taller and taller buildings such as those in all the downtowns of the world's largest cities. The pressures to

build residences on agricultural lands are driven by the economics of the cost-benefit ratio. The choice of whether to build a hotel or a retail store or a mixed use center often hinges on the economics of highest and best use and profitability as well on the predicted trends of the economy.

When there is more money in a project, often there is more time for more thorough programming as well as higher quality of materials. In a recession, the tendency is to do a quick and dirty job to keep the cash flowing. Architects have been fired for doing poor programming jobs because they rushed throughout too fast. Others have been sued because the design did not meet the client's desires.

Sociology

Sociology is the science of human society. Sociology is also impacted by politics and economics. Where an ethnic group lives in a city is somewhat influenced by the economics and the politics. The "rules" of society influence where they live in a major way by implementing prejudices and stereotypes instead of equality.

Tradition has it that the newest immigrant group is on the outside and lives in the shabbiest, poorest part of the city. There is usually another newly arrived immigrant group to replace them when the initial group becomes more established and moves up the economic and social ladders. Boston has seen waves of Irish, Jewish, and African American people move through Dorchester and Roxbury. South central Los Angeles has seen African Americans, Chicanos, and Asian Americans moving through the process of either becoming established as a community within the larger one or becoming integrated into the larger society. The U.S. used to be the great melting pot where everyone who wanted to be successful tried to become integrated into the North American society and culture, but more and more we are giving higher value to other cultures and place emphasis on maintaining the cultural symbols, images, and food, while participating within the social rules of the U.S.

Urban renewal of the 1960s violated many of the social patterns of the people the programs were trying to help so that the building designs that replaced the slums were not a great improvement for people's lives. In the Marseilles block by Corbu, the floor designed to provide neighborhood services such as shops and daycare was not used because it broke up the long-standing social patterns of going to the market.

Pruitt Igoe Example

Bristol (1991) described the political and economic context of the Pruitt Igoe design as the major culprit in the famous failure of this St. Louis housing project. The architectural press has for many years laid the blame for failure squarely on the designers' shoulders because of such features as "skip-stop" elevators (they don't stop on every floor) and internal galleries that were mistakenly thought to create "individual neighborhoods" within the high-rise project. Although these features created opportunities for violent crimes, the real sources of failure stem from the ". . . flawed policies, crises in the local economy, or (from) class oppression and racism . . ." (Bristol 1991, 165). The construction budget was unrealistically low so that materials were not durable, many amenities were eliminated, the density of the project was extreme, and elevator high rises were indicated before the architects came on board. The St. Louis Housing Authority was unable to maintain the project adequately, given the rising costs and the declining market for public

housing. Besides having a high vacancy rate, the project increasingly became the home of ". . . the poorest segment of the black population: primarily female heads of households dependent upon public assistance" (Bristol 1991, 166).

So the failure of Pruitt Igoe that led to its demolition in 1976 was based on the location of the site; the high densities, poor materials and lack of amenities based upon an inadequate budget; the income level of the occupants; the lack of maintenance and repair of mechanical failures; de facto racial discrimination and segregation; and mistaken predictions by the designers regarding how parts of their design would be used.

Method

See Chapters 7 and 8 for a full discussion of methods in architectural research. For understanding people, places, behavior, context, and theory, it is important to understand the methods by which the research was done. If the information was gathered through only observation, then you must be on the lookout for observer bias. If the research depended solely upon interviews and questionnaires, you must be watchful for inaccurate memory and for the desire to please the interviewer by giving the "right" answer.

How we see and understand the interdependence of environment and behavior is colored by the questions we ask. In general, the more anthropological the methods, the more *qualitative* the answers; the more empirical the method, the more *quantitative* the results. It is important to formulate the research questions first, then choose the appropriate methods to answer the questions. Each question should be researched using several methods to avoid biases as much as possible and to increase the reliability of the information.

SUMMARY

In this chapter, the *focus* is on six areas of inquiry: people characteristics, place characteristics, behavioral topics, E/B theories, methods for inquiry, and the influences of context. The more information available to the design team about the issues of behavior and environment that are relevant to the project, the more likely a better solution will be developed. In each of the six categories there are examples of information that influences design.

People's needs vary according to their age, ethnicity, physical ability, gender, personalities, and the roles they take on and should be accommodated as much as possible within the framework of necessary choice and flexibility. Programmers and designers whose designs respond to these people characteristics are much more likely to have satisfied clients.

Considerations of place include scale, geography, building density, degree of urbanization, and the need for environmental controls. A very thorough site analysis usually documents most or all of the place characteristics that are influential in the design.

Behavioral issues include territoriality, personalization, privacy, personal space, perceptions of crowding, wayfinding, design-related accidents, and environmental stressors. For a more complete list, please review Chapter 2. As far as I am concerned, this is the richest area for design response. While the physical configuration of a place does not ensure that people will behave in a certain way, the design can support some activities and behavioral responses and inhibit others.

The E/B theories discussed here were behavior settings, the transactional model of environmental press and competence, sense of place, and Rapoport's several models. Theories are the constructs that relate place to behavior, behavior to people, and people to place. They are especially useful in setting up research study constructs.

The context for design must take into account the intertwined influences of economy, politics, sociology, and culture. Even though these influences may not bring up specific issues in your design project, they will impact the budget, the processing, and/or the community acceptance of your project.

The methods by which you ask your design research questions will determine whether you get quantitative or qualitative answers to your design questions. There are different methods for ascertaining the connections between people and place, place and behavior, and behavior and people. The best methods will be the most comprehensive and include lots of these theory-building connections.

Another important theme of this chapter has been the awareness of the need for flexibility and choice in environments in order to serve many different types of client needs and behaviors. Given the wonderful variety of people, we need to accommodate differences with designed choices.

CHAPTER 10

INFORMATION MANAGEMENT

- INFORMATION MANAGEMENT STRATEGY
  - "BRAIN DUMP" – CLEARING THE DECKS
  - CLARIFY FACTS AND ASSUMPTIONS
  - FIND THE HOLES
  - DESIGN A STRATEGY: STRUCTURES FOR ORDERING AND ORGANIZING DESIGN INFORMATION
  - FIND THE DATA
  - ANALYZE THE DATA
  - DEVELOP GOALS, PERFORMANCE REQUIREMENTS, AND CONCEPTS IN THEIR FINAL FORM
  - EVALUATE
  - SUMMARIZE AND DRAW CONCLUSIONS
  - PRESENT THE INFORMATION

- FINDING THE GAPS: DESIGN BY OVERLAY

INFORMATION MANAGEMENT

Obviously, a man's judgment cannot be better than the information on which he has based it.

A. H. Sulzberger
Address to the New York State
Publishers Association

INFORMATION MANAGEMENT STRATEGY

The programming process outlined in this book suggests that there are design issues that can function as categories for sorting the information into useful sets that are relevant to design. But design problems do not come with their issue categories and priorities all nicely laid out in a perfect hierarchy. In the beginning many designers have only a vague idea about what information is missing. They gather any article, precedent, or bit of data that even vaguely resembles the needs of the problem. That is not the most efficient way to go about it.

The following outline is aimed at information gathering for design and managing those facts so that they are useful at the time in the decision process when they are most relevant. It is presented in a linear manner, but as all design processes, it is cyclical and iterative with much back-tracking, becaues not all information is available when it is desired. Each step may necessitate verification with the client, depending upon the intricacy of the design problem.

The following ten steps illustrate a linear model that lists the processes in rational order. Reality shows that only a few of the steps can be completed independently of each other. Usually several of these steps are going on simultaneously.

1. Do a "brain dump."
2. Clarify all known facts and assumptions.
3. Identify the holes in your knowledge base.
4. Design a strategy for finding out what you need to know.
5. Go for the data.
6. Analyze the data.
7. Develop goals, performance requirements, and concepts in their final form.
8. Evaluate.
9. Summarize and draw conclusions.
10. Present the information.

The following discussion elaborates on these ten rules in much more detail:

1. "Brain Dump"— Clearing the Decks

"Brain dump" is my phrase for writing down or sketching out all of your ideas, thoughts, and assumptions about the problem at hand. To start, lay out all of your preconceptions — start with a list of issues and outline the values associated with any preconceived solutions. What preliminary images or themes immediately present themselves? What solutions do you already have in mind? What do you know about the organization the design will serve? What facts do you have at hand? Who are the people you already know whom you need to contact? What are your other resources?

Here is a preliminary set of questions to start you off on your own brain-dump:

A. What sort of environment do you think your users need to do their best work? Include the qualities that inspire good work, from housework to great bursts of creativity.
B. What is this project trying to say?
C. If I were to work or live here what would I want? How are my client and users different from me and what would they want or need?
D. What are the technical aspects of this project that make it distinctive?

E. What are the opportunities for really creative solutions posed by the functional needs of the client?

F. What inventive strategies must we look at early on because of budget constraints?

G. How will the structure of the client's organization impact the design?

2. Clarify Facts and Assumptions

Clearly articulate your assumptions about the problem, the mission statement as you know it, and goals known to this point. Verify the facts you already have in hand and look at your standard checklist to see what you are you missing. See White (1972), Peña (1987), Palmer (1981), and Chapter 2 for model checklists. Later in this chapter there are examples from some of these lists.

Assumptions are made in order to be tested. Facts are meant to be verified. It is an important facet of information theory that misinformation early in the process geometrically compounds the possibility for mistakes. Be sure to test or verify all facts that are the slightest bit shaky or old. Test all assumptions with the people who can validate or correct your assumptions.

Data Clog (Peña 1987)

This is the situation that occurs when you have too many pieces of unclear information buzzing around in your space to be of any use as you program or design. The strategy here is to categorize and group the information into different issue categories and simplify, simplify, simplify (see Figure 10-1). Get to the essence of the information that will help you make major decisions during programming or schematic

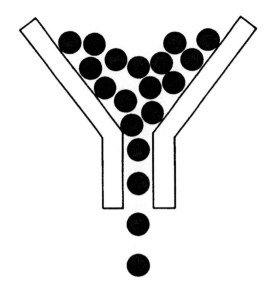

Figure 10-1   Data Clog.
From *Problem Seeking* by William M.Peña. Copyright © 1987 CRSS, Inc. Reproduced by permission of the author.

design and save the smaller particles of data for design development and construction documents. Set priorities for the most important and most impactful issues.

"KISS" Rule

The *KISS* rule works well here: *Keep It Simple, Stupid!* Not that designers are stupid, but we *all* do much better in communicating our ideas if we use a few big ideas to generate the smaller ones. Even Stephen Hawking, the well-known physicist, writes for the popular press in very simple language so that his ideas can be understood.

3. Find the Holes

Once you have found and categorized all the information you have on hand, the next step is to identify what you need to know. Peña (1987) developed a strategy that he called "problem seeking" — looking for the unique, critical problems to be solved that make a design problem distinctive. The most important missing information is the information that will promote a great solution for one of the critical problems in the design project.

As mentioned before, checklists are a good resource for information categories and for discovering what information is missing. You may want to use the lists presented here or develop your own to serve your specific needs. Ask yourself what you need to know to design a top-notch project. Develop the best questions you can! Set your own personal goals for what you want to accomplish with this project.

4. Design a Strategy: Structures for Ordering and Organizing Design Information

Use or develop the methods you need to appropriately answer the questions you have raised. Each question may require a different set of methods — all questions surely cannot be answered by interviewing the client or by observing the users or by group processes. Research may take the form of precedent or other library search, questions to ask the client, workshops with the users, or data to gather from the city, or you may have to design your own research project. The methods chapters (Chapter 6, 7 and 8) deal with asking good research questions and fitting the methods to the questions.

There are many different structures and strategies for ordering information, just as there are many different ways to cut a cake. A strategy for organizing information goes hand-in-hand with finding the holes in your information base. The following discussion shows several relatively well known examples.

Peña's Problem Seeking Model

Peña (1987) used a matrix of Form, Function, Economy, and Time (issue categories) crossed with Goals, Facts, Concepts, Needs, and Problem Statements (aspects of the existing and future states). Within the cell at each intersection is a list of issues or areas of concern that need data to create the appropriate information base for the design. (See Figure 10-2.) During the oil crisis, Energy was a fifth category added to Form, Function, Economy, and Time.

This Information Index serves as a check list for information categories generic to each design problem. It is one way to organize information relevant to and make projections about a design project. During a programming squatters (see Chapter 8) or a client meeting, programmers put all new information on 5 x 7 inch "snow cards" and place them in the appropriate spot in the the matrix. The matrix may be pinned up on a wall or be in a notebook organized by categories of Goals, Facts, Concepts, Needs, and Statement of the Problem. The card method makes it relatively easy to see where there are holes in the information needed.

Palmer's Model

Palmer (1981) uses another set of categories for partitioning and organizing programming information. His matrix is organized with one dimension being the Human Factors, Physical Factors, and External Factors related to a design problem and with the second dimension being Ascertainments (facts about the existing state), Predictions (trends, growth potential, etc.), and Recommendations (for

Information Index

	Goals	Facts	Concepts	Needs	Problem
Function People	Mission Maximum number Individual identity Interaction/privacy Ranking of values	Statistical data Area parameters Manpower/workloads User characteristics Community characteristics	Service grouping People grouping Activity grouping Priority	Space requirements Parking requirements Outdoor space requirements	Unique and important performance requirements which will shape building design
Activities	Exercise of authority Security Progression Segregation Encounters Efficiency	Authority structure Value of potential loss Time-motion study Traffic analysis Behavioral patterns Space adequacy	Hierarchy Security controls Sequential flow Separated flow Mixed flow Relationships	Functional alternatives	Major form considerations which will affect building design
Relationships	Information exchange	Type/intensity	Communication		
Form Site	Bias on site elements Sound structure Efficient land use Physical comfort	Site analysis Soil analysis F.A.R. and G.A.C. Climate analysis	Enhancement Special foundations Density Environmental controls	Site development costs Environmental influences on costs	
Environment	Life safety Sociality Individuality Encoded direction Direct entry Projected image	Code survey Surroundings Psychological implications Point of reference Entry symbols Generic nature	Safety precautions Neighbors Home base Orientation Accessibility Character	Building cost/S.F. Building efficiency Equipment costs	
Quality	Building quality level Spatial quality level Technical quality level Functional quality level	Cost/S.F. Building efficiency Equipment costs Area per unit	Quality control		
Economy Initial Budget	Extent of funds Cost effectiveness Maximum return	Cost parameters Maximum budget Time-use factors	Cost control Efficient allocation Multi-function	Cost estimate analysis	Attitude towards the initial budget and its influence on the fabric and geometry of the building
Operating Costs	Return on investment Minimize operating costs	Market analysis Energy source-costs	Merchandising Energy conservation	Energy budget (if reqd)	
Lifecycle Costs	Maintenance and operating costs Reduce life cycle costs	Activities and climate factors Economic data	Cost control Cost control	Operating costs (if reqd) Life cycle costs (if reqd)	
Time Past	Historic preservation Static/dynamic activities Change	Significance Space parameters Activities	Adaptability Tolerance Convertibility	`	Implications of change/growth on long-range performance
Present	Growth Occupancy date	Projections Durations	Expansibility Linear/concurrent scheduling	Time schedule Time/cost schedule	
Future	Cost controlled growth	Escalation factors	Phasing		

Figure 10-2 Peña's Information Matrix.
From *Problem Seeking* by Willian M. Peña. Copyright © 1987 CRSS, Inc. Reproduced by permission of the author.

the future state). Each of these categories have sub-categories and the cells in the matrix are again specific areas for gathering, organizing, and analyzing information.

The Human Factors category includes such items as: activities, behavior, goals, organization, interactions, policies, preferences, and qualities. The qualities list includes issues such as comfort, efficiency, security, convenience, etc.

The Physical Factors category includes facts about the site, structure, space types, equipment, matrials, durability, and energy use. This category also includes such issues as circulation, comfort, durability, and flexibility.

The External Factors category includes information about the climate, codes, resource availability, economy, time factors, and budgets. A major part of this category is information about the regulatory environment — from solar access and energy standards to land use restrictions and environmental impacts.

My major difficulty with this model as presented is that it blurs the line between categories so that information about behavior is listed in both the Human Factors and Physical Factors categories. Codes are listed under External Factors and Human Factors, etc. This overlap of category content makes it difficult to keep all information organized and readily accessible if you have to look several places for it.

White's Model

White (1972, 7) sees the sequence of programming and design events as follows:

1. Reality (laws, principles)
2. Search for and discovery of laws and principles (fact-making)
3. Known facts
4. Gathering of facts

5. Analysis, evaluation, and organization of facts into meaningful patterns
6. Response to facts in design synthesis
7. Building products
8. Building consequences
9. Evaluation

His emphasis is on facts and his list of traditional facts follows (White 1972). It is used here by permission of the author. This list is at the level of detail required for design development. Many categories are also vital for schematic design. This is a slightly abbreviated version of White's list of the *traditional facts*. See *Appendix A* for the full list with all levels of detail.

TRADITIONAL FACTS

A. Different facts may be pertinent to different types of PROGRAMMING DOCUMENTS. In the same way that we screen facts in terms of their RELEVANCE to building consequences, we also evaluate their PERTINENCE to the purpose of the document where they will be contained. Some of the different types of programming documents in architecture are:
  1. master plan
  2. long range plan
  3. site feasibility
  4. building program
  5. comprehensive plan
  6. project definition.
B. Below are some TYPICAL traditional architectural fact categories. For any specific situation some are more relevant than others. Groupings may also be different depending on the problem (pertain to and involve important building consequences).
  1. Similar projects and critical issues
      a. past projects of similar function, circumstances, and scope
      b. critical issues involved in the building type
      c. trends in the field

2. Client
    a. client goals
    b. philosophy of the organization
    c. goals of the client's process — sub-goals to achieve main goals — user goals
    d. staff organization and framework — personnel diagram
    e. rank and role of personnel
    f. major departmental divisions within the organization — role of each — goals and sub-goals within the overall process
    g. critical issues involved in the organization (people to people relationships, "channels")
    h. does organization usually operate the way it is structured?
    i. divergence of present operations from expressed goals — possible improvements
    j. degree of achievement of sub-goals
    k. individuals of committees responsible for planning with architect — role and responsibility in decision making
    l. related (non-client) organizations which might affect planning
    m. impact of change or growth of related organization
3. Financial
    a. budget — firmness, degree of flexibility
    b. funding methods — bonds, loans, fund raising
    c. timing — construction costs, escalation, interest rates, concurrent similar projects taxing public support
    d. construction phasing — prices, local construction market, strong and weak local trades, incremental construction
    e. design requirements of lending institutions
    f. comparative cost data on similar projects which have been constructed
4. Building codes
    a. occupancy allowed
    b. structural loads allowed
    c. exits required
    d. stairs (number, type, access, fire rating, size, minimum distances to reach stairs)
    e. fire ratings required of materials
    f. ventilation — openings
    g. toilets (number and fixtures of each)

h. fire sprinklers
i. alarm systems
5. Planning by related organizations
    a. duplication of services
    b. review boards
    c. approval boards (regulations, by-laws, planning criteria)
    d. projected construction of similar projects
6. Function
    a. operational system — including links beyond the building
    b. critical issues in ensuring success in the system's operation
    c. needs which are supporting to operation (lounge, waiting, toilet, janitor)
    d. main operational sequences — "feeder sequences" which support main sequences
    e. divisions or departments in the system
    f. general departmental relationship affinities
    g. number and type of people involved (task categories)
    h. operations performed by each type of person
    i. systems of people movement
    j. systems of information movement
    k. systems of material movement
7. Site
    a. legal description of property (boundaries, dimensions, rights of way, deed restrictions, easements, curbs, curb cuts, hydrants, poles)
    b. zoning
    c. utilities
    d. soil conditions
    e. land contours
    f. significant features
    g. existing foliage
    h. sensory
    i. time-distance
    j. existing pedestrian traffic on and around site
    k. existing vehicular traffic on and around the site
    l. surrounding physical environment (edges and heights, axes, walls, modules and rhythms)
    m. surrounding social environment
    n. shadow patterns on the site (trees, adjacent buildings)

o. parking and site circulation
8. Climate
    a. rainfall (frequency, volume, patterns)
    b. sunlight (critical vertical and horizontal angles)
    c. temperatures (seasons, extremes)
    d. wind, breezes (seasons, directions, velocity, extremes)
    e. snow (seasons, percentages)
    f. humidity (seasons, percentages)
    g. potential natural catastrophes (tornado, hurricane, earthquake, flood)
9. Growth and Change
    a. present and projected supporting market of public served
    b. projected staffing (number and type)
    c. projected goals and supporting sub-goals
    d. anticipated deletion of departments and addition of new departments
    e. areas of expected changes in operations (layout and building perimeter implications)

    f. projected changes in information or material systems (disposables)
    g. influence of growth and change of one department on all others
    h. future area needs (construction, cost, design, and parking implications)
    i. projected utility needs — comparison with present and projected supply capacities
C. Each of these fact categories may be EXPANDED to more DETAIL depending on the design requirements. There are also many other fact categories not listed here that pertain to some of the other programming FORMS (long range plan).

Every fact category and specific fact contained under its heading involves CONSEQUENCES which the building has on its environment and contained functions and which the environment has upon the building.

Markus's Model: Markus's (1972) work with the Building Performance Research Unit at the University of Strathclyde in Scotland developed an information model based upon different systems: the Building System, which includes construction and building services (hardware); the Environmental System, which includes spatial and physical considerations; the Activity System, which includes identity, communication, and work flow; and the Objectives System, which includes productivity, morale, and the stability of the organization. The performance of each of these systems is based on cost or value from the cost of provision or maintenance to the value of achieving the objectives of the building program. See Figure 10-3.

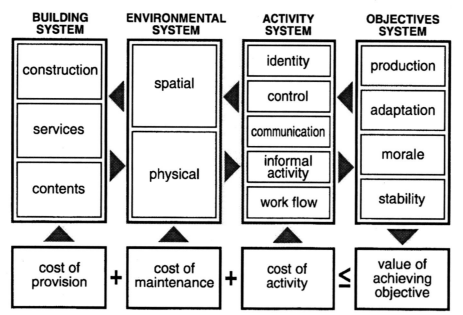

Figure 10- 3 Markus's Building Systems Model

Design issues can be described in terms of their impacts on each of these systems. For example, a maximally energy efficient building will require the use of a combination of specific construction sytems and materials. It will also require certain environmental control systems and particular volumes and orientations of building spaces. Maximum energy efficiency will also require supportive behaviors and activity patterns by the users as well as achieving the goal of making the building part of a sustainable community at low cost. Marcus's model is useful in value engineering and other cost-control systems, especially when the client's budget is tight and the ambition is great.

Traditional Model: Firmness, commodity, and delight have been the three major factors of consideration in architectural design for many, many years — since the famous translation of Vetruvius by Sir Henry Wotton in the late 18th century. Here the design issues are divided into three categories with some small overlap. Firmness includes all considerations of structural strength and life-cycle durability. Commodity includes all factors relating to physical and psychological comfort, including value and usefulness. Delight has to do with pleasure for all the senses. Comfort includes the factors of physical accommodation as well as aesthetic delight. See Figure 10-4.

Duerk's Model: This text offers another way of looking at the array of design data and creating a strategy to

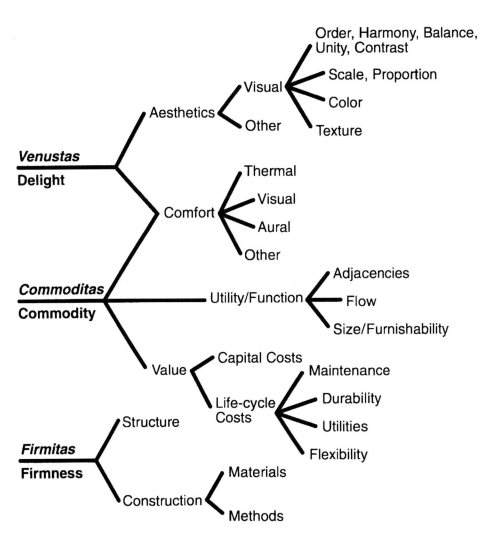

Figure 10-4   Implications in Design of Firmness, Commodity, and Delight.
Developed from diagram by Prof. Don Grant.

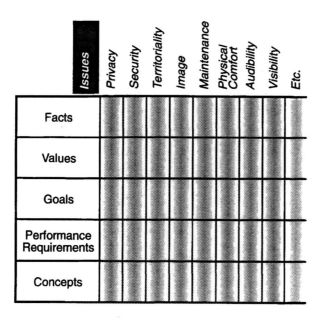

Figure 10-5 Duerk's Model

Issues	Privacy	Security	Territoriality	Image	Maintenance	Physical Comfort	Audibility	Visibility	Etc.
Facts									
Values									
Goals									
Performance Requirements									
Concepts									

make it all comprehensible. See Figure 10-5. The Issue List is on one side of the matrix and Values, Goals, Performance Requirements, and Concepts are on the other axis. This model brings together the best of the above models in that it organizes the design information by issue and allows the programmer to set priorities and organize the issues into larger categories as each project demands. It makes careful distinction between design information that is fact, that which is an issue (or area for making decisions), and that which is a potential solution. Its main strength is the emphasis on performance requirements and the rigor required to make performance requirement statements specific, measurable, and operational.

Each of the other models can be used to expand issue categories as they might be needed by a design project. White's (1972) fact lists add the detail required for programming for design development. Peña (1987) has only one performance requirement per goal or issue and thus simplifies the program. Palmer (1981) adds a category for predictions in addition to the existing (ascertainments) and the future (proposals) states.

5. Find the Data

Identify all sources of information, the players in the game, and the decision makers. Plan out an ideal sequence of information flow, even when you know that scheduling will mess it up every time and you will get some information late in the game that you should have had at the beginning. When the schedule must be changed, replan with current information for the most ideal strategy for gathering the information. See Chapters 7 and 8 for more information on research techniques.

Most programmers find that steps 4 (designing a strategy) and 5 (gathering the data) go hand-in-hand and are often difficult to separate. There is certainly a lot of cycling back and forth between these two steps.

There are three basic types of information for which to look: primary, secondary, and tertiary.

Primary Information

This type of information is your own eyewitness research. It can be most trusted by you because it is open only to your own interpretation and does not have to go through the filter of other peoples' interpretations.

Secondary Information

Secondary information comes from reading someone else's eyewitness research and requires a lot of library time to do a thorough search. Secondary information goes through only one other set of interpretation filters besides your own.

Tertiary Information

Third-hand information is reading about research in a collection of articles read by someone else about another person's research, such as a literature review or survey. Several layers of interpretation are between you and the originally observed data. If you know your sources, these tertiary leads can be very useful to your research plan, especially in helping to establish the boundaries of your research and develop an understanding of what has already been done and what you yourself have to do.

Most designers will use buildings that have already solved a similar problem as design references either as a first-hand visitor or through publications. This precedent research makes available models of what worked and what did not work for similar problems (a somewhat cursory post-occupancy evaluation; see Chapter 13). Other precedent research may inspire an analogy or metaphor to be used to reinvent a new solution to an old problem. Other program documents or evaluations may point up issues or research techniques you would have otherwise ignored.

6. Analyze the Data

Complete the issue list, look for remaining holes in the information, and articulate the values that have been uncovered so far. Draw your conclusions about the constraints and the overall opportunities of the project. Ask yourself what the implications are from the information that has come to light up to this point. Develop a sense of the most important issues that must be solved for this project to be a complete success. Recycle through the above five steps as necessary.

Data gathering gets the facts in hand, and data analysis gives the facts specific meaning that leads to action and program or design decisions. There are many kinds of analysis that are standard for the design process: site analysis, client life-style analysis, work-flow analysis, demographic analysis, organizational analysis, marketing analysis, and other endless possibilities for data analysis. Analysis is making the facts relevant to the particular problem and stating the implications — the opportunities or the problems to be solved by the design.

7. Develop Goals, Performance Requirements, and Concepts in Their Final Form

See Chapters 3, 4, and 5 for the "how to" of developing rigorpus goal statements, performance requirements, and concepts. The sequence for forming goals, performance requirements, and concepts is often woven in to the data gathering phases and does not necessarily happen in a predictable fashion. Once the issues are all identified and the goals, PRs, and concepts are roughed out, then polishing the phrasing and semantics of the goal and PR statements and refining the diagrams for the concepts can be done all at once.

The final revision of the goal and PR statements allows the programmer to insure that all goals are clear statements of the intended quality and that the PRs are measurable. The concepts should be abstract and allow the designer a great deal of freedom in implementation.

8. Evaluate

Look for what's missing, what doesn't feel right; test the validity of assumptions and facts with major design implications. If you are also the designer of the project, reevaluate a parti or major design theme that may have emerged by now. Review with the client any conclusions you have drawn. Check for conflicts between goals and performance requirements.

One of the major difficulties in design is when the designer thinks she has made an accurate interpretation of the client's instructions when, in fact, the information was accurate but the meaning was misinterpreted. See Chapter 13 for more evaluation methods and techniques for every part of the design process.

9. Summarize and Draw Conclusions

Summarize any vital statistics such as room-by-room and total square footage, estimated budget, overall concepts, design direction or emphasis, major problems to be solved, etc. State any specific design implications that have emerged. All summaries and conclusions must be clearly communicated and agreed upon by the client. See Chapter 11 for more on developing summaries.

10. Present the Information

Look at who will receive the information and decide upon an appropriate format for presentation. To gain the client's and user's feedback at the presentation stage, you may need to go back through some of the steps again until it meets your stamp of approval as a complete, appropriately interpreted document. When the program is accepted by the client, the program document is complete.

A program is an evolving entity and the data or client goals may change as the project develops. Documenting these changes is also an important part of information management. The original program is then changed by addenda rather than by rewrite. See Chapter 11 for alternatives for presenting the final program document.

Knowing the client's language and how they best understand information is crucial for a successful presentation to the client group. Most people understand visual information much more readily than verbal or mathematical information. Some people need to see a proposal in three dimensions to be able to understand it. The following examples and exercise are included to make you more aware of these communication issues.

The Translation Trap

Testing interpretations and assumptions as you go along is vital to the success of a programming project. All research is subject to your interpretation and should be verified with the client or user. The vision in the client's head of what the project should be can usually be expressed only in words or in pictures of similar buildings that contain a few of the qualities desired in the final design. These words and cloudy pictures must then be translated into a visualization in the designer's mind so that it can be reconfirmed in words and pictures.

At each step of translation from a visual and emotional image to a verbal picture or from a verbal description to a graphic illustration, there is the danger of a mis-step, a mistranslation. This potential for mistranslation is inherent in the process and in our inability to describe a visual image accurately with a verbal medium.

The Bag Trick

For another way to understand the dilemmas of translating visual images into verbal descriptions more fully, try this. Have someone put a reasonably unusual object (difficult to recognize or name by its shape or texture) into a paper bag without your seeing what it is. Put your hand into the bag without looking at the object. By feeling the object, describe it to a third person who does not know what the object is so that he can draw the object. If you intend to do this exercise, do not read any further until you have done so.

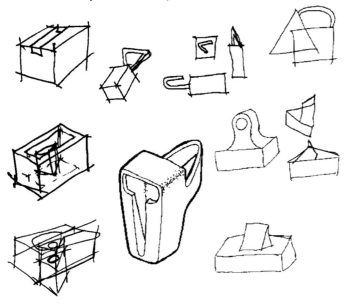

Figure 10-6   Sketches Drawn from Verbal Descriptions and the Cast-Stone Hanger That Was Described

You will very quickly find that this exercise is extremely difficult to do without some guidelines. See Figure 10-6 for some of the solutions produced at a New Year's Eve party using "the bag trick" as a parlor game. The sketch in the center represents an accurate likeness of the cast stone hanger that was in the bag. In this exercise, the people who are most successful in describing the object so that people can draw it adhere to one of the following two strategies:

The first strategy is to describe the object in terms of geometric relationships or Cartesian coordinates. "Imagine a rectangular solid that is 1 ½ inches across, 3 inches long and 1 inch high. It is positioned so that its bottom face is a 1 ½ x 3 inch rectangle and the front rectangle is 1 ½ inches wide by 1 inch high. Now imagine a piece of material ¾ inch wide by ⅛ inch thick by 4 inches long. Imagine that this piece of material is attached to the center of the top face's 3 inch long edges such that the ³⁄₄ inch dimension of each ⅛ x ¾ inch end is parallel to the 3 inch side and the 4 inch long piece of material forms a triangular loop over the top of the rectangular solid as it attaches to each top edge. Now imagine that the rectangular solid is hollow and has a surface thickness of about ⅛ inch. Imagine that the bottom surface has a fat *T*-shaped hole in it." Can you draw it now?

The second strategy consists of using an analogy to give the person drawing the object a known image to modify in her imagination that somewhat matches the object being described. "Imagine a basket that has a V-shaped handle. The handle is ¾ inch wide, ⅛ inch thick, and 4 inches long. Imagine that the body of this basket is a hollow rectangular solid with the opening at the bottom instead of at the top. The body of the basket is 1 inch deep x 1 ½ inches wide x 3 inches long and the hole in the bottom is shaped in the form of a very fat *T*. The handle is connected at the middle of the 3 inche long sides." What is it? Can you draw it this time?

Pi Example
Another example of the power of translating ideas into visual terms in the following use of *pi* (π). Most of us have used pi in geometry since junior high school or earlier. Most of us use it automatically, because it is in a formula, without knowing exactly what it is. It is a mathematical symbol that

we do not usually bother to translate into a visual language, we just plug it into the formula. So, what is pi? In translating it from a verbal word (*pi*) to a mathematical term, we can say that pi is 3.14. But what *is* pi, really? In order to understand what pi actually is, rather than a verbal symbol or a mathematical symbol, we must go to a visual language. This material is derived from *The Relationship Course* presented by Landmark Education Corporation and is reprinted here with the expressed permission of Landmark Education Corporation.

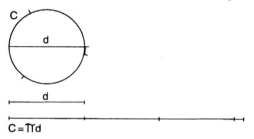

Figure 10-7   Circumference = π x diameter

Imagine a circle made of string with its diameter also made of string. Unroll the circumference string and place it parallel to the diameter. The relationship between the length of the diameter string and the length of the circumference string is such that the circumference string will be pi (or 3.14) times the diameter string for any circle.

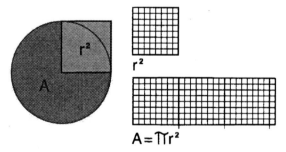

Figure 10-8   Area = π x radius ²

Next imagine a circle superimposed on a square with its sides parallel to and equal to the length of the radii of the circle. The area of the circle is pi times larger than the area of the square with each side as long as the radius of the circle.

The visual description creates an understanding of pi that is not available to us with the word *pi*, the symbol π or the number 3.14159265+. This phenomenon is also true of architectural design. A schematic design alternative shows relationships that are not so easy to understand in their verbal or mathematical forms. This quality of creating new information for the client is a good argument for frequent program and design reviews with the client group.

FINDING THE GAPS: DESIGN BY OVERLAY

The concept of "design by overlay" is based upon the following process:

1. Create your overall design concept (parti) based upon the three to seven major design issues.

2. Overlay the concerns of each of the minor issues, one at a time. Evaluate the concept for how well it performs in each issue area.

3. Adjust the design concept, without losing the ideas or the benefits, to satisfy the performance requirements of these minor issues as well as possible.

Usually the design should be 100 % responsive to the requirements of the top priority issues and can be less than perfect for the lower priority issues. The best of all possible worlds would be to make no trade-offs and have all the issues perform at 100 %.

Using this method, the most important part of information management is having the right information available at the right time. The system of using design issues as categories for organizing all the information necessary to produce a good design allows you to prioritize issues and work on those that are most important first. It also encourages you to work from general, overall design concerns to specific, itemized concerns.

Another vital part of managing design information is to discover what information is missing and what information is most important to the client and to the designer regarding top priority issues. These issues need more in-depth research to discover related facts, clients' and users' values and goals, performance requirements, and concepts required to implement the ideal solution for the top priority issues. Programmers who are also the project designers must guard against jumping to a solution before all the research is done.

Figure 10-9 Section Through Kimball Barrel Vault.
From *Analysis of Precedence* by Clark and Pause. Copyright © 1979 The Student Publication of the School of Design, N.C. State University at Raleigh. Reproduced by permission of the School of Design.

Most of us can only manage to think about a few things at the same time. Miller's (1956) magic number for how many things we can hold in our immediate conscious awareness is seven plus or minus two. One strategy for managing masses of information and a very large number of important design issues is to focus the conceptual

development of a design on a handful of the highest priority issues. Students in the early years of design might try to develop an overall concept that solves the problem for the three highest priority issues. Students in the upper years of design studio might try for five top priority issues. Experienced designers may be able to handle seven to nine major issues, but as the number of major issues increases, the clarity of the design concept usually decreases.

When you have developed the basic concept, based on a small number of the top priority issues, other important, secondary issues can be used as fine-tuning filters overlaid on the design. For example, if the top three issues for a house are security, privacy and energy conservation, then the concept that is developed to solve that problem set must also be evaluated for image, structural stability, territoriality, social interaction, circulation, and all the other issues that will make the design even better. If there is a conflict between the concept that solves the need for energy conservation and the need for a particular image, then the design concept should be modified in order to bring the image as close to ideal as possible without sacrificing energy efficiency or adding too much to the budget.

One of the most difficult pieces of missing information to discover late in the project is a conflict between two different program needs. Major trade-offs become more difficult as the design progresses.

Let's imagine that *the* major design problem for Kahn in the Kimball Museum was the requirement for having natural light in the museum without having the ultraviolet rays damaging the paintings. The solution to this combination of the design issues visibility and maintenance was to bounce the sunlight around in a skylight slit and then bounce it off of a curved ceiling. The structural system of barrel vaults flowed naturally with the concept for the lighting system. See Figure 10-9. The concept had to be molded to accommodate the circulation and service needs of the museum as well as to meet the image desired. See Chapter 5 for the related concept diagrams.

Similarly, the Guggenheim Museum by Wright had circulation as its top priority design issue. The circulation spiral was such a powerful concept that it overruled any possible consideration for "fitting into" the traditional New York City street image, even if Wright had intended it to blend in. The building also had to have services and to create a level of physical comfort as well as deal with the issues of security and maintenance. Artists have criticized the museum because its angled ramp floor gives the rectangular paintings a sense of being skewed and not hanging straight. This is a consideration that was either ignored or not brought up as an important issue.

SUMMARY

The information management strategy proposed here includes ten steps:

1. Do a "brain dump."

2. Clarify all known facts and assumptions.

3. Identify the holes in your knowledge base.

4. Design a strategy for finding out what you need to know.

5. Go for the data.

6. Analyze the data.

7. Develop goals, performance requirements, and concepts in their final form.

8. Evaluate.

9. Summarize and draw conclusions.

10. Present the information.

Each of these steps interacts with the others and it is often possible to be engaged in activities that contribute to the progress of several of these steps at the same time. Although the process is cyclical rather than linear, it is presented in a linear fashion for clarity. Step four is probably most critical for managing design information because the information framework that you use guides your search toward particular categories of information. Each of the models presented (Peña's, White's, Palmer's, Markus's, Duerk's, and traditional) have aspects you might want to include in your own information management framework.

In managing design information it is important to make sure that all participants on the design team are in agreement about what the operational terms mean and the direction of the design. Don't fall into the translation trap by assuming that your interpretation is held by everyone else.

A corollary to the information management strategy is the concept of "design by overlay," which means that the main program and design ideas are generated from the top priority issues and that the minor issues are considered later. The changes required to satisfy these lower priority minor issues should be incidental fine-tuning and should not change the overall concept. Using this approach, the quality and performance level for all issues can be made to be satisfactory, based upon the priority for each issue.

CHAPTER 11

FORMATS: STRUCTURING A PROGRAM DOCUMENT

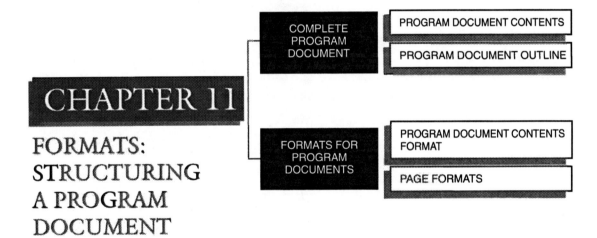

COMPLETE PROGRAM DOCUMENT

PROGRAM DOCUMENT CONTENTS

PROGRAM DOCUMENT OUTLINE

FORMATS FOR PROGRAM DOCUMENTS

PROGRAM DOCUMENT CONTENTS FORMAT

PAGE FORMATS

FORMATS: STRUCTURING A PROGRAM DOCUMENT

The essential thing in form is to be free in whatever form is used. A free form does not assure freedom. As a form, it is just one more form. So that it comes to this, I suppose, that I believe in freedom regardless of form.

Wallace Stevens
A Note on Poetry

COMPLETE PROGRAM DOCUMENT

This section deals with the program *document* as a whole, from introduction to the final summary and appendix. The program document should be a readable story of the project that flows smoothly and logically from beginning to end. Any items that are too detailed for ready consumption by the client or project designer should be put into an appendix.

Figure 11-1 shows the order of information that is the ideal for a program document that uses the process outlined in this book. Different programmers will give specific parts of the program document distinct priorities and emphases and may want to leave some parts out or skim lightly over some of the data. Much depends upon who the client is, what their priorities are, and who is on the programming and design team. The italicized portions in the chart (mission, goals, etc.) are dealt with in other chapters. Graphics play a large role in making a clear communication to your intended audience.

Program Document Contents

The program document presents the facts pertinent to the project's context and constraints so that the client and the design team are clear about all the necessary information. There are many other resources that give constructive information about how to conduct and present site analysis, climate analysis, client organizational analysis, etc. (White 1983; Olgyay 1963; Steele 1981). In this case, I am primarily concerned with presenting categories of useful information for a *complete* program document. The document also presents the analysis of these facts and the requirements for the success of the design along with conceptual proposals for the ideal solution.

Introduction

EXISTING STATE

Background: Cultural, Social, Political, Historical

Physical Conditions: Geography (regional, district, etc.), Site, Climate, Archaeology

Client Profile: Demography, Organizational Analysis, Preferences

Constraints: Codes, Master Plans

FUTURE STATE

Mission
Goals
Performance Requirements
Concepts

Summaries: Budget, Space Summaries

Conclusions: Organizing Concepts, Themes

Phasing Plan, etc.

Appendix: Research Studies, Pro Formas, Client Scenarios

Figure 11-1 Program Document Contents

The first part of a program document organizes all the relevant facts about the existing state into a readable form (the background, site analysis, etc). The meat of the program document is the proposal for the future state — the level of performance and the ideas about the solutions. The final part of the document is composed of the summaries and conclusions that the programmer has reached as a result of the programming research, data gathering, and goal definition work that has developed the program. The appendix gives additional information in greater detail than required by the flow of the story of the building program so that the overall project is made readily coherent in the body of the program document.

The outline shown here works well for simple to moderately complex buildings. Many programmers organize their program documents by functional area or department and use an outline similar to the one presented here to delineate each building section.

Program Document Outline

- *Introduction:* mission statement (Why are we doing this project anyhow?)
- *Analysis* of the *existing state* of affairs: acts of record, site analysis, climate, client/user analysis, codes, background (historical, contextual, political), etc. (the facts of the case)
- *Proposal* for the *future state:* goals/performance requirements/concepts (what the project should turn out to be like)
- *Summary:* parti, concept scenario, space summary, budget, etc. (conclusions drawn from all the preceding facts and proposals)
- *Appendix:* detailed analyses, research data, other relevant information that is too detailed to put into the body of the program document

The following discussion describes each section of a program document in detail:

Introduction

The introduction states the problem in the briefest feasible form, introduces the players, identifies the decision makers, and generally sets the tone of the program document. It includes the mission statement for the project. Often key information about the size, budget, and major organizational aspects of the project will also be included.

Existing State: Setting the Stage

Background: Part of understanding the design problem is to be clear about the context within which the design must be developed. The background of the project needs to be discussed so that the nuances and implications for the current project are not missed. The path to the project's current status may be relevant, especially if there have been several other attempts to develop a similar use or to develop this particular site. The history of the state, city, area, district, or site may be relevant. All the cultural, social, political, and historical factors that will influence the design should be presented for inclusion in the design thinking.

All relevant physical conditions should be delineated including local geography, location in the state, and major circulation routes near the site. Site selection criteria may be important in this part of the document for your project. At the larger scale, Lynch's (1981) categories of district, node, landmark, boundary, and path may be useful.

Site Analysis: The individual project's site analysis can range from mere topographic information for schematic proposals to in-depth studies covering a wide range of topics. The following list of pieces of information will be useful to most designers in developing a comprehensive design. Most site analysis is best presented in a *graphic* manner so that the designer can see how it applies to the site. White's (1983) book is a good place to start as well as other books on landscape architecture (Simonds 1983).

Climate: This includes such facts as seasonal wind speed and direction (a wind rose), sun angles, degree days, humidity, and monthly precipitation amounts and types. This section may also include charts of heating and cooling days, growing cycle, shadow analysis, etc. This would include all the climate information necessary to run an energy analysis

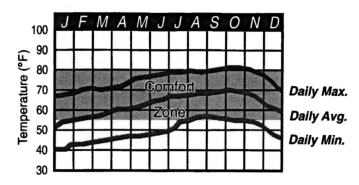

Figure 11-4   Chart of Normal Temperature for San Luis Obispo, California, During One Year

program such as Cal-Pas or Micro-Pas, which are used mainly in California. Also include any information that may indicate the particular microclimate that pertains to the project site.

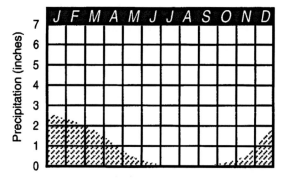

Figure 11-2   Chart of Normal Precipitation for San Luis Obispo, California, During One Year

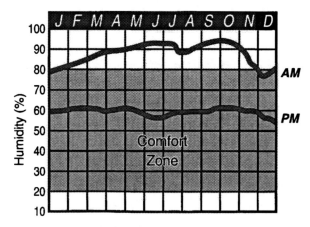

Figure 11-3   Chart of Normal Humidity for San Luis Obispo, California, During One Year

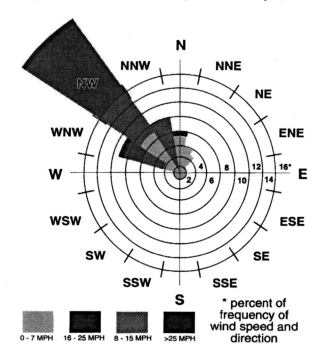

Figure 11-5   Wind Rose for Davenport, California

Topography: This set of facts includes flora, fauna, topography of the land (Figure 11-6), water features, rocks, and other significant geological elements. Archaeological sites may also need to be documented and may become the inspiration for design.

Vital information such as the *actual* location of utilities on site must be accurate. The general location of a sewer pipe is not good enough if the building's foundation is mistakenly designed to go on top of the pipe instead of the required five feet away — because of inaccurate or approximate information.

Context: A contextual analysis includes both the physical context (such as a visual analysis of the character of the surroundings, views into and out of the site (Figure 11-7), and existing buildings) and the intangible context (which will include demography, social structure, history, economics, culture, and politics of the area, if they are relevant to the project). Other information that is a part of the context includes: circulation paths (pedestrian, vehicular, bicycles), location of public transportation, zoning nearby, adjacent land uses, etc.

Visual analysis takes many forms. In San Luis Obispo, California, the downtown has a characteristic ambiance that is largely due to a set of **data lines**. A datum line is a reference line that is relatively consistent and here serves to unify the street front compositions. In San Luis Obispo, the lines are at the base of the store windows, the top of the door jamb, the

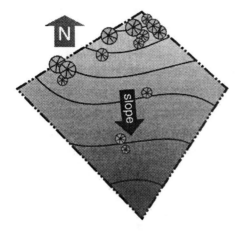

Figure 11-6 Site Slope and Trees

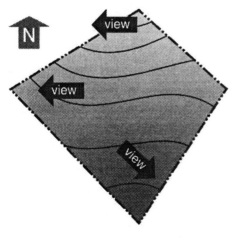

Figure 11-7 Topography and Views

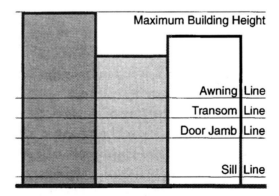

Figure 11-8 Data Lines for Downtown San Luis Obispo, California

top of the transom, and at the top of the awning or sign space. Data lines for the second story are much less consistent and often not permanent. Each building on the street has most of these lines, even though they are not all at exactly the same height above the sidewalk.

Constraints: Sometimes local building codes are much more restrictive than the UBC (Uniform Building Code) and the local zoning codes are an important part of the set of constraints that will set some of the limits of the design. For example, the old New York zoning code required that neighboring buildings be able to get light and air. As a result, the code dictated the wedding cake shape of tall skyscrapers such as the Chrysler and the Empire State Buildings. When the zoning code was changed to encourage plazas, the wedding cake shape disappeared and the glass block buildings took up the new position as the most efficient shape for developers to get their monetary returns on their investments with maximum floor/area ratios.

Another set of constraints may come from existing master plans that need to be reworked or incorporated as a set of working rules for the new project. With a site that has existing buildings or that is an infill site, there are many constraints set up by the adjacent buildings. All constraints serve to confine the range of possible solutions and many times are the impetus for a very creative design that achieves the goals of the project in spite of the constraints.

Client Analysis: To understand the client, the programmer must do some research. Interviews may be enough or, as with Frank Lloyd Wright, extended periods of participant observation may be needed. Otherwise, observation studies, behavior maps (Figure 11-9), time logs, etc., may be necessary to set the quality of information needed for a good design solution.

For many projects, understanding the client's organization may be the key to a good program. Formal organizational hierarchies, informal information networks, other organizational development issues, projected changes in work loads, and job definitions are all useful in understanding an institutional or business client group. For housing and larger community projects, knowing the demographics and the value sets and preferences of the residents/users is vital to the success of the project.

It is important to identify all the user groups — from the casual passerby who is to be impressed with the image of the building to the maintenance personnel and the loan officers at the bank. Different users will have different needs and the programmer, with the client, will have to set priorities that include as many interests as possible, from those of the workers who operate the building to those of the residents who inhabit it.

Future State: What Should Be

The future state is the proposal for what the design *should be* like. This is where the mission statement, goals, performance requirements, and concepts are set out. This segment of the program document is a description of the qualities that a good solution should have as well as a set of yardsticks for measuring those qualities. The concepts are proposals for relationships that create the desired qualities.

Future State Summaries: Polishing the Project Information for Your Client

Space Summaries: Space summaries should include all usable spaces inside the building to be designed as well as all spaces on the exterior that need planning, such as ball fields and other recreational areas for a high school. Targets for net

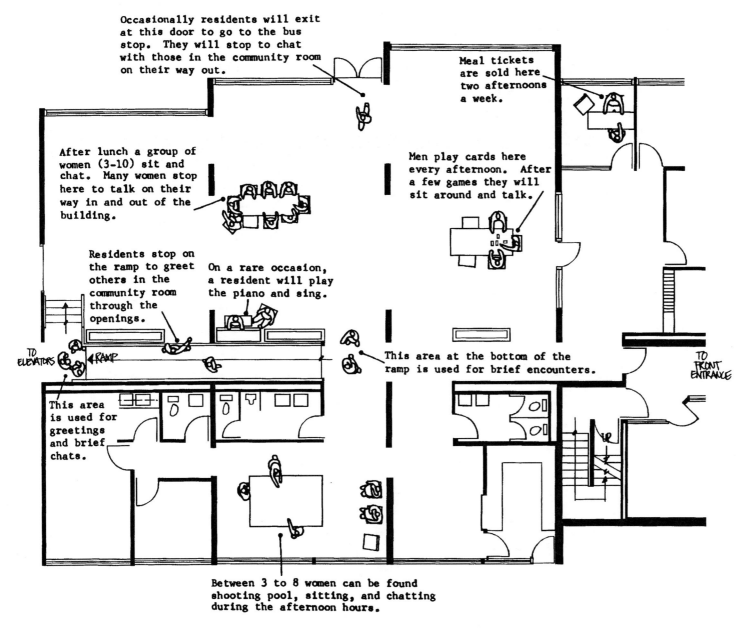

Occasionally residents will exit at this door to go to the bus stop. They will stop to chat with those in the community room on their way out.

Meal tickets are sold here two afternoons a week.

After lunch a group of women (3-10) sit and chat. Many women stop here to talk on their way in and out of the building.

Men play cards here every afternoon. After a few games they will sit around and talk.

Residents stop on the ramp to greet others in the community room through the openings.

On a rare occasion, a resident will play the piano and sing.

TO ELEVATORS

RAMP

This area at the bottom of the ramp is used for brief encounters.

TO FRONT ENTRANCE

This area is used for greetings and brief chats.

Between 3 to 8 women can be found shooting pool, sitting, and chatting during the afternoon hours.

Figure 11- 9   Activity Map Showing User Behaviors.

From *Shared Spaces in Housing for the Elderly* by Sandra C. Howell. Copyright © 1976 Design Evaluation Project, Department of Architecture, MIT.
Reproduced by permission of the author.

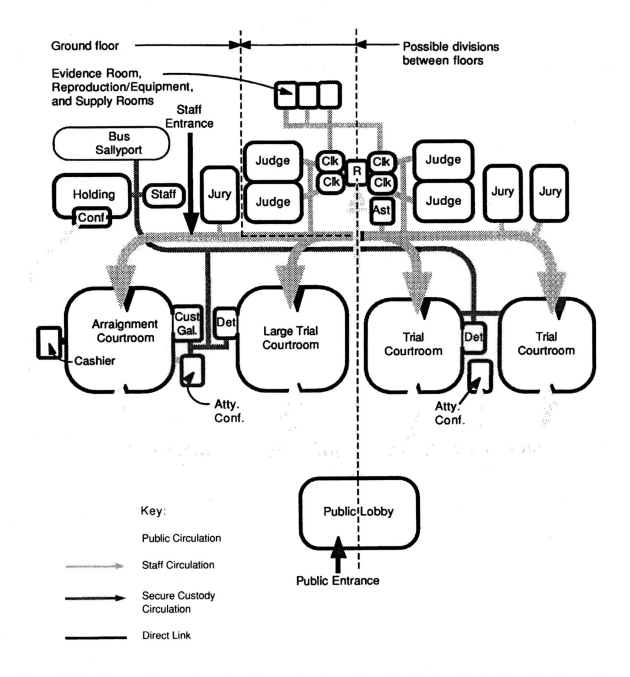

Ground floor ◄━━━━━━━━━━━━━━━━━━► Possible divisions between floors

Evidence Room, Reproduction/Equipment, and Supply Rooms

Staff Entrance

Bus Sallyport

Holding
Conf.
Staff
Jury
Judge
Judge
Clk
Clk
R
Clk
Clk
Ast
Judge
Judge
Jury
Jury

Arraignment Courtroom
Cust. Gal.
Det
Large Trial Courtroom
Trial Courtroom
Det
Trial Courtroom

Cashier
Atty. Conf.
Atty. Conf.

Key:

——— Public Circulation

╌╌╌► Staff Circulation

———► Secure Custody Circulation

━━━ Direct Link

Public Lobby

Public Entrance

Figure 11-10   Adjacency Diagram for a Court House.   Courtesy of Greg Allen Barker, AIA, Jay Farbstein & Associates, Inc.

to gross ratios should also be included so that corridors, toilets, and other non-use areas might be predicted. Any areas that are not full ceiling height (7½ feet), such as basements or attics, may be included if they will have an impact upon the building costs.

Space summaries may be presented in tabular form or in graphic form with a square area indicating the size of each area to scale. The original idea for this format comes from CRSS's "Brown Sheets." Another form of summary is the overall adjacency diagram (Figure 11-10). Exact sizes of spaces may not appear, but relative size or importance is an important visual feature.

Budgets: Budgets should include everything that is required for the completion of the entire project. This includes all consultants' fees, architectural fees, interiors, furniture, equipment, landscaping, and special services or products. Most programmatic budgets do not include budgets for various alternates unless they are part of the original design process. See Figure 11-11.

Major Organizing Concepts and Themes: In the programming process articulated here, most of the concepts are small parts of the whole design and support particular performance requirements. Very seldom does one of these small concepts develop the power to become an overall organizing concept or theme. In the case of the Kimball Museum by Kahn, the barrel vault that was the solution for letting in natural light without the damage of the ultraviolet light rays did become the major organizing idea. Analogies or metaphors can be seen very clearly as organizing themes as well.

Key Elements and Partis: Sometimes a key element that serves as a focal point for the design will be uncovered during programming. Frank Lloyd Wright used geometry

(the hexagon, the 2:1 rectangle, the square, the circle) as a parti for many of his Usonian houses. In ancient Egypt, a key element — the procession to the burial chamber — was the major organizational idea for the funeral ceremony as well as for the design of the complex.

Phasing Plans: Many times a project will be too large or too expensive to be built all at once and the nature of the design will be influenced by the components in each phase. For example, many commercial developments are built initially as a shell and the tenant improvements are built during later phases as the space is rented to particular clients. Sometimes buildings will be built at two stories, requiring the structural capacity for two or more extra stories to be built some years in the future.

Appendix: The Epilogue

The items in the appendix are those things that are too detailed to go into the body of the program document but provide useful design information. The appendix for a schematic design program will include such items as detailed space lists (room by room), detailed cost studies, research reports, and other analytical information that serves to enrich the design information base.

Research Studies: If, during design, specific research is done to reveal particular facts about the user group, the site, or other aspects or issues relating to the design, then the outcomes of those studies should be summarized as a part of the program document in the appropriate spot. The full research report may be useful in the appendix.

Pro Formas: Pro formas contain all the details of generating an appropriate return on investment and the set of assumptions required to develop that level of return. These documents are best included in the appendix because tables of

		CAL POLY CHILDRENS CENTER BUDGET SUMMARY			
NO.	LINE ITEM	SUBCONTRACTOR		SUBCONTRACT $	% TOTAL
1	SUPERVISION	CDSI		$40,000.00	4.44%
2	TEMP FACILITIES & UTILITIES	CDSI	*	$10,000.00	1.11%
3	SOILS REPORT & TOPOGRAPHY MAP	CDSI	*	$5,300.00	0.59%
4	ARCHITECTURE	WEST+DOUBLEDEE ARCHITECT		$55,000.00	6.11%
5	SITEWORK	M J ROSS		$41,235.00	4.58%
6	SITE DISPOSAL	CDSI	*	$3,000.00	0.33%
7	SPRINKLER SYSTEM/UNDERGROUND	ALPHA FIRE/BULLARDS&SONS		$21,800.00	2.42%
8	PLUMBING	M K WILLIAMS PLUMBING		$39,500.00	4.39%
9	ELECTRICAL AND ALARM SYSTEM	P W MANN ELECTRIC		$71,502.00	7.95%
10	CONCRETE FOUNDATION & FLATWORK	MANNING CONSTR.		$55,400.00	6.16%
11	MASONRY	MANNING CONSTR.		$35,900.00	3.99%
12	ROUGH & FINISH CARPENTRY	B J HARVEY CONSTR.		$20,000.00	2.22%
13	ROUGH LUMBER & HARDWARE	CDSI	*	$10,000.00	1.11%
14	TRUSSES	GANG NAIL TRUSS SYSTEMS	*	$8,295.00	0.92%
15	HEATING	RICE HEATING		$21,000.00	2.33%
16	ROOFING	CERTIFIED		$39,295.00	4.37%
17	WINDOWS, SKYLIGHT, & STOREFRONTS	COUNTRY GLASS		$17,846.00	1.98%
18	INSULATION	GEARHART INSUL		$3,000.00	0.33%
19	DRYWALL	WHITES DRYWALL		$51,804.00	5.76%
20	DOORS, FRAMES, AND HARDWARE	CHILDS AND CO.		$14,000.00	1.56%
21	PAINTING	M K BAILEY		$3,000.00	0.33%
22	SUSPENDED ACOUSTIC CEILING	TRI COUNTY INSULATION		$8,953.00	0.99%
23	CANOPY	PACIFIC STEEL SYSTEMS		$9,800.00	1.09%
24	PLASTER	EVANS PLASTERING		$17,418.00	1.94%
25	VINYL, CARPET, & BASE	PHILLIPS FLR COVERINGS		$15,500.00	1.72%
26	WOOD CASEWORK/COUNTERTOPS	PRYOR	*	$30,000.00	3.33%
27	CHALK , MESSAGE, & TACK BOARDS	CDSI	*	$3,000.00	0.33%
28	BATH ACCESSORIES	PENCE BLDG SPECIALTIES	*	$4,000.00	0.44%
29	KITCHEN EQUIPMENT	CDSI	*	$8,000.00	0.89%
30	STAINLESS STEEL KITCHEN TOPS	A & J REFRIGERATION		$7,200.00	0.80%
31	BLINDS	3 DAY BLINDS		$781.00	0.09%
32	TELEPHONE SYSTEM	CENCOM		$3,000.00	0.33%
33	PLAY AREA CHAIN LINK FENCE	FENCE FACTORY	*	$5,000.00	0.56%
34	LANDSCAPE	OASIS LANDSCAPING		$30,000.00	3.33%
35	PAVING	TOSTE /APODOCA	*	$10,000.00	1.11%
36	CLEAN UP	CDSI		$5,000.00	0.56%
37	CONTINGENCY	CDSI		$37,000.00	4.11%
38	BOND FEE/MOBILIZATION			$25,000.00	2.78%
		SUBCONTRACT TOTAL		$786,529.00	87.40%
		PROFIT/OVERHEAD		$113,420.00	12.60%
		TOTAL CONTRACT AMOUNT		$899,949.00	100.00%

Figure 11-11   Contractor's Design-Build Spread Sheet Budget. Used by permission of Terry Simons, Development Services.

numbers are very boring to most people and they interrupt the information flow of the program document. Only the most significant numbers should go into the body of the program document and should also be highlighted in the full pro forma in the appendix. If possible, the numerical data should be converted into graphic form.

Client Scenarios: The main points from client scenarios should also be included in the program document, but a more in-depth look at the client's procedures and lifestyle should find a place in the appendix. Client scenarios may take the form of timelogs and diaries or may be the expected user flow through the client's service delivery system. If you have to imagine a typical client or create a composite "generic client," then the scenario is crucial to the designer's understanding of the needs of the client or user. See Appendix B for examples.

the format accordingly. If the program is to be used to obtain a loan, the financial information must play a prominent role. If the program is for presentation to various user groups, then the functional aspects need to be primary. If the program is for a government agency, then the format must conform to the specifications given.

Regardless of format, the document should be easy to read and to reference different aspects. My favorite analogy is that the program is the story of the building to come and should be as easy to read as a novel. Obviously this is not true for a document that is filled with page after page of room requirements. My suggestion is that the detailed room requirements be a part of the appendix or in a special section of the program document so that the body of the program document is easier to read.

FORMATS FOR PROGRAM DOCUMENTS

When you have all the parts and pieces of the program document, then you must decide upon the graphic format for presentation. Since a program document is a compilation of the client's and the programmer's intentions for the project, including all the relevant facts and constraints that must be considered, the format should reflect that intention. The program document is the conceptual basis for design and is the basis for the contractual agreement regarding the direction of schematic design. The form that the document takes should support and easily convey the essence of the ideas manifested in the program. The following format structure for a program document is one that works and that can be adjusted to suit your particular presentation. It is important to know who the audience will be for the document and to tailor

Program Document Contents Format

The following format briefly describes the order and the contents of each section. Chapter 12 shows parts of this format in detail in a presentation of case studies.

Introduction

The introduction includes a statement about why the project is being undertaken and why it is important. It should include the mission statement (megagoal). It might also include some summary information such as overall square footage, the main ideas for the design, the major problems to be resolved by the design, and the important decision makers in the process. The introduction acts as the executive summary would in a larger report.

Existing State — Context

This includes all the facts that outline the context within which the design must be completed successfully. This includes the constraints, the appropriate codes, the site analysis, client analysis, a description of the physical context, and the socio-political context.

Future State — Goals, Performance Requirements, Concepts

The following outline for the relationship of goals, performance requirements, and concepts is easy to read and follows the ideas from general qualities to specific implementation.

1. Goal Statement

1.1 Performance Requirement Statement

    1.1.1 Concept Diagram

    1.1.2 Concept Diagram

    1.1.3 Concept Diagram

    1.1.4 Concept Diagram

2. Goal Statement

2.1 Performance Requirement

    2.1.1 Concept

    2.1.2 Concept

    2.1.3 Concept

2.2 Performance Requirement

    2.2.1 Concept

    2.2.2 Concept

    2.2.3 Concept

2.3 Performance Requirement

    2.3.1 Concept

    2.3.2 Concept

    2.3.3 Concept

    2.3.4 Concept

3. Goal Statement

3.1 Performance Requirement

    3.1.1 Concept

Performance requirements and concepts continue as necessary for each following goal.

Summaries and Conclusions

Summaries include space summaries, budgets, overall adjacency diagrams, organizing concepts and themes, any phasing plans, and any overall conclusions reached by the client and the programmer.

Appendix

All material that interrupts the flow of the program document or is too detailed for the body of the document goes in this section.

Page Formats

Page formats can be used to make the presentation of your program a graphically interesting document. With today's desk top publishing techniques, there is no limit to your potential layout. Each page format has its advantages and disadvantages, which can be used to suit your purposes.

Three Columns Wide

The landscape format (wide) is being used more and more for books that have a great deal of graphic content. The columns are narrow so that they are easy to read. This is good for pages that are mostly text. Three columns give a great deal of choice about how to integrate the graphics — from in-line column graphics to whole page diagrams or photos. Several alternatives for this format are shown at the end of this chapter. See Figure 11-12.

Two Columns Wide

Two columns in a landscape format make the columns just about as wide as is comfortable to read. If the lines of type get any longer, they are hard to track from the end of one line back across the page to the beginning of the next line. Here, too, the multiple columns give a fairly wide variety of possible ways to integrate text and graphics. See Figure 11-13.

Two Columns Wide with Sidebar

This format is the one used for this book. It incorporates many of the advantages of a three-column format with narrow text columns and a variety of graphic integration potentials. The sidebar (a narrow column used for auxiliary information) allows information to be presented in a way that does not interfere with the flow of the main text. See Figure 11-14.

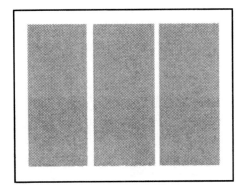

Figure 11-12   Three Columns Wide Format

Figure 11-14   Two Columns Wide with Sidebar

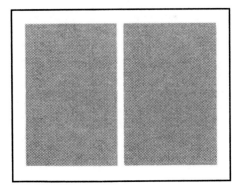

Figure 11-13   Two Columns Wide Format

One Column Vertical with Wide Gutter

This format overcomes some of the difficulty of one column by making it narrower due to the wide gutter. Integration of graphics into the text can take on either the in-line format or text-wrap format. The gutter is the inboard space on the page, toward the spine of the book, that allows for the pages to be bound together and still be read without being "lost in the gutter." See Figure 11-15.

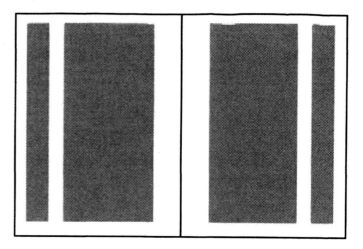

Figure 11-16 One Column Vertical with Sidebar

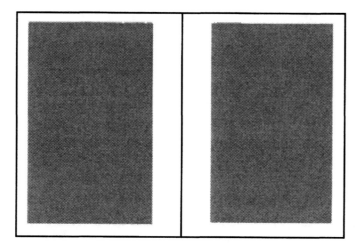

Figure 11-15 One Column Vertical with Wide Gutter

One Column Vertical with Sidebar

This is my personal favorite of the one column vertical formats. The sidebar is used to present graphic or other information that is supplementary to the text or to accommodate large graphics. See Figures 11-16.

Two Column Vertical

This format is fairly easy to read because of the shorter lines of text. It looks a bit awkward in the 8 $1/2$ x 11 inch format because of the proportion of the page length to the width. See Figure 11-17.

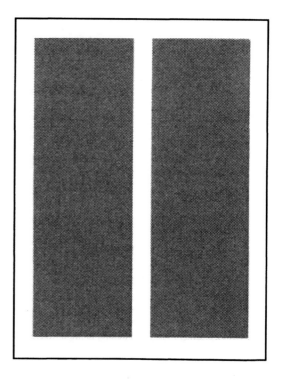

Figure 11-17 Two Column Vertical

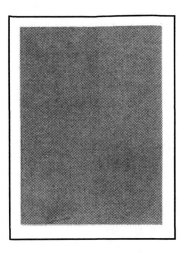

Figure 11-18   One Column Vertical

One Column Vertical

This is the hardest to read of all formats unless the page is small or the type is large. Long lines of text make it hard for the eye to catch the next appropriate line of text without skipping or repeating a line. See Figure 11-18.

Potential Layouts for Pictures Integrated with Text

Figures 11-19 to 11-23 show the wide variety of page layouts possible with a three column horizontal page format.

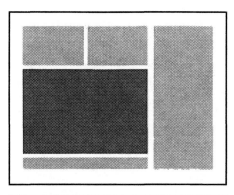

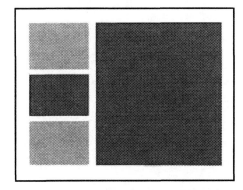

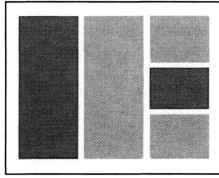

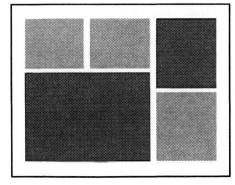

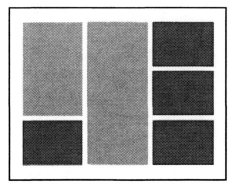

Figures 11-19 and 11-20 Page Layouts on a Three-by-Three Grid

Figures 11-21, 11-22, and 11-23   Other Potential Layouts

Figure 11-24 Page Format: One Column Vertical with Sidebar.
From *Site Planning,* 3rd Edition, by Kevin Lynch and Gary Hack. Copyright © 1984 MIT Press. Reproduced by permission of the publisher.

SUMMARY

A program document should be as easy to read as a novella about your project. The description of the background and the context for the project (existing state) should flow easily into the proposal for the future state. A program document should be as graphic as possible from the site analysis to the parti. Any necessary information that is so detailed that it interferes with the flow of the document's "story" should go into the appendix.

A complete program document consists of the following items:

1. *Introduction:* mission statement (Why are we doing this project anyhow?)

2. *Analysis* of the *existing state* of affairs: acts of record, site analysis, climate, client/user analysis, codes, background (historical, contextual, political), etc., the facts of the case

3. *Proposal for the future state:* goals/performance requirements/concepts (what the project should turn out to be like)

4. *Summary:* parti, concept scenario, space summary, budget, etc. (conclusions drawn from all the preceding facts and proposals)

5. *Appendix:* detailed analyses, research data, other relevant information that is too detailed to put into the body of the program document

The ideal format for describing the program proposal (future state) as described in this text is as follows:

Mission Statement

1. Goal Statement

1.1 Performance Requirement Statement

    1.1.1 Concept Diagram

    1.1.2 Concept Diagram

    1.1.3 Concept Diagram

    1.1.4 Concept Diagram

2. Goal Statement

2.1 Performance Requirement

    2.1.1 Concept Diagram

    2.1.2 Concept Diagram

    etc.

Each subsequent performance requirement and goal would follow in the same format. This format is the easiest way to display the tree format of the information hierarchy. See Figures 1-1 and 5-7, examples in Chapter 5, and Case I in Chapter 12.

Program document page formats complement the message of the program document and help to engage the reader in the story of the document. Graphics for content and layout are very important to the success of your program document for your audience. They should be the highest quality possible. A page format should be chosen to complement the program information and be easily understood by your client group or design team. With the wide variety of formats available, you might choose a different one for each program document, or you might make up one standard, flexible format. If there are lots of small graphics, a narrow column seems to give the most versatility in page layout. I prefer the wide page format with three columns or wide format with two columns and a sidebar like this book. Remember that a very wide column makes your document harder to read because the eye has a hard time tracking accurately to the beginning of the next line. Very narrow columns only work well with small type like newspapers. Balance the type size and the column width for easy reading.

A mixture of text and graphics makes the page look more interesting. If the page is only type, then the headings should create contrast and white space to enhance the graphic quality and interest of the page.

CHAPTER 12

CASE STUDIES: PROGRAM EXAMPLES

**CASE I:
PROGRAM FOR A
NEW
ARCHITECTURE
BUILDING**

**CASE II:
PROGRAM FOR
YOUTH MODEL
RESIDENTIAL
FACILITY**

CASE STUDIES: PROGRAM EXAMPLES

CASE I: PARTIAL PROGRAM FOR AN ADDITION TO THE SCHOOL OF ARCHITECTURE, CALIFORNIA POLYTECHNIC STATE UNIVERSITY, SAN LUIS OBISPO, CALIFORNIA

The following portion of a program document is the compilation of the work done by one fifth year programming class for a proposed addition to the College of Architecture and Environmental Design (CAED) for the School of Architecture at Cal Poly, San Luis Obispo, California. A partial program is illustrated here that includes the Goals, Performance Requirements, and Concepts for six different Issues. In this version some unpolished work is included in order to maintain the sense of student work. Mutually exclusive alternative concepts would not be included in a final program document.

In order for this example to be a complete program document, it would have to include a thorough site analysis — locating existing buildings, utilities, circulation, and activities; climate and energy studies; topography, views, odors, noises, and soil data. The size of the building would have been determined by utilization and class size predictions. It would also include the history of the school and how it grew to become one of the largest schools of architecture in the U.S. Code requirements particular to a building for architecture studios, assembly, offices, and computer rooms plus the constraints imposed by working with the State Architect's Office and the Campus Master Plan would also be included.

The introduction would elaborate on the school's philosophy and the types of students who can be expected to attend. It is hoped that a programming process involving students, faculty,

and staff would be implemented and reported in the program document. Summaries would include space summaries, adjacency diagrams, a budget, and a site zoning plan. The appendix would include the results of any research done plus a more detailed report of the participatory programming process.

This type of program document is good for programmers who are also designers and who need to do a thorough job of programming to create client agreement on design direction. It is also good for developing your knowledge of a building type you have never done before or for an aspect of building design that is new to you.

The part of the program document that is illustrated here is the section dealing with the future state — the goals, performance requirements (PRs), and concepts. Many of the students' concerns focused upon the College of Architecture and Environmental Design rather than just the School of Architecture. At Cal Poly, labs and studios are synonymous.

PROGRAM GOALS, PERFORMANCE REQUIREMENTS, AND CONCEPTS FOR THE SCHOOL OF ARCHITECTURE

Circulation Goal: The facility should provide an extremely clear, simple, and exciting circulation system for College of Architecture and Environmental Design members as well as for visitors.

Circulation

PR: The facility should encourage maximum information flow between departments.

Computer Networking

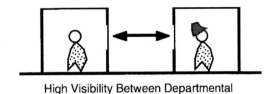

High Visibility Between Departmental Territories

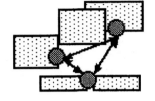

Easy, Direct Paths Between Departments

Some PRs will have more concepts than others. In these examples, there are some alternative concepts that would not be in the final program document.

Circulation

PR: Circulation system should be self-explanatory for first time visitors and should provide for its users a clear sense of orientation.

Circulation Directly Through Different Spaces

Entry Icons

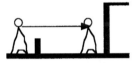

Activity Patios and Elements Along the Main Paths

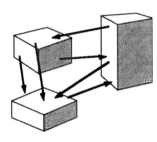

Three-Dimensional Views to Other Areas

Circulation "Spine"

Sculptural Focal Point

Readily Identifiable Landscape Elements

Windows into Activity Areas

Circulation

PR: Major circulation paths should easily accommodate the handicapped and those with minor mobility difficulties.

Many Ramps with a Maximum Slope of 1 to 12

Wide Paths with Traction Surfaces

Other Potential Concepts:
Curb Cuts and Direct Access to All Offices and Labs

In a final program document, the concepts would all be diagrammed rather than verbalized.

When doing computer graphics, leave the text caption out of the graphic if at all possible. "Curved paths" shows up as the wrong type style and size in the adjacent graphic. Add captions later so that the graphic can be appropriately sized.

Circulation
PR: All major circulation paths should be pleasant and visually stimulating.

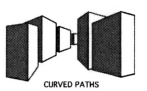

CURVED PATHS

Display Cases
Along Paths

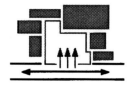

Views into
Common Spaces

Ramps   Stairs   Change in Direction

A Variety of Ways to Move Through the Complex

Circulation
PR: Circulation system should be very efficient and handle class-change crowds with ease and safety.

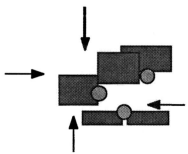

Service Access Separated from
Pedestrian Traffic

Shortcuts Across Corners

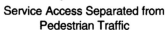

Wide Paths

Image Goal: The facility should clearly promote a vivid image of all five individual departments united with the common purpose of instilling the values of creativity, productivity, and resourcefulness.

Image
PR: The new structure should be a recognizable landmark from other parts of the campus.

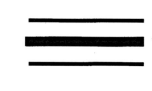 

Open Space/Landscape Focal Point   Tall Building as Marker

Image
PR: *The new construction should clearly improve the overall sense of unification of the five departments while maintaining each department's autonomy.*

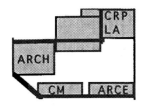

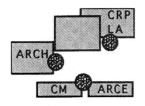

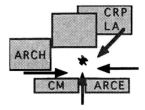

Create a CAED Precinct   Define Departmental Entries   Visual Focal Point for the Entire School

Image
PR: *The new building should be visually unified with the existing structure(s).*

Align Heads

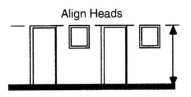

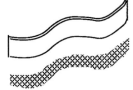

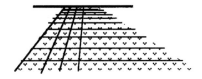

Standardize Functional Elements   Paths Go in the Direction of Walls   Repeat Details from Existing Buildings   Similar Floor and Ground Surfaces

Image
PR: *The facility should promote a strong and instantaneous sense of welcome upon the arrival of CAED members and visitors.*

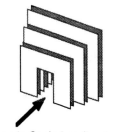

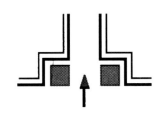

Other Potential Concepts:
Clear Direct Path to Entry, Welcoming Building "Arms" Views into Public Spaces from the Outside

Change in Scale Leading to Entry   Exhibition Cases at Entry   Landscape Dramatizes Entry

Image goals are the most difficult to state with specific, measurable, and operational performance requirements. Image is subjective and can be evaluated only through judgment. Concepts that give the designer freedom to create new ideas are also somewhat difficult.

Privacy Goal: The facility should provide CAED members with a high degree of control of interaction and distraction within their work/ study places.

Privacy
PR: *Visibility into the work/study place should be high, with controls to allow for times when the area should not be disturbed in order to increase productivity.*

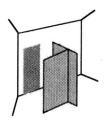

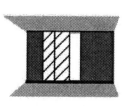
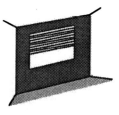
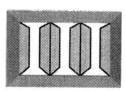

| Moveable Tackboards | Tall Slit Windows | Sliding Glass Doors with Drapes | Big Windows with Moveable Covering | French Doors with Pinup Surfaces |

Privacy
PR: *Sound transmission into work/study place should be minimized to ±35 db.*

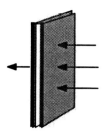

Other Concepts:
Wall Insulation,
Mass Walls,
Thick Tack Boards

Sound Absorbing Materials in Exterior Corridor

Double Glazed Windows

Security Goal: All people using the facility should feel safe to come and go at any hour of the day or night without fear of theft, vandalism, or assault.

Most PRs should have at least three or more concepts to implement their function.

Security
PR: All grounds of the facility and support areas should have good visual access to and from at least one frequently occupied area. ALL AREAS SHOULD FEEL LIKE SOMEONE IS WATCHING IT.

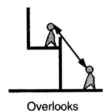

Other Concepts:
Large Windows to
Paths, Glass Doors

Overlooks

Security
PR: Studios should be organized to concentrate the density of observant people responsible for each studio area.

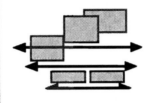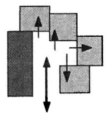

Studios and Offices Along
Regularly Traveled Paths

Common Entry to Studio Clusters
and Studio Social Space/ Courtyard

Security
PR: All pathways should have clear lines of sight and should be lit so that faces are recognizable at 20 feet and areas where someone could remain concealed are brightly lit.

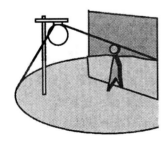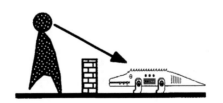

Side Lighting

Low Barriers, Enabling Inspection

Pools of Light at Corners,
Bends in Path and Nooks

Final program documents should have precise graphics rather than having corners that are not square.

Social and Academic Interaction Goal: The facility should promote spontaneous social interaction between students of all years and departments and with faculty and administrators to exchange information, ideas, and techniques on a frequent basis.

The diagrams for the CAED focal point concepts could be greatly improved by making them relational rather than subjective. For example, the coffee cup could be replaced by a diagram of the relationship between the place to drink coffee and the rest of the CAED.

Interaction
PR: The CAED focal point should attract a majority of students and faculty to pass through it every day.

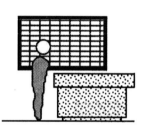
Central Mail, Copying

A Place to Drink
Good Coffee

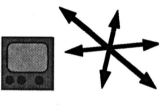
Bulletin Boards and Electronic Information at
Pedestrian Crossroads

Sunny Spot with a
Gallery at the Center

Interaction
PR: The precinct should encourage a high incidence of chance meetings and conversations.

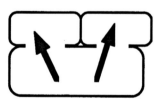
Display Areas Near Work Areas

Places to Sit Near Major Circulation Paths

Comfortable Places to Sit and Major
Displays to Talk About

Interaction

PR: The faculty should be integrated into the lab environment with visual and physical access to the studios.

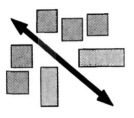

Through Circulation

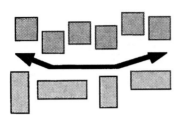

Parallel Arrangement of
Offices and Studios

Central Offices and
Circulation

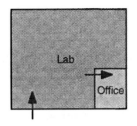

Faculty Offices in Labs

Interaction

PR: The building should encourage a wide variety of academic, social, auxiliary, and extra-curricular activities for all CAED students.

Student Organization Kiosks
and Glass Bulletin Boards

Highly Visible Student
Organization Spaces

Interaction

PR: Studios should facilitate interaction between class years.

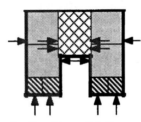

Studios Share Crit Space
and Faculty Offices

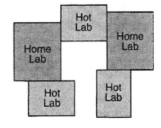

Mix Home Labs and
Hot Labs

Interaction

PR: The facility's "center" should be designed so as not to feel empty or desolate when not being used for events.

Irregular Plan

Change Floor Levels

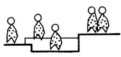

Flexibility

Dedicated Space for Traveling Exhibits

Visibility Goal: The facility and the activities within it should be highly visible to visitors and inhabitants of the facility from adjoining areas on campus and identified as the CAED.

Visibility
PR: On-going work (students __and__ instructors) should be highly visible at all times to both users and visitors.

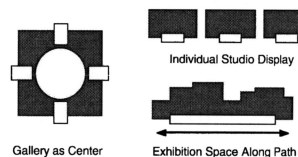

Individual Studio Display

Gallery as Center   Exhibition Space Along Path

Other Concepts: Views into Activity Spaces, Lobby Displays, School and Departmental Office Displays

Visibility
PR: All schools should have visual access to each other.

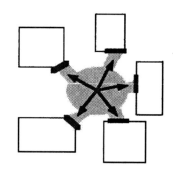

Other Concepts:
Shared Open Spaces,
Windows Facing Other
Parts of the CAED,
Balconies

Entries Visible to
Each Other

Visibility
PR: Visitors should have a sense of being in a school of architecture by what they see going on around them

 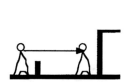 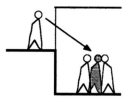 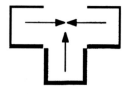 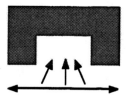

Outdoor Classrooms   Activity Patio Along
Busy Path   Activities Viewed from
Above   Orient Spaces Toward
Each Other   Views from Paths

CASE II: NEW YORK STATE DIVISION FOR YOUTH MODEL RESIDENTIAL FACILITY ARCHITECTURAL PROGRAM AND CONCEPT DESIGN

Excerpted from the Final Report:
February 1, 1991
By Jay Farbstein & Associates, Inc.
Used by permission of Jay Farbstein and New York State Division for Youth.

The following excerpts are presented to show a design development program that was written to be handed off from a programming consultant team to a design firm. All italics in the body of this section and in the sidebar are my comments. All plain and bold type is from the Program Document. The "• • • • •" symbol indicates a body of material left out of the ±200 page document. The excerpts are intended to follow the example of one issue through the various levels of detail. Bold type in this section is for emphasis in the original document, rather than indicating glossary terms as in previous chapters.

This program is similar to the schematic design protocol in this text in that it clearly states the mission, goals, and performance requirements for the facility. These are valuable examples for students of programming who will be doing design development programming as well as schematic design (SD) programming.

This program is different from the schematic design protocol in that it includes a functional program that is a clarification of the client's service delivery program. The architectural program is always a statement of the facility implications of the functional program, but very often the functional program is not included in the architectural program document. It is also different from the SD

programming protocol because it does not include diagrams of design concepts to implement the performance requirements. Instead, the programming consultant team was asked to complete a conceptual design of the site and building to test out their programming concepts. The programming team consisted of Jay Farbstein and Associates as lead programmers, Rich Wener as special consultant, and Patrick Sullivan as design consultant.

The final noteworthy difference is the level of detail specified by the performance requirements in this example. Schematic design performance requirements are more functional and do not necessarily dictate materials or equipment.

PROGRAM STRUCTURE/CONTENTS

I. Introduction and Summary

II. Functional Program

> Mission, Goals, and Objectives
>
> Facility Users
>
> Psychological and Sociocultural Factors
>
> The Habilitation Program
>
> Habilitation Schedule and Daily Routines
>
> Policies and Procedures
>
> Future Trends

III. Architectural Program

> Facility-Wide Design Requirements
>
> Facility Organization and Layout
>
> Space Requirements
>
> Safety and Security
>
> Design and Performance Requirements

FACILITY ORGANIZATION AND LAYOUT

Excerpted from the Introduction and Summary. This section gives an overview of each of the building's main elements and the most basic requirements. DFY stands for Division for Youth.

Public users (visitors, salespersons, etc.) are normally restricted to a semi-secure zone near the entry. Immediately **inside the secure area** are functions such as central services, administration, conference rooms, teacher preparation area, counseling offices, and the "spiritual center," all of which need convenient external access and serve the entire facility.

Youth **housing** areas are divided into pairs of 15 bed units with contiguous classrooms and teaching labs. Vocational classrooms and labs are clustered elsewhere in an area with vehicular access.

Recreation facilities will be located for easy youth access, as will the three **dining** rooms, which will be adjacent to the **kitchen** (which also must have vehicular access).

There will be **handicapped access** throughout the building.

The major relationships within the facility are illustrated in the diagram near the beginning of the chapter titled *Architectural Program* and more concretely in the concept design. The design evolved the concept of a **major spine** which organizes all movement within the building in a pleasant, but controlled mall-like environment. The mall organizes a **one-way movement** system (to separate groups of youth) on either side of common activity spaces. All main functional areas used by youth are directly accessed off the spine. Central control, the central services desk, and all five housing unit control stations directly observe movement on the spine.

• • • • •

SAFETY AND SECURITY

There are two primary security goals: first, to protect youth from each other and themselves; and second, to ensure staff safety. Inside the facility, security must be present, but not obtrusive. Maximum reliance will be placed on direct contact with or observation of youth by staff. Security systems will be used to support this direct involvement; thus, audio and closed circuit television systems will be limited. There will be obvious security measures such as perimeter walls of the building and fences around the site that are robust and make escape attempts unlikely and difficult.

DESIGN AND PERFORMANCE REQUIREMENTS

Design of the facility shall meet the technical and performance requirements outlined in the following paragraphs.

Building design shall meet American Correctional Association **standards** as well as applicable building **codes** and related standards.

Certain portions of the building will have to be constructed of **materials** that make escapes very difficult. Exterior walls must not only be resistant to penetration, but must meet energy conservation standards and should be attractive, durable and require little maintenance. Windows must meet security requirements as well as building and fire codes, and energy conservation requirements

Interior design materials and surfaces must meet tests of both **practicality and durability** and must also meet certain **psychological** needs. Colors in living areas should be bright and cheerful; in classrooms and service areas light and neutral with brighter accents.

Floor coverings in residential areas will be carpet; in work areas, resilient flooring; in wet areas, ceramic tile will be used. Vocational shops will have polished concrete floors. Interior **walls** may be masonry or of plywood and sheetrock over steel studs. Walls within reach of youth shall be **finished** with durable, easily cleanable paint, such as epoxy. It should be anticipated that walls will have posters, signs and other objects taped to them, and should be sufficiently durable to endure such treatment. **Ceilings** in youth areas must be out of reach; at least 9' high. **Doors** are painted metal in metal frames.

Furnishings must be selected so that they are difficult to use as weapons, yet are comfortable, durable, and attractive.

Various types of **signage** must be provided, with wording verified by DFY prior to fabrication. Signage shall be readable by the visually impaired.

Natural light and view should be provided whereever possible, provided they do not compromise required security. Lighting fixtures that can be reached must be of a secure type, but those which cannot be reached by youth may be standard types. All lighting must meet applicable correctional, energy, and school standards.

Communications systems will include a telephone system linking all staff workstations, with built-in provisions for a computer network. An independent portable communications system (walkie talkie) will also be provided. Pay phones will be available in appropriate locations for public, visitors, and staff.

Acoustical controls, and acoustical privacy where needed, will be designed into the facility.

The major design issues for the design of a youth correctional facility are safety and security. The statement of the other issues was left out for brevity.

These design and performance requirements are stated in the most general terms. Other parts of the program develop them at greater levels of specificity for each building area. Notice how some of these PRs are issue-based and others are building system-based.

The HVAC system must provide excellent thermal comfort throughout the facility while also being energy efficient and economical to operate. Most spaces will be cooled as well as heated. It is likely that a central boiler with decentralized heating and air handling systems will be provided. Backup systems must be provided.

Fire detection and suppression systems will be provided (although the building is probably not required to be sprinklered). While smoke evacuation systems may not be required by code, they should also be considered for installation in certain areas. Other building system requirements cover plumbing, electrical service, mechanical rooms, and provision of utilities including domestic and fire suppression water systems. An emergency generator will be provided to meet essential power requirements.

• • • • •

II. FUNCTIONAL PROGRAM

INTRODUCTION

This chapter reports on the functional program; that is, the functions and operations expected to be carried out in the new facility. Only by defining what the Division for Youth wants to happen in the facility can an appropriate basis be developed for architectural programming and design. Subsequent sections of the functional program define:

- The **mission** of and objectives for the facility.
- Who the **users** of the facility will be.
- **Psychological** and sociocultural factors that need to be taken into account in design.

- An overview of the habilitation **programs** to be offered at the facility
- The more detailed habitation **schedules** and daily routines that will be carried out.
- The **policies and procedures** that will need to be developed for the facility.
- **Future trends** that the facility may have to respond to.

• • • • •

MISSION STATEMENT, GOALS AND OBJECTIVES

MISSION STATEMENT

Overall Agency Mission (Source: DFY *Master Plan Update '87-'89*, Draft, August 1990)

The overall mission of the DFY is "preventing delinquency through positive youth development." This is achieved through a continuum of programs, from prevention, through custody, to aftercare.

For youth committed to its custody, the Division seeks to provide "an environment and services that promote positive development." Programs are designed to "foster the attitudes, skills, and behaviors these youth will need to function as law-abiding, productive members of their communities." Stabilization is a first step, followed by habilitation. Habilitation stresses the development of personal competencies (skills, successes, etc.) and social integration (values, attitudes, and the replacement of external direction with self-direction and control). The final step is reintegration

The Functional Program is a restatement of the client's service delivery program and, as such, guides the direction of the architectural program.

to the community. (Note: the term "habilitation" is used rather than "rehabilitation" because these youth are seen as needing to develop skills and attitudes they have never had, rather than being returned to conditions which they have abandoned.)

FACILITY MISSION

Youth Served. The facility will be designed to serve a range of youth, but it is primarily targeted toward juvenile delinquents who require the structured setting of a "limited secure" facility based upon DFY's classification system. These are youth who have demonstrated that they require removal from the community.

Program. The mission of the facility's program is to transform the youth into capable, law-abiding citizens who will be able to function within society upon their return to it. Each youth's particular needs are identified within a treatment plan, and specific services in areas such as education, medical treatment, and counseling are directed toward meeting his needs. Within the program, youth will progress through three stages or progress levels: orientation (transition into the program), habilitation (or the main program), and preparation for release and reintegration. The program is intensive and highly organized, using a wide variety of techniques to build skills and to change patterns of thinking and behaving described in detail later in this report.

GOALS AND OBJECTIVES

Habilitation and Order

Habilitation is the primary mission of the facility. However, the maintenance of order is also important, since it allows consistency in the operation of the facility, which permits programs to function dependably. Without their safety guaranteed, youth and staff would not be able to work toward achieving habilitation.

MEASURES OF SUCCESS

For the facility to be a success, the following types of outcomes would be found:

- Youth would leave the facility with more skills (e.g., they would have attained their GED; they would have improved vocational skills, job readiness, and life and career skills).
- Youth would have **improved "personal capital"** (skills) **and "social capital"** (socialization).
- There would be a **lower cost of care** (that is, the facility would be able to operate effectively with a lower staff ratio than other DFY facilities; as a result, there would be a lower cost per bed or per youth-day; other operating costs, such as for energy, would also be lower).
- There would be a **lower rate of reincarceration** (this was recognized as an important but difficult measure given such variables as length of stay, the milieu to which the youth returns, and the critical role of aftercare).

• • • • •

FACILITY IMAGE/MESSAGE

The building design should communicate a clear message about expectations of youth and staff. These are the messages,

Please note that the facility mission is written in terms of the youth served and that the use of the word "program" in these paragraphs means the service delivery program.

as articulated by the DFY design team, that should be communicated (by the building, staff, and program):

- "Welcome" (note the meaning for youth, staff, and visitors first impressions).
- "Be calm."
- "I want you to like me and take care of me." (says the building), and "I like this place" (says youth and staff).
- "I'm nice and well kept up."
- "I'm a refuge for you."
- "I can take care of your needs."
- "Here's your chance to get it together."
- "Respect me" ("I respect you").
- "I'm not threatening."
- "I'm functional and uncomplicated."
- "It's not easy to get out (escape)."
- "I look soft —but, I can take it."

The overall image that the facility should convey is that of a benign, collaborative institution. Still, it is recognized that there is a degree of conflict between the desired image of comfort and hospitality on the one hand and the need for security and observation on the other.

• • • • •

SAFETY AND SECURITY

Security is a primary goal of the facility. Safety of youth, staff, and the community must be assured.

- Protect youth from each other and themselves. Suicide prevention is extremely important.

- Protect staff through back-up systems (e.g., electronics), communications with other staff (including staff on different units being able to see each other), living units being fully visible, and teamwork.

Security should be present, but not obtrusive. Circulation should be easy, but controlled, with a secure perimeter. Excellent visual observation is required of all main circulation systems.

• • • • •

ARCHITECTURAL PROGRAM

The next section is excerpted from the architectural program for the DFY Model Residential Facility. I have left out the portions that deal with the overall facility and the other functional areas.

SAFETY AND SECURITY

Goals and Objectives

Security is a primary goal of the facility which, by its mission, must assure the safety of staff, youth, and the community. Key security goals are:

- To protect youth from each other and themselves. Suicide prevention is extremely important as is the prevention of sexual assault.
- To protect staff through appropriate staff to youth ratios, ease of communications with other staff, teamwork, and back-up systems (such as electronics).

Security depends first on the staff and operational procedures (e.g., escorted movement, counts). Physical security is there to communicate expectations (to say, for example, "it's not worth trying to get out"), and as a fall-back. The facility perimeter is the last resort and is there to slow youth down, to reassure the community, and to keep unauthorized people out.

Security should be present, but not obtrusive. Circulation should be easy, but controlled, within the secure perimeter. Youth movement will be escorted or accompanied. Excellent visual observation of circulation spaces will facilitate unaccompanied movement, when or if appropriate. After bedtime, control will be tighter, with corridors and sub-areas closed off. Movement within the housing unit should be easier than movement among parts of the facility.

Crisis Management Situations and Responses

The kinds of crisis or emergency situations which may be experienced by the institution and thus should be included in planning include:

- Power failure.
- Fire/emergency evacuation.
- Natural disaster.
- Medical emergency.
- Escape.
- Passive demonstration.
- Hunger strike.
- Group disturbance.
- Riot.
- Hostage taking.

- Bomb threat.
- Employee job action.
- Suicide.
- Perimeter violation.
- Water or sewage system disruption.
- Miscellaneous (sniper, toxic fumes, etc.).

I have summarized the following sections for brevity.

Of these, the most important and likely events fall into three broad categories.

Internal Disruption. The main need is to be able to segment and contain the population (by zoning). In any one of these events, the steps to a response include:

- Become aware of problem (communications and visibility).
- Get staff there quickly (simple and visible circulation).
- Confine the problem (by segmenting one area).
- Set up an intervention strategy. This is benefited by having visual preview into the trouble area, as well as the use of electronic surveillance aids and audible alarms.
- A location is needed to break down the group, that is to remove the problem kids to another area (a separate area or the disciplinary isolation rooms, if only a few youth are involved).

Evacuation. When evacuation is needed, the most desirable response is to be able to move youth to a safe haven within the perimeter.

Perimeter Intrusion. The principles that govern design are prevention of the event, detection if an attempt occurs, and intervention or response to curtail it.

Physical Security

In response to the above listed concerns, the overall strategy is as follows:

- The **perimeter** of the building will be robust and make escape difficult.
- The **exterior enclosure** of the building will be secure, with security windows and doors/locks.
- **Within the facility,** there will be a greater degree of freedom and less security, though materials and systems will be of durable construction.
- **Locking Systems.** DFY policy prevents locking sleeping room doors in limited secure facilities. Sleeping room doors are key operated from the outside to unlock them, but the youth can open the door at any time from the inside. An ergonomically designed control panel will display the controls and status for each lock on a plan of the site and facility.

• • • • •

RESIDENTIAL AREAS

OVERVIEW

Living units are the focus of activity during evenings and weekends as well as being the locus for portions of many program activities, such as counseling and education. Living units house 15 youths, with pairs of living units sharing one staff office/control room for supervision of 30 youths by one staff at night.

Participation in activities outside of the living unit provides daily variety in the youths' surroundings. Youths will generally be escorted to daily activities with their entire living unit group. Only illness will prevent a youth from participating in scheduled group activities (in which case, he will be in the medical area), so the living unit will not be occupied during activities scheduled at his/her locations. Youths will have some choices regarding participation in activities at the living unit.

• • • • •

RELATIONSHIPS

The following relationships govern the layout of this area (refer to the relationship diagram on page 203):

- All spaces within the living unit are accessed from the activity area/dayroom.
- Provide ongoing visual surveillance between normally staffed positions during evening hours. Each staff office/control room shall have direct visual contact with another office or with central control.
- Classroom directly adjacent to each living unit. Provide direct visual access to classroom from dayroom and staff office/control.
- Convenient access to outside recreation area and other spaces shared between two living units.

UNIT LOCKING

During normal daytime and evening hours, the living unit perimeter will be secured by doors with *communicating locksets* that either knob can be locked or unlocked

A large number of potentially dangerous situations create the conditions requiring the security performance requirements.

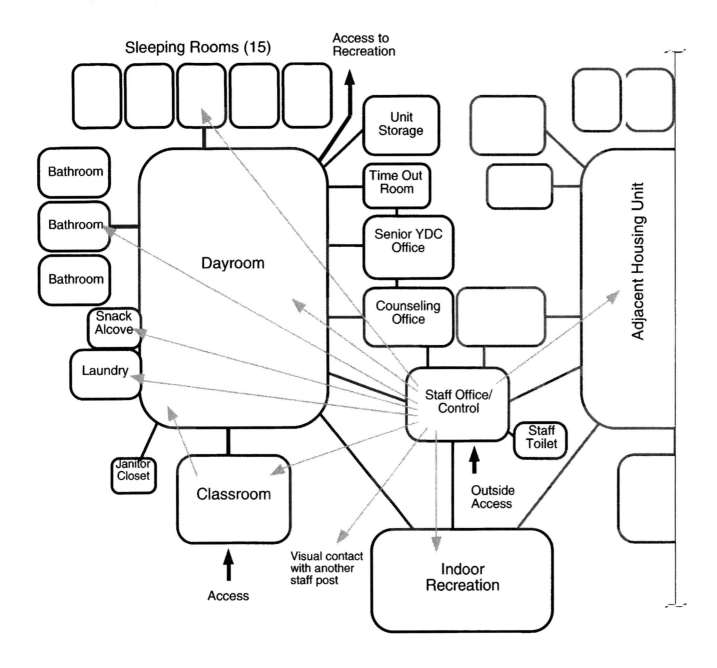

Sleeping Rooms (15)

Access to Recreation

Bathroom

Bathroom

Bathroom

Dayroom

Snack Alcove

Laundry

Janitor Closet

Classroom

Access

Unit Storage

Time Out Room

Senior YDC Office

Counseling Office

Staff Office/ Control

Staff Toilet

Outside Access

Adjacent Housing Unit

Visual contact with another staff post

Indoor Recreation

Figure 12-1   Relationship Diagram for the Residential Areas

Unit locking specifications are one of the aspects of implementing the performance requirements for security.

Here, in the architectural program specifically describing the sleeping rooms, the issues of safety and security are dealt with at the very finest level of detail. Many of the requirements are much closer to material specifications than performance requirements. For example, the vision panel in the door is specified to be 4 inches wide and approximately 2 feet high. Many requirements point out conditions that must be avoided.

independently by staff. These doors additionally have electrified mortised deadbolts remotely operated by central control. The dead bolts are activated during the night shift or emergencies, and control of the living unit perimeter reverts to central control. The living unit perimeter doors have the following requirements:

- Call button and intercom to central control at each side of door.
- Indicator lights for door status with operation buttons at central control. A living unit's deadbolts can be activated individually or as a group.
- Each door numbered.
- Electronic deadbolt retracts in fire or with power failure.
- No control of deadbolts from living unit.
- No control of locksets from central control. There shall be no way of remotely unlocking door unless living unit staff have unlocked the living unit doors previously.
- All perimeter doors to all living units can be operated by all YDA keys. Locking doors within living units shall all be operable by that unit's staff but not staff from another living unit.
- Paired units sleeping room doors shall be keyed the same.
- Teachers' keys operate the living unit perimeters, but don't operate doors to sleeping rooms.

COMMON REQUIREMENTS

Residential areas have the following common requirements:

- Drinking fountain in each unit, recessed, tamper resistant, handicapped accessible.

- Natural lighting and view are required in sleeping rooms and dayrooms; desirable in other spaces.
- Acoustical control is required to assure normal conversational levels are not disturbed. Provide low reverberation time in larger spaces.
- Color corrected fluorescent lighting is desirable, controlled for differential lighting in parts of the unit.
- Documented bed check process; locate check-in stations to assure staff movement.

• • • • •

ROOM REQUIREMENTS FOR SLEEPING ROOM

SIZE OF THIS ROOM: 70 NET SQUARE FEET.

NUMBER OF ROOMS OF THIS TYPE: 150 (15 PER HOUSING UNIT).

Description/Function: All sleeping rooms are single occupancy for sleeping and individual activities. Youths cannot be locked into their rooms.

Code and Agency Requirements: ACA: All sleeping rooms are single occupancy (no dormitories) and have at least 35 square feet of "unencumbered" space (exclusive of furnishings). Furnishings include a bed, desk, seat, and storage. Building Code: minimum area 70 square feet with a minimum dimension of 7 feet. One sleeping room in each living unit shall be handicapped accessible.

Behavioral Issues/Response: The individual sleeping room is an essential ingredient in the treatment program, offering youth greater potential for self -control, self-expression, privacy, and a place to retreat to when pressures become great (rather than acting out violently). Youth will be able to personalize their rooms through having personal belongings, photos, and other decorative items.

OCCUPANTS/USERS

Staff: Housing unit staff enter the youth's room as necessary for private conversations, inspections, searches.

> **Youth:** One occupant per room.
>
> **Others:** None.

Activities: Sleeping, dressing, reading, studying, some individual counseling, use of cordless phone for incoming private calls.

Days and Hours of Operation: Intermittent use 24 hours per day, seven days per week.

LINKAGES:

- Direct access to dayroom.
- Convenient access to bathrooms.

Room Shape: Generally rectangular rooms are preferred (at least one straight wall with a minimum of 8 feet is needed for placement of the bed).

Enclosure: Fully enclosed.

SAFETY AND SECURITY

> **Objectives:** Room, hardware, and furnishings should be suicide proof. Exterior wall and its window should be secure.
>
> **Locks/Doors:** Classroom lock, outside knob locked or unlocked by key, inside knob always unlocked.

Door opens in with hinges accessible from outside (for emergency door removal).

Alarm/Detection: Smoke alarms are located in room return air ducts.

Visual Observation: Vision panel in the door, 4 inches wide by approximately 2 feet high.

Monitoring System: Intercom with "listen-in" capability.

Furniture: Fixed, so cannot be used as a weapon or for a barricade. No sharp edges or corners. No places to hide contraband. No way to attach cord (etc.) to attempt to hang self.

Fenestration:

- Security glazing and frames.
- Not operable.
- No security screens.
- Avoid direct view to other rooms, if possible.
- Larger area than provided by narrow slits.

Ambient Environment

HVAC:

- High quality, finely zoned heating and air conditioning.
- Secure mesh or performed plate air grilles.
- More than minimum CFM air movement required by code is preferred.

Lighting: Provide overall lighting for general illumination and reading with switch in room (override by unit control). Provide 5 foot candles night lighting in with pressure switch to illuminate immediately outside sleeping room door.

Acoustics: No special requirements.

View: View to exterior; without direct view into other sleeping rooms.

Equipment and Systems

    Power: Provide power outlet near desk with override switch from unit control.

    Plumbing: None.

    Communications/Information: Intercom to unit control room.

MATERIALS/FINISHES

    Floor: Carpet meeting flame-spread requirements.

    Walls: Gypsum board with semigloss, washable painted surface.

    Ceiling: 9 foot height. Gypsum board with semigloss, washable painted surface.

    Display: Designated area of wall with high gloss finish for personalization.

    Colors: Light colored walls and ceiling; medium colored floor.

Furnishings and Fixtures (In Contract)

- Fixed desk and seat.
- Open storage shelves or pigeon holes, 3 shelves, 24" wide x 12" deep (no provision for hanging clothes). (The need for storage in the sleeping room is reduced by the policy to issue clean clothes and towels every time youths shower.)
- Bed:
  Vermin resistant.

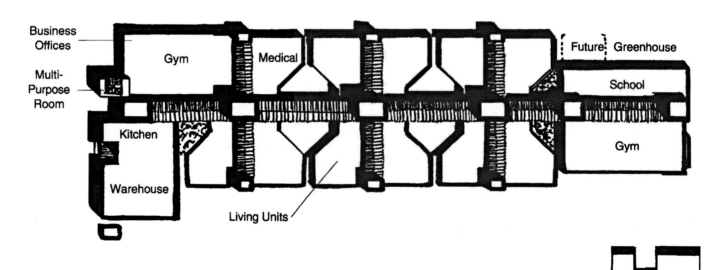

Figure 12-2 Concept Design for the Facility

- At least 36" x 7'.
- No places to hide contraband.
- Not a concrete slab.
- No drawers underneath.
- Fixed to floor.
- "Homelike" feeling.
- No sharp corners.
- Space to store shoes beneath bed.
- No use of restraints on beds.

Other Requirements: None.

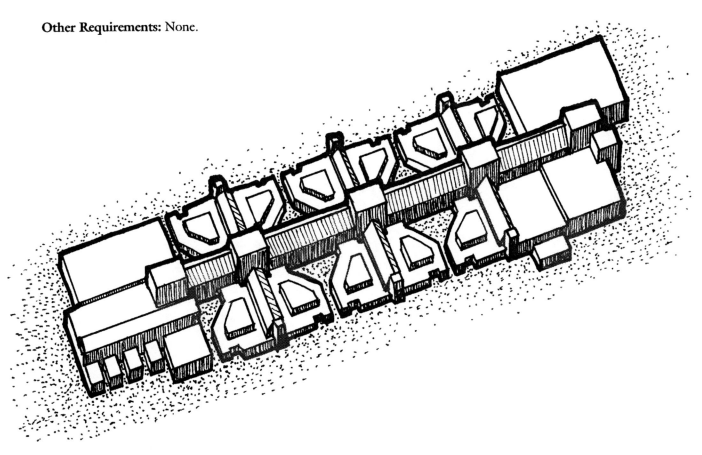

Figure 12-3 Model of the Proposed Conceptual Design. Note the Changes from the Drawing as the Design Evolved.

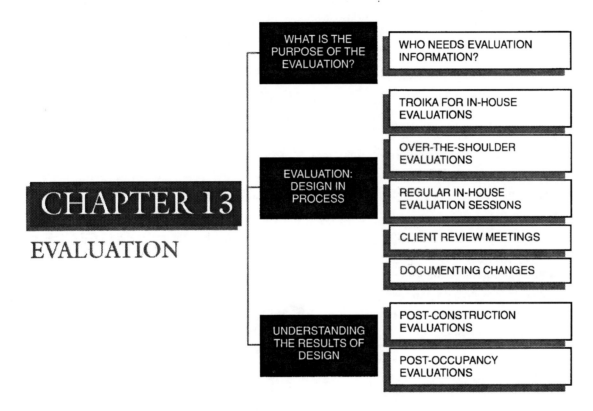

CHAPTER 13

EVALUATION

WHAT IS THE PURPOSE OF THE EVALUATION?

WHO NEEDS EVALUATION INFORMATION?

EVALUATION: DESIGN IN PROCESS

TROIKA FOR IN-HOUSE EVALUATIONS

OVER-THE-SHOULDER EVALUATIONS

REGULAR IN-HOUSE EVALUATION SESSIONS

CLIENT REVIEW MEETINGS

DOCUMENTING CHANGES

UNDERSTANDING THE RESULTS OF DESIGN

POST-CONSTRUCTION EVALUATIONS

POST-OCCUPANCY EVALUATIONS

EVALUATION

I am bound by my own definition of criticism: a disinterested endeavor to learn and propagate the best that is known and thought in the world.

Mathew Arnold
The Function of Criticism at the Present Time

WHAT IS THE PURPOSE OF THE EVALUATION?

Under the primary purpose of repeating successes and avoiding mistakes, there are four general purposes for doing design evaluation:

1. To test how well the project is making progress toward meeting its goals.
2. To test how well a built project implemented its goals, to fine-tune the building's performance, and make corrections for the rest of the building's life-cycle.
3. To gather information that will be valuable in the programming and design of a new building, to test new concepts, or to use the generalizable information in adding to the knowledge base for a building type.
4. In extreme cases of disastrous building failures such as in an earthquake, fire, or social failure, such as Pruitt Igoe, evaluation contributes to creating new building code requirements, new policies, and/or new programming processes. Other extreme cases that benefit from evaluation are buildings that succeed far beyond expectations

Parshall (in Preiser 1989) has suggested that evaluation procedures are also useful in educating new building personnel about the building. In some cases, evaluations are done to test the validity of the intentions of the program rather than how well the program was implemented.

The four main evaluation purposes each have a different time line. The first one, evaluation of goal accomplishment, happens during the design process and can start during programming. The second, evaluation to fine-tune a

building's performance, is usually done within the first two years after the occupants have moved in (technical post-construction evaluation or functional post-occupancy evaluation (PCE/POE). See Figure 13-1 for a diagram showing evaluation as part of the normal design process. The third, evaluation to gather information for a new building, is usually done after the evaluated building has been occupied for a larger number of years and during the programming process for the new building (also PCE/POE). The fourth, evaluation of a building failure, is done after the building is no longer usable, in the most disastrous cases, or when a problem becomes notably serious enough to investigate its success or failure.

At this point in time, most evaluation research of built projects is carried out by academicians or by government agencies. Corporations with large physical plants and facility managers sometimes carry out systematic evaluations as well. Very few clients are currently willing to pay for PCE/POEs as

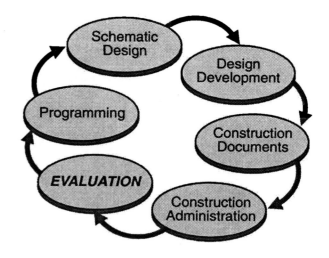

Figure 13-1 Evaluation in the Design Process

a regular part of the design cycle. They are more willing to fund such research as a part of programming for a new building. It is my belief that good programming allows for good evaluation of the building during the design process and makes POEs much easier to manage if the goals and performance requirements are well developed and documented. As the need for ongoing building performance feedback becomes critical to facilities design and management, then PCE/POEs will become a normal part of the design process.

Who Needs Evaluation Information?

In each of the different types of evaluation, the people who want to know the results of the evaluation are different. Designers, programmers, and clients want to know how well the building design is progressing toward the goals set for it during the design phase. Users and owners want to know how to fine-tune a building when they move in and settle down to business. Programmers, designers, and design students want to know the results of building-type POEs. And many people want to know the results of a disaster post-mortem — from code writers to lawyers, designers, city officials, and design students.

One of the most important sets of questions you can ask in preparing to evaluate a design at any stage in the process is, "Who is asking for the information?" "How are they going to use the information?" "What are the questions they need answered?" Each type of person who wants information about the performance of a building has certain biases and expectations about the utility of the information gathered. My particular bias is that evaluation information should always

be used to improve the building as a product or to improve the design and programming processes. When the purposes for evaluation are established, the process of designing the research is much the same as other programming research described in Chapters 7 and 8. The task is to choose the appropriate methods for the questions being asked.

I do not believe that the evaluation process should be used to fix blame on any of the participants in the building process for the ordinary failures of a building to meet the original expectations. If a client wants to mount an evaluation process solely for the purpose of finding someone to blame or to sue, I would not participate because the myriad of possible contributing factors are much too difficult to assess in terms of a direct cause. In the case of a major failure, the situation is different and the nature of lawsuits and fixing blame is in a completely different arena. White (in Preiser 1989) cautions that there are many factors that should be taken into consideration when doing an evaluation study. He lists the planning factors as, "purpose, building sample, content, rigor, tools and techniques, participants, cost, and reporting methods responsive to client concerns such as avoiding embarrassment, defending results, satisfying administrative superiors, boosting morale, minimizing disruption, resolving conflicts, and obtaining maximum public relations benefit from the POE study" (Preiser 1989, 19).

Post-occupancy evaluations are research and must be as rigorously designed as possible. The starting point is to create a hypothesis or hypotheses. Casual observation and interviews with key players in the building's use patterns should give the evaluator a good idea of the major programming issues that need to be tested. It is generally impossible to test every aspect of a building's performance, so with the budget in mind, choose those themes that are most critical to the success of the building or those issues that are most likely to yield the information that will answer the questions that were posed by the client. The categories of Person, Place, and Behavioral Issues as illustrated in Chapter 10 are good places to start looking for questions.

As in any good research, you need to know what you are going to do with the data before you go out to gather it. Be sure that you have at your command analysis techniques that are suited to making sense of the data you collect. Simple means or averages are probably not enough to get meaningful information from some POE data, depending on what you are evaluating. Sometimes correlation studies are sufficient, other times multivariate studies are necessary. The data must be collected in a manner that facilitates the best possible analysis. Discussions of how to manage many analysis techniques are presented in several books directed toward students of building evaluation, such as Preiser, Rabinowitz, and White (1988) and Kirk and Spreckelmeyer (1988). Both these books have bibliographies that point to more sophisticated analysis techniques. Another book that gives a broad perspective is Preiser (1989).

In the process of design, as the details of the building become more and more specific, the involvement of the programmer becomes diminished until the post-occupancy evaluation (POE) phase. Not all firms do systematic evaluations of their projects, but it is posited here as the ideal completion to the design process. During the POE, it is usually the programmer who is best suited to use the program as the tool for evaluating the building in use. Sometimes special research teams of social scientists and programmers may be the best bet, especially if the major questions are about how the people and the building work together. If the questions have to do with building systems (HVAC

performance, lighting, etc.), then it will be the engineers and technicians who are best suited to do the post-construction evaluation. Some clients will want both POE and PCE information.

EVALUATION: DESIGN IN PROCESS

One of the major values of programming is to have the best information available at the best possible time so that mistakes can be avoided as early in the design process as possible. Correcting mistakes gets to be more expensive at each successive stage of the building process. Evaluation during the design process, based upon a good program, can save a great deal of money and time. In a parallel situation, computer flight simulations that train pilots to cope with unusual situations cost *one tenth* of what it would cost to train pilots in real airplanes (Bechtel, in Preiser 1989). Evaluating the utility of buildings before they are built can only save money.

Besides getting regular feedback from the client/user it is also a good idea to have scheduled evaluations along the way. See Figure 13-2. I suggest that evaluations (some more formal than others) should happen fairly frequently:

1. At the end of programming: evaluate completeness and internal consistency.
2. As alternatives are generated for schematic design: the program can be the yardstick to help choose the best alternative.
3. At the end of schematic design: to see if there is any fine-tuning that needs to be done to improve the design and make it more consistent with the program.
4. In the middle of design development: to check that any new information has been incorporated, to

update any program changes, and to make sure the program is still being clearly followed.

5. At the end of design development: again for fine-tuning and consistency.

6. At the end of construction documents: for more fine-tuning. This assumes that the most glaring errors have been corrected in earlier evaluations.

7. During construction: to make sure that all is as intended.

8. Post-occupancy evaluation: to check how well the program was followed and to test out the validity of assumptions made in the program.

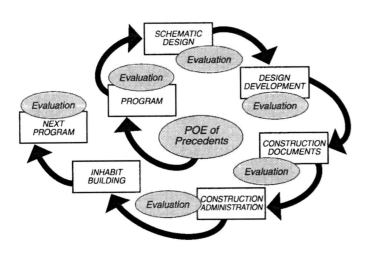

Figure 13-2 Systematic Evaluation as a Part of the Cycle

There are a number of processes that have been used successfully by a number of design firms. The following is a description of some of these processes and is intended to be a set of suggestions upon which to build your own evaluation processes.

Troika for In-House Evaluations

There are many forms that the design evaluation process might take. The CRS-Sirrine model has been the "troika," meaning that three different groups of players in the design process participate in the evaluation: designers, managers, and technologists in the firm jury the design on its merits in terms of Form, Function, Economy, and Time (Figure 13-3). Each member of the evaluation team gives the project a score in each category, based on a standardized set of criteria. These

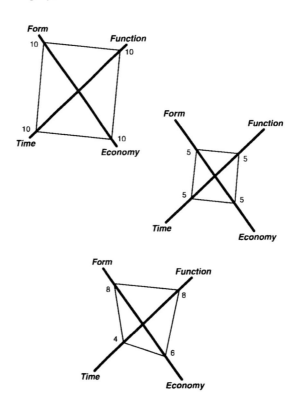

Figure 13-3 Troika Scoring for a Perfect Building, a Barely Passing Building, and a Normal Building Score. Adapted from Parshall, in Preiser 1989.

scores are then converted into an overall score that is the area of the diamond created by each leg of the quartet of concerns.

Ten points for each area of concern (Form, Function, Time, and Economy) gives a diamond with an area of 200 units, the perfect building. A diamond with five points for each area of concern is the absolute minimum acceptable, the beginning point of architecture. According to Parshall (in Preiser 1989) there are five steps in the CRSS process:

1. Establish a purpose.
2. Collect and analyze quantitative information.
3. Identify and examine qualitative information.
4. Make an *assessment*.
5. State the *lessons learned*.

Over-the-Shoulder Evaluations

Another option for the evaluation process includes having the programmer meet with the designer on a regular basis for over-the-shoulder design critiques or for team design sessions. This technique works very well if the programmer maintains extensive contact with a group client or if the programmer is the client's representative for the project. It also works well when the designer is uncertain of the most appropriate of several alternatives to a specific design problem. Clear communication keeps all parties on track and keeps the goals of the project fresh in the minds of the design team members.

Often the designer will uncover questions that were not formally addressed in the program document. As these arise, consultation with the programmer and client/user is useful to clarify the questions, if possible. If this is not possible and the questions have a large impact upon the design, go back and do more programming. This technique provides a good opportunity for input on both formal and functional issues.

Regular In-House Evaluation Sessions

Some firms present their projects to the entire work force on a regular basis for a free-for-all evaluation/discussion that ranges from how well the design meets the program to any other topic that will help to improve the design and educate the teams. Another technique is for the design team to review the program with the programmer at specified intervals and check for any missing items or any places in the design that need to be polished to meet the standards set by the program. This is one of the most exciting ways I know to update the firm's knowledge-base and share the firm's wisdom with new employees.

Client Review Meetings

It almost goes without saying that there should also be regular meetings with the client to insure that the program and/or design is going in the right direction, that some critical piece of information has not been left out, and that the programmer's and/or designer's interpretations are in line with the client/user's needs and expectations. After the programming and design team has made their evaluations, it is a good idea to check in with the client to see if the direction the project is going is the best one for all concerned.

Documenting Changes

During these evaluation sessions, whatever form they take, there may be discoveries of new issues, new information or alternative assumptions that require another look at the program document. Sometimes information discovered during the inquiry of the design process requires that the program be revised and updated. The program is not a document that is immutable and cast in concrete, but it should be a clear focus for the direction of the project and lay out the scope as clearly as possible so that when it is revised, all parties (client, designer, and programmer) are aware of the changes and agree to them.

Documentation of the changes produced by on-going design evaluations may take several forms. If they are discovered early enough in the process, the program document can be updated. After the program document has been finalized, changes may take the form of addenda to the program, memos documenting changes, and new decisions or an entry into a design log of the process. If the changes are significant, a supplement to the program document may need to be issued.

UNDERSTANDING THE RESULTS OF DESIGN

Post-Construction Evaluations

There are basically two kinds of evaluation of design results, post-construction evaluation (PCE) and post-occupancy evaluation (POE). Post-construction evaluation deals with the technical measures of a building's systems' performance. The types of information gained from these studies cover such topics as structural stability and integrity, watertightness, HVAC function, and material durability or maintenance. Post-occupancy evaluation deals with functional measures. POE information deals with the fit between the building's use and its form, perceptions of the building environment, enhancement of activities, and the physical comfort of the building occupants. Since the focus of this text is mainly on

the interaction of behavior and environment, rather than on the technics of building, it will concentrate on post-occupancy evaluation.

Post-Occupancy Evaluations

There are generally two major reasons why architectural firms do post-occupancy evaluations (POEs): to fine-tune the building and test how well it met the program and to evaluate an existing building as a model for a design in process. Those POE studies that are done to create more general knowledge about a particular building type are usually done by academics. It is my feeling that POEs are a normal extension of the design process — from programming, schematic design, design development, construction documents, bid, construction, and move-in to post-occupancy evaluation.

The post-occupancy evaluation is a research study that develops and tests hypotheses just as any programming research study does. Topics likely to arise as POE subjects are: life-cycle costs, users' perceptions of satisfaction about particular aspects of the building, building support for activities, mechanical system performance relative to comfort levels reported, safety requirements, users' behavior in certain building conditions, and outcome of particular design issues such as privacy, circulation, security.

A good POE will include the following steps:
1. Brief the current building managers about the purposes and the content of the evaluation.
2. Conduct a tour to orient the research team members and introduce the participants.
3. Conduct specific research studies, from interviews and surveys to observation studies and photodocumentation.

4. Analyze the data.
5. Debrief the research team.
6. Debrief the client participants.
7. Document and present the results of the process.

Preiser (1989, 5) has distinguished three levels of effort that characterize POEs.

"1. Indicative POEs give an indication of major strengths and weaknesses of a particular building performance.

"2. Investigative POEs go into more depth whereby objective evaluation criteria are explicitly stated.

"3. Diagnostic POEs require considerable effort and expense, are time consuming, and utilize sophisticated measurement techniques. They correlate physical environmental measures with subjective occupant response measures, thus providing a higher degree of credibility for the results."

Examples

The literature is wide and multifaceted. A good deal of the POE work is unpublished and proprietary. The following is not an attempt to do a thorough literature survey, but to give you a feel for the variety of work that has been done in POE and some resources for your own further research.

Van der Ryn's (1967) monograph, is one of the seminal POEs. It could probably be characterized as an investigative POE. It undertook to discover why students were not particularly happy with the dorms at UC Berkeley and preferred to live in apartments. The Building Performance Research Unit at Strathclyde has produced other evaluative studies of schools (Markus et al. 1972).

One of the largest POEs was by Newman (1972). It examined 100 different housing projects and has been very influential in making designers aware of the interaction between housing form and people's sense of ownership and security. Marcus's (1975) studies are unusual because Marcus was a participant observer living in the Easter Hill Village housing project that she studied.

Brill's (1984) office research clearly made the point that good design has a very large payback in terms of user satisfaction, lower turnover, and higher worker productivity. It is one of the very clear indicators that architectural design can influence ongoing building costs.

Bechtel and Srivastava (1978) produced a bibliography on housing POEs for the Department of Housing and Urban Development that was quite extensive. The pattern was clearly that most POEs were done by academicians and government and that very few private firms were doing POEs in housing.

In 1983 with several students, I conducted an indicative POE of the Juvenile Services Center in San Luis Obispo, California. We developed the hypothesis that in the Center the residents would feel a great need for privacy, since they were always under surveillance. To our surprise, we found that the major issue for these young inmates was loneliness. Having a roommate was a prize worth working for. All POEs will have hypotheses and should allow for potential disproof as well as confirmation of the hypotheses.

Other good resources on building evaluation are IFMA (International Facilities Management Association) which produces benchmarks for office building performance; EDRA (Environmental Design Research Association) which has an annual conference with many papers on POEs and programming; NBS 361 (National Bureau of Standards Technical Report #361, 1972) for a collection of many papers on building performance; ISO (International Standards Organization), CIB (Centre Internationale de Batément) and

BOMA (Building Owners and Managers Association), for information on office building income and expense.

Adding to the Knowledge Base

In order to create a shareable data base of evaluation studies, there needs to be some standardization of POE methods and measuring instruments so that studies can be compared from building to building and across time. It would be well to establish some performance requirements that are standard over a building type. Issue-based programming could contribute to that end. It would also be useful to have a standardized data base format so that all researchers could contribute to the store of information in ways that would be retrievable by designers. The ICADS project (Pohl 1992), at California Polytechnic State University, is a large step in the direction of creating a format for an expert CAD system, but the structure needs more building data in order to be complete.

similar to CRS-Sirrine's "troika" system, requires that a scoring system be developed that can be used consistently for a large variety of projects. If the programmer meets regularly with the designer to discuss the progress of the design, the programmer can evaluate the design in progress over the shoulder of the designer as he develops the project. Evaluation meetings with other design teams within the firm or with various client representatives also give good feedback.

There are two types of evaluations that are gathered after a building is built: post-construction evaluations, which deal with the technical specifications of the building, and post-occupancy evaluations, which deal with the fit between the building form and the needs of the occupants. Both should be carefully formulated to answer the questions asked by the users of the evaluation.

Any evaluation should be designed to fill the needs of the people using the information. Clients, programmers, and code officials all have needs for different information from a

SUMMARY

All evaluations are based on the premise that we will get better, less costly buildings if we repeat our successes and avoid making the same mistakes over and over again. During the design, evaluation is used to measure a project's progress toward its goals. After a project is built, evaluation can be used to fine-tune the building's performance, gather information that will help to program a similar project, or to document situations that help create new codes or standards. See Figure 13-4 for the place of evaluation in all design processes.

There are a number of evaluation techniques that can be used during the design process. A by-the-numbers approach,

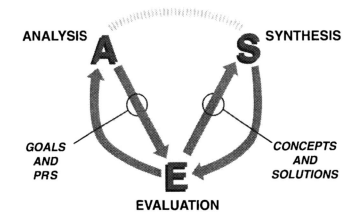

Figure 13-4 Evaluation in the Design Cycle

design project evaluation. Clients might want to know if they got their money's worth and if they can improve the efficient use of their building. Programmers want to know anything that will help them program the next similar building. Code officials want to know what to prohibit so that known mistakes will not reoccur. In evaluation, as in initial programming, the art of asking good relevant questions is paramount. Questions to be answered include: "What is the purpose of the evaluation?" "Who is the audience for the evaluation information?" "How will they use the information?" Research questions beyond fine-tuning of a design need to be rigorously formulated. Once these questions are formulated, the research and data analysis methods need to be carefully developed to gather and interpret the information most accurately and efficiently. Finally the evaluation report needs to be crafted as carefully as a program document. Graphics should be used as much as possible to convey the evaluation results.

Appendix A

FACTS LIST

From *Introduction to Architectural Programming* by Edward T. White. Copyright © 1972 Edward T. White. Reproduced by permission of the author.

TRADITIONAL FACTS

A. Different facts may be pertinent to different types of PROGRAMMING DOCUMENTS. In the same way that we screen facts in terms of their *RELEVANCE* to building consequences, we also evaluate their PERTINENCE to the purpose of the document where they will be contained. Some of the different types of programming documents in architecture are:
  1. master plan
  2. long range plan
  3. site feasibility
  4. building program
  5. comprehensive plan
  6. project definition

B. Below are some *TYPICAL* traditional architectural fact categories. For any specific situation some are more relevant than others. Groupings may also be different depending on the problem (pertain to and involve important building consequences).
  1. Similar projects and critical issues
    a. past projects of similar function, circumstances and scope
    b. critical issues involved in the building type
    c. trends in the field
  2. Client
    a. client goals

b. philosophy of the organization

c. goals of the client's process — sub-goals to achieve main goals — user goals

d. staff organization and framework — personnel diagram

e. rank and role of personnel

f. major departmental divisions within the organization — role of each — goals and sub-goals within the overall process

g. critical issues involved in the organization (people to people relationships, "channels")

h. does organization usually operate the way it is structured?

i. divergence of present operations form expressed goals — possible improvements

j. degree of achievement of sub-goals

k. individuals of committees responsible for planning with architect — role and responsibility in decision making

l. related (non-client) organizations which might affect planning

m. impact of change or growth of related organization

3. Financial

a. budget — firmness, degree of flexibility

b. funding methods — bonds, loans, fund raising

c. timing — construction costs, escalation, interest rates, concurrent similar projects taxing public support

d. construction phasing — prices, local construction market, strong and weak local trades, incremental construction

e. design requirements of lending institutions

f. comparative cost data on similar projects which have been constructed

4. Building Codes

a. occupancy allowed

b. structural loads allowed

c. exits required

d. stairs (number, type, access, fire rating, size, minimum distances to reach stairs)

e. fire ratings required of materials

f. ventilation — openings

g. toilets (number and fixtures of each)

h. fire sprinklers

i. alarm systems

5. Planning by related organizations

a. duplication of services

b. review boards

c. approval boards (regulations, by-laws, planning criteria)

d. projected construction of similar projects

6. Function

a. operational system — including links beyond the building

b. critical issues in insuring success in the system's operation

c. needs which are supporting to operation (lounge, waiting, toilet, janitor)

d. main operational sequences — "feeder sequences" which support main sequences

e. divisions or departments in the system

f. general departmental relationship affinities

g. number and type of people involved (task categories)

h. operations performed by each type of person

i. systems of people movement
    (1) points of origin and destination
    (2) frequency and pattern (continual or intermittent)
    (3) degree of urgency
    (4) role in the overall operation
    (5) peak loads
j. systems of information movement
    (1) points of origin and destination
    (2) frequency and pattern (continual or intermittent)
    (3) degree of urgency (speed required)
    (4) role in the overall operation
    (5) form
    (6) storage implications
    (7) operations performed on information (including production and removal of trash)
    (8) peak loads
k. systems of material movement
    (1) points of origin and destination (including delivery and pickup)
    (2) frequency and pattern (continual or intermittent)
    (3) degree of urgency (speed required)
    (4) role in the overall operation
    (5) form (size, weight)
    (6) special considerations (fragile)
    (7) operations performed on information (including production and removal of trash)
    (8) storage implications
    (9) peak loads
l. work nodes (stations where work is performed)
    (1) number, type, and relationships

    (2) number and type of people at each
    (3) nature of tasks performed
        (a) key issues in successful performance of tasks
        (b) identification of possible sources of strain in performing tasks
    (4) furniture and equipment required for each person (including visitors, clients)
    (5) accessories required for each person
    (6) sizes, electrical requirements, and other considerations regarding furniture, equipment or accessories
    (7) area requirements of each node
    (8) circulation patterns within each node (people, material, information)
    (9) security requirements (open, closed, locked)
    (10) general electrical requirements at each node
    (11) criteria for selecting architectural surfaces and detailing
    (12) special relationships with other work nodes (visual control)
    (13) lighting requirements
        (a) intensity required at task
        (b) incandescent vs. fluorescent
        (c) direct vs. indirect
        (d) skylight vs. window
        (e) need for total darkness
        (f) need for controlled lighting
    (14) sensory
        (a) type and intensity of stimuli produced (noise, odors, vibration,

dust, electro-magnetism, bacteria)

(b) type and intensity of stimuli which must be excluded or screened (including visual privacy)

(c) important environmental situations (mood, atmosphere)

(15) air conditioning requirements

(a) heat generated by equipment and people

(b) special air circulation or ventilation requirements (isolation, 100 % exhaust, decontamination)

(c) special temperature requirements

(d) air additives

(e) special controls over air conditioning

(f) groupings of similar air conditioning requirements

(g) total needs

(h) space required for mechanical

(i) vibration control

(j) heating and cooling seasons

7. Site

a. legal description of property (boundaries, dimensions, rights of way, deed restrictions, easements, curbs, curb cuts, hydrants, poles)

b. zoning

(1) present allowable uses

(2) setbacks

(3) access points

(4) relation to street lights and median breaks

(5) density

(6) heights allowed

(7) parking required

c. utilities

(1) locations

(2) distances to site

(3) depths

(4) telephone, gas, water, sewer, electrical

(5) capacities (present and projected)

d. soil conditions

(1) percolation

(2) bearing

(3) chemicals

(4) density

e. land contours

(1) elevations

(2) drainage patterns (including from and to adjacent land)

(3) flood basins (tides)

(4) blocked visual access due to mound and ridges

(5) points of visual emphasis

(6) flat areas

(7) slope orientation to surrounding areas (visually)

f. significant features

(1) rock outcroppings

(2) existing buildings

(3) ditches

(4) water

(5) trees

g. existing foliage

    (1) tree types

    (2) limb spread

    (3) height

    (4) ground cover (where drainage
    may be affected)

h. sensory

    (1) noise (direction, intensity, frequency,
    pattern, probability of continuance)

    (2) odors (direction, intensity, pattern, type,
    probability for continuance)

    (3) visual (poor views, good views, public
    and private zones, reliability of continuance
    of views)

i. time-distance

    (1) car-pedestrian

    (2) to and from significant points
    on and around site

    (3) time-distance on site

j. existing pedestrian traffic on and around site

    (1) volume

    (2) location

    (3) frequency and pattern (time of day,
    continual, intermittent)

    (4) nature (to work, school, lunch, random
    stroll)

    (5) possible contribution to these activities

k. existing vehicular traffic on and around the site

    (1) volume

    (2) location

    (3) frequency and pattern

    (4) nature

    (5) possible contribution to these activities

l. surrounding physical environment

    (1) surrounding zoning

    (2) possible development on adjacent and
    surrounding property

    (3) profile (skyline)

    (4) scale

    (5) image

    (6) materials

    (7) forms

    (8) density

    (9) light (shade and shadow)

    (10) orientation (views of the site from other
    points)

    (11) landscaping forms

    (12) details

    (13) geometry (existing paving patterns,
    building edges and heights, axes, walls,
    modules and rhythms)

m. surrounding social environment

    (1) identifiable patterns

    (2) ethnic groups and values

    (3) relationships between groups

n. shadow patterns on the site (trees, adjacent
buildings

o. parking and site circulation

    (1) needs (present and projected)

    (2) area required

    (3) dropoffs required at entry

    (4) lighting

    (5) special controls (restricted parking)

    (6) on-site circulation required (between
    buildings)

    (7) supporting circulation (to lunch, to

work)

(8) volume and frequency patterns (peak loads)

(9) patterns of direction of entry approach and departure (people and cars)

(10) existing roads

(11) points of logical access-egress (all types of traffic)

(12) surrounding land values

8. Climate

   a. rainfall (frequency, volume, patterns)

   b. sunlight (critical vertical and horizontal angles)

   c. temperatures (seasons, extremes)

   d. wind, breezes (seasons, directions, velocity, extremes)

   e. snow (seasons, percentages)

   f. humidity (seasons, percentages)

   g. potential natural catastrophes (tornado, hurricane, earthquake, flood)

9. Growth and Change

   a. present and projected supporting market of public served

   b. projected staffing (number and type)

   c. projected goals and supporting sub-goals

d. anticipated deletion of departments and addition of new departments

e. areas of expected changes in operations (layout and building perimeter implications)

f. projected changes in information or material systems (disposables)

g. influence of growth and change of one department on all others

h. future area needs (construction, cost, design and parking implications)

i. projected utility needs — comparison with present and projected supply capacities

C. Each of these fact categories may be EXPANDED to more DETAIL depending on the design requirements. There are also many other fact categories not listed here that pertain to some of the other programming FORMS (long range plan).

Every fact category and specific fact contained under its heading involves CONSEQUENCES that the building has on its environment and contained functions and which the environment has upon the building.

Appendix B

SCENARIOS

The first four scenarios were written by a group of third year design students to help them picture clients for a co-housing scheme based upon a studio course titled "Living Lightly on the Earth."

The Harris Family

Early in the morning, Harvey and Eudora Harris begin their day. As most retired people will, they prefer to use as much of the day as possible. Turning on the thermostat is the first order of the day, allowing the hot water to flow from the solar heated tanks to the showers and sinks. The solar panels heat up about enough water for four short showers, or enough hot water for the entire day for two people. When the showering is done, the thermostat is turned back down to conserve energy. As Grandma finishes preparing for the day, Grandpa makes his way out to the chicken coop to collect that day's eggs, as well as the rather lengthy trip down to the mailbox at the end of the driveway. There's a letter today, tucked in under the regular junk mail, from their grandson down in San Luis Obispo. Keeping that letter on top, Grandpa climbs the driveway back to the house, looking forward to the morning meal.

The typical breakfast consists of either ham and eggs, if the chickens have been especially generous, or Grandpa's famous flapjacks, covered with some homemade olallieberry jam. Today, flapjacks are the choice with some special homegrown raspberries to top them off. Both Grandma and Grandpa enjoy cooking, either for each other or for others. While Grandpa cooks breakfast, Grandma reads the letter.

Apparently, there's a new community effort emerging in San Luis Obispo, consisting of people gathering together to "live lightly on the earth." The kids were involved, and were wondering if Grandma and Grandpa would be interested in moving down to join them? The letter went on to talk about what that "living lightly on the earth" theme meant, and strongly emphasized having people nearby in case something happened, rather than being isolated on five acres beyond the edge of town, as Grandma and Grandpa are now. The kids even teased that a chicken coop on the property could be arranged so that Grandma could keep her hens. In town there's a smaller chance of predatory coyotes attacking the fowl. Chuckling, Grandma had to agree. Discussing the pros and cons, Grandma and Grandpa agree to think about it through the day, and discuss it at dinner. After the meal, they take the dishes to the sink, where they usually sit all day, so water needs to be used only once in the day to wash them.

The cooler mornings usually find Grandma outside in her gardens. Ornamental flowers are grown in carefully tended beds to the side of the house as well as in the greenhouse next to the garage. Vegetables are grown in abundance in her one-quarter acre plot in front of the house, mostly green beans and tomatoes, with a fair share of corn and squash thrown in. Every once in a while, Grandma looks around at her beloved garden, knowing that she'll miss all this space if they move down to San Luis Obispo. But, she tells herself, the kids mentioned something about a garden on the property, or at least small individual gardens for everybody. She wouldn't have to do without her gardens. Maybe, if it turned out to be a larger community garden, she wouldn't find herself with so many jars of canned beans and things, since she could give them to the community. Besides, this vegetable garden gets bigger as she gets older. At least it

seems that way. Smiling, Grandma gets back to work, realizing she was leaning more towards this move the more she thought about it.

Grandpa will spend his morning working on one of the many vehicles his sons and grandsons bring him to fix, as well as adjusting the two windmills on the property. The tall, sophisticated-looking wind generator is used to generate electricity and is located right in the middle of Grandma's vegetable garden, much to her consternation. There are two electric meters on the property; both connect to PG&E, but one measures the electricity from PG&E to the property when the wind isn't strong enough to turn the blades, and the other meter measures how much Grandpa sends back to PG&E. This system works out so well that the monthly electric bill is somewhere around $8. The second windmill, smaller and looking like something stolen from a run-down barn, is used to pump the property's water from underground wells. Today, a belt is loose on the smaller windmill, which is quite a serious problem. Sometimes, it's a hassle to maintain this little windmill, but the water wells are really the only way to get water to the property. Grandpa really wouldn't mind giving it up for the convenience of a water line in town, like San Luis Obispo could offer. Pondering this thought, Grandpa looks back toward the tall wind generator. His grandson, knowing about the wind generator, had mentioned something about the proposed site being well protected by trees and a mountain. Maybe the wind generator wouldn't work as well as it did here, but it was worth it to look into possibilities. His mind churning, Grandpa focuses again on his project at hand. For heaven's sake, they hadn't even decided to move yet.

Lunch consists partially of vegetables from the garden, perhaps a little homemade bread. Any meat they wish to eat must be purchased from the nearby town of Aromas, eight miles away, or even from Watsonville, 15 miles away. They tried once to grow their own beef, by way of one steer Grandma fondly named HOF, or Hamburger On Foot. Unfortunately, they both became fond of HOF, but especially Grandma. When it came time to butcher HOF, he very generously provided them with a large amount of meat, but Grandma refused to eat any of it, and even became a partial vegetarian for six months, refusing to eat any kind of beef. They haven't tried to grow their own beef since then, although the chickens, when they become too old to lay, become candidates for the dinner table. Anyway, as isolated as they are, their car is very important to them. They usually shop for groceries in town only once a week in large quantities. They might consider walking more if they were in town, but since Grandma's recent problem with reoccurrence of arthritis, and Grandpa's recent bout with prostate cancer and chemotherapy, they aren't as active anymore.

After lunch, when the wind picks up too much to be outside comfortably, Grandma will either bake in the kitchen, or go upstairs to paint her landscapes in the natural daylight from the front windows. The kitchen is simple, consisting primarily of a conventional oven and microwave, as well as the basic kitchen appliances, like a blender and mixer. Dry goods are stored in the large pantry, but more space is constantly needed for storing many of the jars of canned vegetables and jams that come out of the gardens. More storage areas are needed throughout the house for knickknacks and painted canvases lying everywhere. During these afternoons, Grandpa will either read a book or go back outside to "play" with his cars and other household repairs.

Their dinner consists of more vegetables from the gardens, some meat from town, and possibly some homemade hominy. Dinner conversation tonight draws back to the issue at hand: the possible move to San Luis Obispo and the grandkids. Grandma's green thumb would be put to good use in the garden, and Grandpa's knowledge of cars and general fun personality would also make him an asset to the group. Besides, both of them realize, but don't like to say, five acres is a little much to manage at their age. And moving south would get them closer to family members. There would be small children to enjoy, as well as friends constantly close by in case something happened. The idea sounds good. Smiling at each other, Grandma and Grandpa admit that they are close to a move. At the end of the meal the entire day's dishes are washed at once, and any edible wastes are given to the chickens to eat. After all, those chickens must be given a fighting chance against the animals at night.

Evening activities consist of either visiting with friends or driving into town for various activities, such as square dancing, Grange Hall meetings, or church gatherings. They really do like people, and Grandma surprises herself by realizing she would be happier with more friends nearby. Maybe she'll call her grandkids tomorrow and talk some more about this "living lightly on the earth" community. The end of the day finds them quietly reading in bed, and lights go out early.

The Diskette Family

"Thirty thousand dollars, I hope it's worth it." Nick Diskette had never thought it would be possible, but just last month the city made it legal. Almost immediately he convinced the owner that a gray-water system for the hotel would be valuable considering the terrible price of water these days. As manager of the hotel for some 15 years, Nick had seen water consumption go up, as well as seen the water costs go up throughout the city. Always trying to convince other businesses of the importance of conservation, this day was indeed a victory.

"Just finished up, Mr. Diskette," says the evening manager as she finishes her checklist. Good, it's almost 7:00 PM, and he can go home to another wonderful meal with Nora. It never ceases to amaze him how over 30 years of marriage he has never grown tired of his wife's cooking. Probably because she's a gourmet or that he loves her to death. Who's to say? Nora should have been home from her job at the library for a few hours now, and the house is probably almost cleaned for the kids' arrival tonight.

Nora is in great shape for a woman in her 50s and that's probably due to her riding her bike back and forth to the library every day, but it is also due to the fact the her cooking has always been good tasting as well as good for you. It's low in fat and cholesterol. She has always been disgruntled at the average American's diet. Why use sugar and oils for taste when a few key herbs and spices can easily do the job better? She had tried to teach her three children, two girls and a boy, about proper nutrition, but like most young adults it was all forgotten once college rolled around. But now that the girls are somewhat older and married, they have become quite interested in proper eating. Mother knows best.

Every Friday, this being no exception, Diane and her husband, Jack, with the grandchildren, Wally and Theodore, come to dinner. At 5:00, Nora hadn't separated the trash for the week or gathered the vegetables for the meal. "The vegetables," Nora muses, "I can't believe what a wonderful garden we have. It only took a small amount of time and the

rewards are great! Now that it's been a few years, we are producing probably 80-90 % of our vegetables right here. And oh, how they taste! Sometimes it's hard to believe how many chemicals we consumed at one time." But the best part about the garden is the herbs. You name it and Nora grows it, plus she knows how to use it. "Hold it! Enough day dreaming. Nick's bus will be here soon and the kids wouldn't be too far behind."

The bus trip generally took about 30 to 40 minutes, depending upon the day, but rarely did Nick mind. At 57, he had done more than enough driving to work — plus the new bus lines were clean and safe. That's a great departure from the years before. Thanks to the shift in City Planning attitudes and their new, more environmental point of view, the citizens have really taken to public transport. "It's about time."

"Where to this year?" Nick pondered as he sat back and pulled out a few brochures on Alaska. Every year for the past ten or so, the Diskettes travelled for a month somewhere. They have been to Europe, the South Pacific, Asia, and throughout much of the U.S., but they had not travelled to Alaska. Maybe this year? "The kids are coming tonight; I almost forgot! The grandchildren will be staying the weekend again. I always enjoy that; they tend to keep me young. Maybe tomorrow we can take them out to the lake for some swimming, fishing, and a picnic. Better yet, maybe they're old enough for golfing. No, I don't think they're old enough yet to watch their Grandfather be slaughtered by their Grandmother. Probably mess up their psyches for life. Better not do that. Definitely make it the lake."

• • • • •

"How was your day?"

"Good. I finished off the water recycling stuff. It sure seemed complicated. I forgot the kids were coming today. I lost track of the days."

For the three thousand fifty-sixth time in their marriage, not that she was counting, Nora told her husband that she had reminded him that very morning of the fact.

By the time the kids arrived, the tensions of the week had subsided and they were both in the mood for company.

The Junkerson Family

It was a typical weekday for the Junkerson family. At half past six, Sandra, 30 years old and mother of two, got up quietly and carefully, trying not to wake up Ward. She knew that her husband must have been burning the midnight oil in his attempt to finish his novel for his deadline. Sandra tiptoed to the kitchen, silently poured herself a glass of nonfat milk, and cut a slice of freshly baked bread from the bread machine. She always enjoyed this time of the morning by herself, eating her breakfast in the filtered sunshine without the daily distractions from the kids.

At 7:30, her workmate and car pool companion, Sue, came over and picked her up for work. The usual 45 minute commute found the two friends talking about nothing but their kids. Half an hour later, the second radio alarm sounded. Ward jumped up from the bed, his head still spinning from the late night session. At 34, he felt he was getting too old to wait until the last minute to finish his work. He proceeded to the kitchen to fix breakfast for himself and his two small children. Jamie, six years old and halfway through first grade, was getting ready for her show-and-tell

day at school. As usual, her daddy started her right with a nutritious meal and a tall glass of orange juice. Jamie wolfed down her food and hurried out to meet her friend Samantha for their four-block walk to school. After Jamie left, Ward ate with his four year-old, Marvin, while Bugs Bunny cartoons played in the background. Ward had wanted to get rid of the T.V., but his wife would have no part of it. She saw the tube as an educational tool for the children, a source of news, and an entertaining way to wind down after a hard day of accounting work. After doing the breakfast dishes, Ward prepared to spend the day running errands. He walked Marvin to his Grandma's, which was on the way to town. Although the Junkerson's had one reliable car and Sandra had carpooled with a friend, Ward still did not drive that often, almost always preferring to walk. While he walked, ideas almost always flowed freely into his train of thought and thus surfaced for his literary creations. Grandma lived only four streets over and often took care of the children when she was not playing bridge. Ward continued on to downtown where he dropped off the rough draft of his new novel. His publisher would be very pleased with the environmentalist approach Ward took in his newest work. After walking back home and mailing a week and a half's worth of bills, it was off to the nursery for Ward. He needed to pick up a package of ladybugs to combat the aphids that were feasting on his roses. Ward did not have a lot of time to devote to his garden, but that was alright as it was a small manageable plot of land. Still, there was nothing he liked better after a good novel than to work outdoors in the sun and the greenery.

Today was much like a holiday for Ward, since he had finished all his chores by noon. His return trip took him back to Grandma's for a delicious lunch of chicken soup and crackers. Grandma never kept much food on hand. Ward took Marvin and strolled on home, stopping by a city playground to play on the swings with his son. He liked his new town much better than where he had previously lived. There the playgrounds were littered with crack vials and dirty syringes. Ward decided to just say no and move away. His new life featured better living conditions, although sometimes he felt he was in a time warp. Arriving home in plenty of time before his daughter came home from school, Ward put Marvin down for a nap and went to work in the garden. Tonight he planned to bake a fresh apple pie. The fruit trees were full and ripe. Ward also cleaned out the tomato and lettuce reserves for a fresh dinner salad. Ward loved going to the garden to watch Wenona, his new neighbor, work in her bikini. It was great entertainment for the whole family, if Jamie and Marvin were around. Presently, Jamie came home with a couple of her friends and a day's full of stories to tell her dad. She also forgot to mention that her Brownie troop was meeting at the Junkerson's to discuss the sale of their Brownie cookies.

The aroma of Ward's apple pie filled the warm evening air as the kids played another round of afternoon hide-and-seek. As the dinner hour approached, Sandra called home to say she had to work overtime again. Ward and the children consumed their supper together, wishing mommy could be with them. At 7:00 PM, Sandra came home with her microwavable Weight Watchers meal, knowing that Ward had cooked dinner. "But Mommy, his cooking's getting better," assured Jamie. Ward added, "Look out Julia Child. But until then, no pie while you're on your diet." Sandra could only cringe. After dinner she made her weekly food run to the all natural food store while Ward maintained order at the Brownie convention. Later that night found Ward and Sandra winding down in an entertaining way watching T.V. of course!

The Page Family

John and Wenona Page have been married 5 years. John is 35 years old and currently works as a disc jockey for a local classic rock radio station. Wenona, 32, is a nurse at Sierra Vista Hospital. Wenona is six months pregnant. John and Wenona sometimes have night shifts, which can create conflicts with their other activities and social life.

John is especially environmentally conscious; although Wenona shares some of her husband's views, she is mostly indifferent. John refuses to drive his car unless he absolutely has to, however, he is glad that Wenona drives at night. They only own one car, a Geo Metro. Some of the things that John and Wenona would want in a new home are passive solar heating, maximum daylighting, recycling bins built into kitchen cabinets, possible use of a gray-water system, and maybe even a clivus multrum waterless toilet (given the severe water shortage in San Luis Obispo).

The Pages like to entertain small groups of friends about once a week. Occasionally, they have larger parties for 30 or more. They would like a kitchen large enough to cook large meals in, but also one that conserves space and is very efficient. The appliances most often used are the microwave, refrigerator, gas stove/oven, and the clothes washer.

John enjoys woodworking and spends much of his spare time making or repairing furniture. He would like some kind of a workshop space in his new home. He also has a large collection of record albums and needs about 15 feet of shelving to store them.

He also has a large stereo/entertainment system. Wenona spends much of her spare time gardening and sewing. She would like an outdoor space for gardening and potting plants.

The Pages understand that if they join a group of five other families and try to "live lightly on the earth" with them, there will be drawbacks. However, they tend to think that the benefits will far outweigh any sacrifices made. The Pages also want to live in a more communal atmosphere; they tend to feel isolated with their night-time jobs. They also have little Shawn to think about. What kind of atmosphere will this new place provide for their child(ren)?

A typical daily schedule for the Pages is:

9:00 AM	Wenona and John wake up and get ready for work
10:00	Wenona starts work
11:00	John starts work
12:00	Lamaze class
6:00 PM	Wenona goes home and starts to prepare "dinner"
7:00	John starts bicycling home for dinner
8:00	Relaxation, read paper, talk
9:00	Free time to spend together or enjoy hobbies
1:30	Bedtime snack
2:00 AM	Bedtime/sleep

The students involved in creating these scenarios were Mike Fields, Freeman Leung, Clay Little, John Luddy, Karl Chan, Robin Gates, Katie Hou, Tom Lane, Dan McCauley, Sharon Janssen, Derek Knowles, Patrice Langevin, Steve Olander, Marne Bridges, Jim Garcia, Scott Jones, Lorenzo Lopez, and Frank Phanton.

The next scenario is probably the funniest one I have ever received as a class assignment. It was written by a second year student to create a sense of what an artist's life could be like.

Steve's Scenario

A typical work day in Jim's studio might go something like this. He would sleep in a little, say 9 or 10, having been up late the night before doing some nighttime photography. After turning on some RUSH, he would shower or relax in the sauna. Euripides would need to be fed, so he would have to go to the kitchen for dog food, and while there, fix himself something to eat (not dog food). After putting on the CARS he would go down to his studio, taking time to view his previous work in the gallery and the other areas throughout the house. By now it would be 11 or 12. While working he might want to change to U-2 and get some munchies or coffee. But that's OK because he would have to step back and view his work in progress and see how he feels about it. Around 4 or 5 it would be time to have a sandwich or open a can of SpaggettiOs (with franks). Time to go back to the kitchen. When he gets there he finds he only has SpagettiOs in cheese sauce, so he calls Euripides and gets in his '57 Buick and heads for town. After going to four different markets to find SpaggettiOs with franks, he cruises back to the studio. Now it is around 6 and he isn't hungry any more because he bought a Snickers at the third market, so he feeds the SpaggettiOs to Euripides (with franks). He notices his answering machine is blinking and finds out Patti called. He tries to call her, but gets her answering machine and hangs up. Now it is around 7. Back to work in the studio on his latest creation. At 9 the Snickers wore off, so he heads to the kitchen and realizes that his SpaggettiOs are long gone. The hell with it, he decides Bob's Burnt Bunnies sound pretty good, and he sneaks out leaving Euripides at home, because Euripides always begs for the bunny bones and Jim's afraid the poor mutt will choke. It's a beautiful evening, so he leaves the top down on the gas hog. While driving down the hill he notices that the sun is doing some unusual things in the trees, so he whips out his camera and takes a few. Jim is so zoned out by the experience that while driving he doesn't see the porcupine in the road and runs right over it. Looking in his rear view mirror, he notices the sun is doing some unusual things to the dead porcupine, so he stops and whips out his camera and runs back to take a few. When he returns to his car, both of the right side tires are flat. Of course he had only one spare tire and it was flat anyway. Jim sticks out his thumb and catches a ride with Farmer Bob (who just happens to be the owner of Bob's Burnt Bunnies). Farmer Bob recognizes Jim as a regular customer (there's only five in the town), and decides to give him an extra order for free because he felt sorry for him. After stuffing himself Jim calls the towing company and tells them his story. Now it's 10:30 and they charge double time after 6. Jim spent his last eight dollars on Bunnies, but finds out they take American Express. The driver picks Jim up at Bob's and drives over to the car. Mel, the driver, brought two spare tires. After jacking up the car he finds that the lug bolts don't match with Jim's Buick. Jim calls him a few names and Mel jumps in the truck and peels out leaving Jim in the dust. Jim notices that the moon is doing some unusual things in the dust, so he whips out his camera and takes a few. It's a long walk back to the studio, but Jim doesn't have much choice. Jim picks up his camera and the porcupine and heads up the road. Luckily he was wearing his Reeboks. Upon approaching the studio, he hears Euripides barking and bounding down the road. Euripides was happy to see the present Jim brought him. It's now 12:30. Jim goes in and relaxes in the sauna, and puts on Van Halen, because he's hate'n life. Eddie gets him back in the mood though, and it's back to the studio. First he has to develop the pictures he took. They turned out great, so he takes off with his new ideas into the wee hours of the morning.

By Steve Townley

Appendix C

DEFINITIONS OF ISSUES

Notice that many of the issue areas interact and some overlap. In any given design problem, the definition of the issue areas of highest priority may need to be clearly articulated and operationally defined.

AUDIBILITY - the acoustic properties of an environment that contributes to one's ability to hear what needs to be heard and to mask unwanted sounds

BEHAVIOR SETTINGS - the units for describing the interdependencies of activity and physical setting. See Chapter 9 for a full description.

CIRCULATION - movement or flow of people, objects, information or substances
  Information - includes, paper flow, phones, computer hookups, multi-media, conversations, etc.
  Material - raw and finished materials; services such as water, gas, electrical energy; supplies such as paper goods and food; equipment, etc.
  Parking - temporary storage of vehicles from trucks and buses to cars and bicycles
  Pedestrians - people walking, skating, pushing a wheelchair, on crutches, or otherwise moving without a vehicle
  Vehicles - cars, trucks, buses, motorcycles, mopeds, trolleys, rickshaws, bicycles; trains, boats, planes

COMFORT - providing ease and enjoyment
  Physical - accommodation of physical needs to allow ease: thermal, tactile, fit, fresh air, appropriate level of physical stimulation (noise, glare, etc.)

COMFORT - providing ease and enjoyment

    Psychological - conditions for mental ease: appropriate shapes, colors, meanings, light levels conducive to the task at hand

CONVENIENCE - ease of access to places, materials, and information

DURABILITY - ability to endure the designed use over time

ECONOMY - maximum benefit for minimum means

    Elegant means - getting the task done simply and well

    Phasing - the expansion from minimum size to maximum size with appropriate intervals and functions

    Quality - attribute or degree of excellence required for success

ENERGY EFFICIENCY - amount and/or percentage of available energy that is used

FLEXIBILITY - ability to change easily

    Adaptability - ability to change from one use to another

    Choice/Variety - ability to interpret or use environments in different ways at the same time

    Expansion/Contraction - ability to enlarge or shrink a space with ease

    Multi-use - ability to use an environment in different ways at different times

IMAGE - how a place looks and is interpreted by the observer; the visual impression

    Identity - how a place is recognized visually

Message - what a place is trying to "say" to its users

Ordering/proportion - recognizable visual patterns and relationships

Status/hierarchy - the communicated value or importance of a place or a person occupying a place

Symbolism - the meaning or representation to be communicated

INTERACTION - mutual action and interchange: social, academic, team work

    Group participation - groups of people engaged in a common activity

    Social - friendly interchange for its own sake

LEGIBILITY - quality of the environment as readable

    Layering -foreground, midground, and distant view giving a sense of what is near and what is far

    Orientation - sense of direction: either cardinal or in relationship to a destination

    Plan recognition - ability to recognize where one is in a building in relationship to its plan

    Sequence - the order in which spaces occur, procession

MAINTENANCE - keeping things and places clean and in good condition

MOOD/AMBIENCE - the emotional sensation in response to a place

    Attitude - one's mental state or disposition

    Emotional response - one's change in emotional state as a result of being in a particular place

    Spirit of place - rich experience of a place as being recognizable and whole

OLFACTORY - the sense of smell and the smells of an environment

PERSONALIZATION - marking a space to claim it as reserved territory
> **Group** - creating the symbols of ownership by a group
> **Individual** - decorating or marking a space as one's own

PRIVACY - the ability to control the comings and goings of people across one's boundaries, the regulation of interaction
> **Group** - ability to control who participates in the group's activities and who or what is excluded
> **Individual** - ability to equate actual privacy level to the desired privacy level

RESOURCE MANAGEMENT - careful use of resources such as water, materials, energy, fuels, and personnel; includes concepts of recycling and minimum use of embodied energy

SAFETY - protection from harm or danger
> **Accidents** - known causes of accidents are eliminated
> **Hazards** - barriers are created to separate people from potentially dangerous places

SECURITY - protection from unwanted aggression by another person
> **Assault** - conditions created to protect from the possibility of personal assault
> **Robbery** - protection from the potential for robbery
> **Unauthorized access/entry** - protection from the possibility of unauthorized access
> **Vandalism** - elimination of the conditions that invite vandalism

TERRITORY - claiming a space as belonging to a person or group
> **Group** - physically proclaiming temporary or permanent ownership of a place by the group's marking boundaries
> **Individual** - physically proclaiming temporary or permanent ownership of a place by one's marking boundaries

VISIBILITY - ability to see, includes light levels and sight lines as well.

GLOSSARY

abrasion - rubbing off; grinding, polishing a surface; evidence for measuring where activities were

accretion - a collection of matter, the addition of material; also evidence for measuring where activities were

AIA - American Institute of Architects, 1735 New York Avenue, NW, Washington, DC 20003

algorithm - a step-by-step method for finding the answer to a problem; a formula for action

analogy - comparing of something point by point to something else; useful in design for generating concepts

analysis - breaking the whole into parts to discover its nature or function

ANSI - American National Standards Institute

anthropometrics - the study of the measurements of the human body

architectural determinism - the philosophy that architecture determines people's behavior

behavior setting - the social/physical situations in which human behavior occurs; units for describing, analyzing, and understanding the interdependence of activity and setting

bidding - the process of getting competitive prices on a contract

binary decisions - the answer can only be one of two answers — either yes or no, 1 or 0, this or that

briefing - the British term for architectural programming

case study - an in-depth study of several situations (cases) that answers the "how" and "why" questions in field situations

casual observation - observation focused on understanding the general issues of a situation and for raising questions that can be answered by other methods

charette - 1. waiting until the last minute to get the design project finished as in the case of the French art students who were still working on their paintings as they rode the cart (*en charette*) to the studio to be critiqued 2. an intense workshop involving a community design problem, community residents, a series of experts, and students, all trying to get the best design to solve the problem

"chicken test" - the most critical test for the success or failure of a project

clerestories - high windows that let in light but no view except sky and trees, often at the top of a wall at the high side of a sloped roof

concepts - physical relationships appropriate to get the job done

conceptual scenarios - several paragraphs that explain the main ideas behind a design

construct - a definition of the rules and important variables in a research study; a definition of "the way the world works" relevant to the study

contract documents - those drawings and specifications that are the legal contract for the accurate production of a building project including site work, landscaping, interiors, equipment and all structure and building systems

CPM - *c*ritical *p*ath *m*ethod for developing a project schedule

crowding - the perception that there are too many people — from an elevator to a city

data lines - an architectural reference line that gives consistency to the design; in cities, buildings, and landscapes

degree days - a unit of measurement caluclated by comparing the mean daily temperature to a standard (normally 65°F) — positive numbers indicate cooling loads; negative numbers indicate heating load

density - number of people per unit area

design development - the second stage of physical design; an alternative has been chosen and a more specific, detailed design is developed

design issue - see "issue"

design log - a method for recording all design decisions and research on a project so that they can be retrieved on call

EDRA - Environmental Design Research Association: 733 Northeast 18th Street, Oklahoma City, OK 73105

environment/behavior interaction - the interdependence of behavior and environment; for the purposes of design, you cannot have one without the other

environmental press - the forces in the environment that demand an individual response; degree of press varies with individual competence and the environment

ergonomics - the study of the human body at work

esquisse - a brief sketch or modeling problem that is based upon and expresses the essence of the design problem

evaluation - the act of judging the positive and negative aspects of a project or design alternative to see if it measures up to expectation

extrovert - a person who directs his/her attention to phenomena outside him/herself; one who is energized by other people

existing state - the set of facts and constraints within which a design is developed

experimenter bias - faulty research results from the researcher designing a study such that the results are most likely to be what was expected rather than allowing for the hypothesis to be proven false

facts - things or events that have occurred in reality; true things

focus group - a group of people gathered together to discuss a topic in order to share their opinions on a specific topic; in design a source of programming information

future state - the situation that the design proposes to create to solve the problems posed to the designer

goals - the qualities of outcome desired for design issues

gutter - the blank space on the inside edge of a page of print that is wide enough to allow space for the binding of a book or report

heuristic method - working by a "rule of thumb" to skip steps normally required in an algorithm; using intuition

hierarchy - a group of things arranged in order of rank, grade, or size

home range - the area covered by the places where one feels at home and known

hypotheses - the educated guesses about what the answer to a research question might be

imaging - making a design idea visible — in any medium

incrementalism - building up an idea or a design project by small parts to create the whole

introvert - a person who directs attention inside himself/herself and is energized by ideas

issues - situations or sets of concerns that demand design decisions or responses

issue-based programming - a programming process that uses design issues as categories for organizing information for the design process

judgment measures - making decisions based on the relative goodness of solutions

JND - *just noticeable difference*: the point at which a change in some phenomenon becomes barely noticeable in human perception

life space - the area covered by the memories of places one has been and is familiar with

MBTI - *Meyers Briggs Type Indicator*: a scale that measures the extroversion/introversion, intuitive/sensate, feeling/thinking, and judgment/perception aspects of a person's personality

megaconcept - another word for parti, the major organizing idea of a design

metaphor - a figure of speech in which one thing is compared to another, in design the comparison can be on a point by point basis a well as general function

mission - the overall purpose for a project

naturalistic observation - observation in the field when the observer has no control over the actions of the events being observed

NIMBY - *Not In My Back Yard!* - a planning term for people who do not want certain landuses or inhabitants near their property

open system - a system open to inputs from the outside

operationalizing a definition - the process of defining terms such that all parties using them are clear about the meaning and use them in the same way

paired comparisons - a technique for choosing an alternative; done by comparing each possibility with each other possibility, one at a time, and adding up total paired wins to choose the final top choice; usually done in a matrix

parti - an overall organizing idea for a design; its source could be a particular geometry or analogy or relationship between objects; it is site specific and pulls together the main concerns of the project

pattern - a recognizable relationship between components; the next in the series is predictable

performance requirement - a measurable level of function

PERT - *Program Evaluation Review Technique* for scheduling

photodocumentation - a process of systematically gathering information through photographs — still photos or movies and video

pilot study - a preliminary research trial run where the bugs are worked out and, hopefully, all major mistakes are made so that they can be corrected

pre-design services - include feasibility studies, master planning, programming (the conceptual stage of design), research for a design project

privacy gradient - the transition from one zone of privacy to another; the ideal is a gradual transition from most public to most private unless there are sufficient barriers between zones of very different intensities

post-construction evaluations - technical building or project evaluations that focus on the mechanical function of the project such as leaks and plumbing or HVAC system performance

post-design services - include user's manuals, post-occupancy evaluation, building fine-tuning, research

post-occupancy evaluations - building or project evaluations that focus on the satisfaction and behavior of the project's users

program document - the document produced as a report on the decisions and process of programming a design project

programming - the orderly process of gathering, interpreting, and presenting information to define the scope, nature, and direction of a design problem

quality circle - an on-going discussion group that has as its purpose improving a specific product or process

range measures - measures of function that have a scale such as temperature, decibels, feet, angles, cfm, etc.

regionalism - the tendency for designers to repeat a similar set of design responses in a region such that the architecture has a distinct visual character

research question - in this text I use this term to describe any question that has an answer with design consequences and can be researched to find data useful for making decisions

RUDAT - *Regional Urban Assistance Team*: the acronym also stands for the event during which the team puts together a plan for revamping a city or town; usually sponsored by the AIA and a student design team

scalar measures - measurment by a scale such as a thermometer, yardstick, light meter, or anemometer

scale - the relationship of things to each other, most commonly in architectural design the term refers to the relationship of objects and buildings to the human body

schema - an outline, diagram, or plan of an idea

schematic design - the beginning of physical design, when alternative solutions are developed; general, broad-brush decisions are made at this stage

semantic differential - sets of paired words used to rate specific situations on the scales created by the paired opposite words (i.e., warm to cool)

shelf list - shows all the books in the library in order by call number

simile - a figure of speech in which one thing is likened to another in whole rather than in part

simulations - the creation of circumstances that replicate situations in critical aspects so that these aspects might be studied

snow cards - at the design firm of CRS-Sirrine, they are 5" x 7" cards that each hold one programming goal, concept, or important fact; pinned to the wall they form an information matrix and serve to organize the data as well as "snow" the client.

specification, functional - a performance specification that states how the product should function

specification, object - a specification that states the materials and dimensions of the product

squatters (programming and design squatters) - a process of gathering together the programming or design team with the client and working together until the programming or schematic design is conceptually complete; rarely used for design development. Developed by W. M. Peña

statistical observation - techniques of observation that gather data that is rigorous and specific enough to be put to statistical tests

superorganizing idea - a parti, an idea that is the overall organizing idea of a design, a megaconcept

synomorphic - actions and objects fit compatibly together

synthesis - the act of combining parts to make a whole

system - a set of objects and processes that work together so that the sum is greater than the sum of its parts

systematic observation - an observation technique that collects data in measurable units so that the units can be counted and tabulated

territoriality - the sense of ownership of a place

theme - an idea that permeates the design and helps to generate the parti or overall organizing idea

units of analysis - organized categories of information that allow for the design research problem to be studied in component parts

users' manual - a booklet put together by the design project's programmers and designers to record the intentions of the design and to guide users as to how to get the most out of the building as it was designed

value - principle or standard of what is good or worthwhile or desirable

value system - the set of values that a client or client group holds that determines what they hold dear and how they evaluate the design

variable - aspects of a research situation that are studied because their changing values or actions will change the outcome; independent variables are those that can be manipulated by the researcher, dependent variables are those that are measured as outcomes of changes in the independent variables

white noise - a continuous, non-specific noise that is loud enough to mask other sounds, but not distinct enough to be distracting information

Bibliography

Adams, James L. 1986. *The Care and Feeding of Ideas: A Guide to Encouraging Creativity.* Reading, Mass.: Addison-Wesley Publishing Company, Inc.

This is an expansion to *Conceptual Blockbusting.* It covers "thinking" from the machinery of thinking to memory and habits. It has lots of exercises for "doing" from recognizing the ruts we get into to creating rewards and decision strategies.

——— 1979. *Conceptual Blockbusting: A Guide to Better Ideas,* 2nd ed. New York: W. W. Norton and Company.

This book is an in-depth discussion of the major blocks to creativity: perceptual blocks, emotional blocks, cultural and environmental blocks, intellectual and expressive blocks, and the several languages of thinking. It gives many specific ways to break through these conceptual blocks. The readers' guide at the end gives an introduction to many other resources.

Alexander, Christopher. 1964. *Notes on the Synthesis of Form.* Cambridge, Mass.: Harvard University Press.

The treatise on rationally decomposing a design problem into its component parts and forming a solution from the integration of the solutions to the separate parts of the problem.

Alger, John, R. M., and Carl V. Hays. 1964. *Creative Synthesis in Design.* Fundamentals of Engineering Design Series, ed. James B. Reswick. Englewood Cliffs, N. J.: Prentice-Hall.

A discussion of the design process from the engineering point of view. A good introduction to morphological analysis and critical path scheduling.

Altman, Irwin. 1975. *The Environment and Social Behavior: Privacy • Personal Space • Territory • Crowding.* Monterey, Cal.: Brooks/Cole Publishing Company.

This book gives a theoretical and practical understanding of privacy, personal space, territory, and crowding that is vital to designers who aspire to serve the needs of their clients in these areas.

——— and Martin Chemers. 1980. *Culture and Environment.* Basic Concepts in Environment and

Behavior Series, eds. Irwin Altman, Dan Stokols, and Leonard S. Wrightsman, Monterey, Cal.: Brooks/Cole Publishing Company.

Expounds on the research of privacy, personal space, and territory in different cultures with chapters on world views, cognition, and perception. It also explores the places created to support these behaviors: homes, neighborhoods, and communities. Good background for designers doing cross-cultural work.

American National Standards Institute. 1977. *Specifications for Making Buildings Accessible to and Useable by Physically Handicapped People*. A 117.1-1977. Washington, D.C.: U.S. Government Printing Office.

Americans with Disabilities Act Handbook. 1991. Washington, D.C.: Equal Employment Opportunity Commission: U.S. Department of Justice.

The *ADA Handbook* is the architect's guide to the federal legislation on making buildings accessible to the handicapped. No architectural office should be without one.

Archea, John, et al. 1979. *Guidelines for Stair Safety*. Washington, D.C.: National Bureau of Standards, Center for Building Technology, NBS-BSS 120.

Archer, L. Bruce. 1965. *Systematic Method for Designers*. London: Council of Industrial Design. Reprinted from *Design*, No. 172-188, April 1963 to August 1964.

Architectural Psychology Research Unit. 1974. *A Short Course in Architectural Psychology*. No dates. Sydney, Australia: Department of Architecture, University of Sydney.

The results of a five-day course designed by David Canter that included thematic talks, discussions, and exercises. Includes a wide variety of topics mostly in the realms of perception.

Barker, Roger G. 1968. *Ecological Psychology: Concepts and Methods for Studying the Environment of Human Behavior*. Stanford, Cal.: Stanford University Press.

The premier work on behavior settings from the definitions to the theory to the application. This is not a text for the casual reader of social science, for it is the culmination of 20 years of Roger Barker's research and is steeped in the jargon and appropriate academic language of social science research.

Barnes, Edward Larrabee. 1966. From *Architects on Architecture*. In *Introduction to Architecture*. See Snyder 1979, 19-20.

Baum, Andrew, Jerome Singer, and Carlene S. Baum. 1982. Stress and the Environment. 15-44. In Gary Evans, ed., *Environmental Stress*. Cambridge, England: Cambridge University Press.

Beaumont, Peter, et al. 1984. Orientation and Wayfinding in Tauranga Departmental Building: A Focused Post-Occupancy Evaluation. In *The Challenge of Diversity*, eds. Donna P. Duerk and David Campbell, 77-90. EDRA 15; June 28-July 2, at San Luis Obispo, Cal.: EDRA, Inc.

Bechtel, Robert B. 1977. *Enclosing Behavior*. Community Development Series, vol. 31, ed. Richard P. Dober. Stroudsburg, Penn.: Dowden, Hutchinson, and Ross.

An early book on the integration of social science methods into design processes. Easy reading and another good place to get one's introduction to the field of environment and behavior studies.

———— and R. Srivastava. 1978. *Post Occupancy Evaluation in Housing*. Washington, D.C.: Department of Housing and Urban Development.

A very complete bibliography of most of the housing POEs done up until 1978.

Becker, Franklin D. 1977. *Housing Messages*. Community Development Series, vol. 30, ed. Richard P. Dober. Stroudsburg, Penn.: Dowden, Hutchinson, and Ross.

Housing form as a communication: for public housing, for vandalism, for personalization, for images of home and pride in where one lives. All physical changes advocated in the hope of creating an atmosphere for social change.

Benedikt, Michael. 1991. *Deconstructing the Kimball*. New York: Lumen Books.

Boudon, Philippe. 1969. *Lived-in Architecture: Le Corbusier's Pessac Revisited*. Cambridge, Mass.: MIT Press.

A look at the history of intention, implementation, and use of workers' housing in Pessac, France. An illuminating illustration of the differences between Corbu's vision of housing and the residents' actual inhabitation. The upside is that the buildings lent themselves very well to user modification.

Brill, Michael. 1970. PAK: Planning Aid Kit. Paper presented at the Session on Environmental Architecture and Psychiatry, 123rd annual meeting of the American Psychiatric Association, San Francisco, Cal., 12 May.

——— 1984. *Using Office Design to Increase Productivity*, vol. 1 and 2. Buffalo, N.Y.: Workplace Design and Productivity.

One of the first major studies to use environment and behavior research to create applications for a specific building type. A very valuable resource for anyone designing offices.

Bristol, Catharine. 1991. The Pruitt-Igoe Myth. *Journal of Architectural Education*. May: 44(3): 163-167.

Broadbent, Geoffrey. 1973. *Design in Architecture: Architecture and the Human Sciences*. Chichester, U. K.: John Wiley and Sons Ltd.

One of the early works that helped to popularize design methods in its more scientific bent. An excellent resource for design methods from the dual graph to an understanding of the role of climatic factors in programming.

Brolin, Brent C. 1976. *The Failure of Modern Architecture*. New York: Van Nostrand Reinhold.

An indictment of the clean, square, ornamentless style called "modern" architecture with a call for understanding the needs of the users and behavioral information.

Burden, Ernest. 1992. *Grid Systems and Formats Sourcebook*. New York: Van Nostrand Reinhold.

A resource for page formats and layout grids.

Campbell, Donald T., and Julian C. Stanley. 1963. *Experimental and Quasi-Experimental Designs for Research*. Chicago. Ill.: Rand McNally College Publishing Company.

A great little handbook for the serious researcher.

Chadwick, Alex. Report on Sick Buildings. July 21, 1992. Washington, D.C.: *Morning Edition*, National Public Radio.

Clark, Roger H., and Michael I. Pause. 1979. *Analysis of Precedent: An Investigation of Elements, Relationships, and Ordering Ideas in the Work of Eight Architects*, vol. 28. Raleigh, N.C.: The Student Publication of the School of Design, North Carolina State University.

A thorough graphic analysis of the basic concepts that are embedded in the work of eight different architects using four different works per architect as examples.

Clark, Sam. 1983. *The Motion-Minded Kitchen: Step-by-Step Procedures for Designing and Building the Kitchen You Want with the Space and Money You Have*. Boston, Mass.: Houghton Mifflin Company.

How to design the "user friendly" kitchen, from planning to construction. Good measurements for planning counter heights for various tasks considering user height. Based on a lot of the work by Lillian and Frank Gilbreth, the efficiency experts.

Cohen, Sheldon, and Neil Weinstein. 1982. Nonauditory Effects of Noise on Behavior and Health. In *Environmental Stress*, ed. Gary Evans, 45-74. Cambridge, England: Cambridge University Press.

Dahl, Dan, and Randolph Sykes. 1983. *Charting Your Goals: Personal Life-Goals Planner*. New York: Harper & Row Publishers, Inc.

A workbook for getting your life's goals together that can give useful insights about creating goals for architectural projects. Topics covered are viewpoints, resources, charting goals, and commitment. Each topic covers needs, wants, values, images, tactics, and strategies.

De Chiara, Joseph, and John Callender. 1980. *Time-Saver Standards for Building Types*, 2nd ed. New York: McGraw-Hill, Inc.

Examples of the standard and/or recommended sizes and relationships of rooms, furniture, and equipment used in a wide variety of building types. Although it is a very good place to start, some of the information is dated and all of it is to be questioned rather than blindly applied to any particular design situation.

Drefuss, Henry. 1967. *The Measure of Man: Human Factors in Design*. New York: Whitney Library of Design.

A reference guide for anthropometrics — the measure of man and woman. With lots of charts for easy reference.

Duerk, Donna P. 1980. *Enabling Environments: People, Wheelchairs, and Standards*. Unpublished Masters Thesis, MIT, MarchAS Program, Cambridge, Mass.

A case study showing how seven families, with at least one member confined to a wheelchair, modified and remodeled their homes to accommodate that member. The conclusion is that handicapped people are substantially accommodated when the entry, the circulation from room to room, and the bathrooms are made accessible — all other modifications are individual preferences. The ANSI Standards (A117.1-1977) for making buildings accessible were not followed when the remodeling job would be too expensive for the benefit derived or when little benefit was perceived for the handicapped resident.

———— and Beatrice E. Lewis. 1979. *Joslin Clinic: A Preliminary Investigation*. Unpublished manuscript.

A post-occupancy study of a diabetes clinic in Brookline, Massachusetts, developed as part of course work at MIT.

EDRA Conference Proceedings. Various Editors. P. O. Box 24083, Oklahoma City, Okla. 73124; 1971 forward.

Environmental Design Group for the Department of Mental Health. 1976. *Design Guidelines: Intermediate Care Facilities for the Mentally Retarded*. Boston: Commonwealth of Massachusetts.

Evans, Gary, ed. 1982. *Environmental Stress*. Cambridge, England: Cambridge University Press.

This book brings together a lot of research on environmental stress from the actual physical results on health to the psychological results and our perceptions and appraisals of our environment as well as theories about stress. The major stressors covered are noise, air pollution, crowding, architectural dysfunction, and heat.

Farbstein, Jay, and Min Kantrowitz. 1987. *Retail Design Guidelines*. Washington, D. C.: USPS Facilities Department, Philatelic and Retail Services Department.

Franck, Karen A., and Sherry Ahrentzen, eds. 1989. *New Households, New Housing*. New York: Van Nostrand Reinhold.

Fuller, R. Buckminster. 1963. *Ideas and Integrities: A Spontaneous Autobiographical Discourse*. Englewood Cliffs, N.J.: Prentice-Hall.

A great introduction to what makes Bucky Fuller, the problem-solver, run. Keep your dictionary close at hand.

Garling, Tommy, and Eric Lindberg. 1984. Postoccupancy Evaluation of Spatial Orientation and Wayfinding. In *The Challenge of Diversity*, eds. Donna P. Duerk and David Campbell, 91-99. EDRA 15; June 28-July 2, at San Luis Obispo, Cal.: EDRA, Inc.

Gehl, Jan. 1987. *Life Between Buildings: Using Public Space*. New York: Van Nostrand Reinhold.

A fully illustrated study of activities that occur in the public realm with international examples. Planning guidelines for enlivening the public spaces between buildings.

Gregory, R. L. 1966. *Eye and Brain: The Psychology of Seeing*. London: Weidenfeld and Nicholson.

Guralnik, David B. 1966. *Webster's New World Dictionary of the American Language*. Cleveland and New York: The World Publishing Company.

Hall, Edward T. 1977. *Beyond Culture*. Garden City, N.Y.: Doubleday & Company.

A further look at how space and culture are connected. Creates an awareness that we are so much a part of our own culture that we assume it to be universal much as a fish would have a hard time discovering water. A call to be aware of the cultural rules that our clients live by so that our designs will be appropriately supportive.

—— 1969. *The Hidden Dimension*. Garden City, N.Y.: Doubleday & Company.
A classic reference for the ideas of culture as communication in terms of proxemics, or personal distances, and how these show up in our designed environment and as different dimensions in different cultures.

—— 1959. *Silent Language*. Garden City, N.Y.: Doubleday & Company.
The first of Hall's books to call out the *language* of proxemics and its importance in human culture.

Hanna, Paul R., and Jean S. Hanna. 1987. *Frank Lloyd Wright's Hanna House: The Client's Report*, 2nd ed. Carbondale, Ill.: Southern Illinois University Press.
An interesting insight into the relationship between Frank Lloyd Wright and one of his clients.

Harris, Robert. 1975. Bootstrap Essence-Seeking, *Journal of Architectural Education*. 29:30-32.

Harvey, Joan, and Jacqueline Vischer. 1984. Environmental Design Research in Canada: Innovative Government Intervention. In *The Challenge of Diversity*, eds. Donna P. Duerk and David Campbell, 278. EDRA 15; June 28-July 2, at San Luis Obispo, Cal.: EDRA, Inc.

Hawking, Stephen W. 1988. *A Brief History of Time: From the Big Bang to Black Holes*. New York: Bantam Doubleday Dell Publishing Group, Inc.
A truly delightful look at the scientific model of thought and of the state of modern physics for the lay reader.

Hershberger, Robert G. 1972. Toward a Set of Semantic Scales to Measure the Meaning of Architectural Environments. In *Environmental Design: Research and Practice,* ed. William J. Mitchell, 6-4-1 to 6-4-10. EDRA 3/AR, January 24-27, at UCLA, Los Angeles, Cal.: Regents of the University of California.

Howell, Sandra C. 1976. *Shared Spaces in Housing for the Elderly*. Cambridge, Mass.: Design Evaluation Project, Department of Architecture, Massachusetts Institute of Technology.

—— 1980. *Design for Aging: Patterns of Use*. Cambridge, Mass.: MIT Press.
Case studies and design guidelines for housing for the elderly. Explores furnishability and other issues of great interest to architects.

Jacobs, Jane. 1961. *The Death and Life of Great American Cities*. New York: Vintage Books.
One of the classic case studies of a city, with astute observations as to the relationship between the design of a city and its vitality. Still as poignant today as it was over 20 years ago.

Kiersey, David, and Marilyn Bates. 1984. *Please Understand Me: Character and Temperament Types*. Del Mar, Cal.: Prometheus Nemesis Book Company.
A quick and easy introduction to the idea of personality types with a short, self-administered scale similar to the longer MBTI. Different personality types make different demands upon the environment and this book will help in beginning an understanding of these valuable differences.

Kirk, Stephen J., and Kent F. Spreckelmeyer. 1988. *Creative Design Decisions: A Systematic Approach to Problem Solving in Architecture*. New York: Van Nostrand Reinhold.
Design process as a decision model. Each chapter covers the history, theory, and methods of a particular topic ranging from group creativity to design communication and then draws conclusions about the topic.

Koberg, Don, and Jim Bagnall. 1991. *The Universal Traveler: A Soft-Systems Guide to Creativity, Problem-Solving, and the Process of Reaching Goals*. Los Altos, Cal.: Crisp Publications, Inc.
An all-purpose guide to the design process. This updated version uses space travel analogies to highlight the design process as a great adventure.

Laseau, Paul. 1980. *Graphic Thinking for Architects and Designers*. New York: Van Nostrand Reinhold.
An introductory text that stresses the graphic aspects of the

design process and gives multiple examples of processes and techniques. A good place to start for understanding the relationship between graphics of all kinds and the thinking/decision process.

Lawson, Bryan. 1980. *How Designers Think*. London, England: The Architectural Press, Ltd.
A delightful book on thinking and designing from the British point of view. Lawson speaks of the changing role of the designer in our society and how the design process has been explained in different ways as well. The bulk of the book is a section on different ways of thinking and designing that most programmers or designers will find useful.

Lawton, M. Powell, and Lucille Nahemow. 1973. Ecology and the Aging Process. In *Psychology of Adult Development and Aging*, ed. C. Eisendorfer and M. Powell Lawton, 619-674. Washington, D.C.: American Psychological Association.

Lazarus, R. S., and J. B. Cohen. 1977. Environmental Stress. In *Human Behavior and Environment*, vol. 1, eds. I. Altman and J. F. Wohlwill. New York: Plenum Press.

Le Corbusier, Jeanneret-Gris, and Edouard Charles. 1980. *The Modulor*, 2nd ed. Cambridge, Mass.: Harvard University Press.
Corbu's attempt to bring the science of measures to the same level of harmony as the science of sound, i.e., music. This book is filled with Corbu's sketches, projects, and thoughts about the art and science of proportion.

Lewin, Kurt. 1935. *A Dynamic Theory of Personality*. New York: McGraw-Hill, Inc.

Loo, Chalsa, and Paul Ong. 1984. Crowding Perceptions, Attitudes, and Consequences Among the Chinese. *Environment and Behavior* 16(1): 55-87.

Luckiesh, M. 1965. *Visual Illusions: Their Causes, Characteristics and Applications*. New York: Dover Publications, Inc.
A compelling introduction to the power of visual illusions and their applications in many fields from art to architecture.

Lynch, Kevin. 1981. *A Theory of Good City Form*. Cambridge, Mass.: MIT Press.
Guidelines for what it takes to create good urban environments. Basic theory.

——— and Gary Hack. 1984. *Site Planning*, 3rd ed. Cambridge, Mass.: MIT Press.
The definitive work of site planning.

Marcus, Clare Cooper. 1975. *Easter Hill Village: Some Social Implications*. New York: Free Press.
A classic in the area of participant observation in design research. A post-occupancy evaluation of public housing in Richmond, California, with a depth that few, if any, other studies have ever managed to produce.

——— 1976. The House as Symbol of Self. In *Environmental Psychology: People and Their Physical Settings*, 2 ed., ed. Harold M. Proshansky, William H. Ittelson, and Leanne G. Rivlin, 435-48. New York: Holt, Rinehart and Winston.

——— and Wendy Sarkissian. 1986. *Housing as If People Mattered: Site Design Guidelines for Medium-Density Family Housing*. Berkeley and Los Angeles, Cal.: University of California Press.
This is a necessary resource for anyone designing medium-density housing. Issues and performance requirements are presented in a thoughtful and well-illustrated format. There are many ideas for improving design. One of the better resources on programming for housing.

Markus, Thomas, et al. 1972. *Building Performance*. New York: Halstead Press.
Documents the work of the Building Performance Research Unit of the University of Strathclyde in Scotland. The research unit was started in 1967 and has contributed a great deal to the descriptive and theoretical knowledge base for the interface between people and building design.

McGinty, Tim. 1979. Design and the Design Process. In *Introduction to Architecture*, ed. James C. Snyder and Anthony J. Catanese, 152-190. New York: McGraw-Hill, Inc.

McHarg, Ian L. 1971. *Design with Nature*. Garden City, New York: Doubleday & Company.
Profusely illustrated and eloquently written treatise on creating man-made designs in harmony with earth's nature. A personal quest to which Ian McHarg has devoted most of his adult life. The book rings for me with echoes of his dramatic Scottish brogue and his passion for knowing what the earth has to offer before building.

Michaelson, William, ed. 1975. *Behavioral Research Methods in Environmental Design*. Stroudsburg, Penn.: Hutchinson Ross Publishing Company.
Seven essays covering topics from planning games and surveys to photodocumentation and behavior settings.

Miller, George. 1956. The Magical Number Seven, Plus or Minus Two: Some Limits on Our Capacity for Processing Information. *Psychological Review*. 63: 81-97.

Moore, Gary T., ed. 1973. *Emerging Methods in Environmental Design and Planning*. Cambridge, Mass.: MIT Press.
This is one of the early works filled with the hope and expectations of what the computer could do to facilitate better design — much of which is just now coming into common practice. There are papers on the design process, evaluation, and systems engineering as well. Based on the Proceedings of The Design Methods Group First International Conference, June 1968.

———— Paul D. Tuttle, and Sandra C. Howell. 1985. *Environmental Design Research Directions: Process and Prospects*. Ervin H. Zube and Gary T. Moore, consulting editors, Praeger Special Studies. New York: Praeger Publishers.
The purpose of this volume is to delineate the field of environment and human behavior studies and to state the aspects most needing attention — those issues at the cutting edge in 1981.

Moos, Rudolf H. 1974. *Evaluating Treatment Environments: A Social Ecological Approach*. New York: John Wiley and Sons.

———— 1979. *Evaluating Educational Environments*, 1st ed. San Francisco, Cal.: Jossey Bass Publishers.

Müller-Brockman, Josef. *Grid Systems in Graphic Design*, 2nd ed. New York: Hastings House Publishers.
A reference for the graphics of page layout.

Myers, Isabel Briggs. 1980. *Gifts Differing*. Palo Alto, Cal.: Consulting Psychologist Press, Inc.
The Myers-Briggs Type Indicator (MBTI) is a tool for evaluation of one's personality based on Jungian typology. There are four rating scales: introvert-extrovert, intuitive-sensate, thinking-feeling, and judging-perceiving. The study of personality types leads one to savor the valuable differences between people and to appreciate the need for choices in designing for a wide range of people.

National Aeronautics and Space Administration. 1989. *Man-Systems Integration Standards*. Houston, Tex.: National Aeronautics and Space Administration. NASA-STD 3000, Rev. A.
This is a great resource for anthropometric data and ergonomic requirements for the design of many things from switches and control panels to specifications for microgravity working accommodations.

NBS 361. 1972. National Bureau of Standards Technical Report #361. Washington, D.C.: U.S. Government Printing Office.
A collection of early work on building performance which is useful to programmers.

Newman, Oscar. 1972. *Defensible Space: Crime Prevention Through Urban Design*. New York: Macmillan Publishing Co., Inc.
Full of valuable insights into designing buildings so that people know their neighbors and want to take care of their larger territory. Known for its flawed statistics, but valuable for its perspective and design guidelines.

Nowlis, D. P., E. C. Wortz, and H. Waters. 1972. *Tektite II: Habitability Research Program*, Los Angeles, Cal.: Airesearch Manufacturing Company for NASA.

Olgyay, Victor. 1963. *Design with Climate: Bioclimatic Approach to Architectural Regionalism*. Princeton, N. J.: Princeton University Press.
One of the first easily comprehended volumes that point out the need for energy efficient design.

Olsen, Richard, Janet R. Carpman, and Gary Winkel. 1984. Hospital Design Research, Implementation and Evaluation: Workshop #1 — Planning and Programming Research. In *The Challenge of Diversity*, eds. Donna P. Duerk and David Campbell, 295. EDRA 15; June 28-July 2, at San Luis Obispo, Cal.: EDRA, Inc.

Osgood, Charles E., George J. Suci, and Percy H. Tannenbaum. 1967. *The Measurement of Meaning*. Urbana, Chicago, and London: University of Illinois Press.
For those readers serious about understanding and using the semantic differential. Very technical, covers the statistical chore of choosing and testing paired opposite words that are effective in eliciting evaluation, potency, and activity.

Palmer, Mickey A. 1981. *The Architect's Guide to Facility Programming*. Washington, D.C.: The American Institute of Architects.
A survey of programming processes by different firms as well as an information management structure proposed by the author. About one third of the book is dedicated to case studies that show parts of actual program documents. Currently out of print.

Pauls, Jake. 1985. Research and Applications Related to Building Code Requirements for Means of Egress. In *Research and Design 85: Applications of Design and Technology Research*, 235-40, March 14-18, Los Angeles, Cal., Washington, D.C.: AIA Foundation.

Peña, William M., Stephen A. Parshall, and Kevin A. Kelly. 1987. *Problem Seeking: An Architectural Programming Primer*. 3d ed., Washington, D. C..: AIA Press.
This is the first book to share the "how to" of programming.

The CRS methods have probably influenced more programmers than any other way of thinking about programming. It is deceptively simple in format and holds a great deal of information for the beginning programmer. The most current edition of this book is published by the AIA.

Perin, Constance. 1970. *With Man in Mind: An Interdisciplinary Prospectus for Environmental Design*. Cambridge, Mass.: MIT Press.
An early proponent of programming as "the instrument of collaboration" so that the human sciences are involved to create more fit environments. Also a proponent of the dramatic analogy for creating environments as stage sets for human expression. Shares a vision of a responsive environment as one that is smaller in scale, greater in variety and flexibility, dominated by home environments, and reflective of what we know about ourselves.

Pohl, Jens, et al. 1992. *AEDOT Prototype (1.1): An Implementation of the ICADS Model*. San Luis Obispo, Cal.: CAD Research Center, College of Architecture and Environmental Design.

Preiser, Wolfgang F. E., ed. 1985. *Programming the Built Environment*. New York: Van Nostrand Reinhold.
Ten essays on different aspects of programming.

——— ed. 1989. *Building Evaluation*. New York: Plenum Press.
Based upon the Symposium on Advances in Building Evaluation: Knowledge, Methods, and Applications, held as part of the Tenth Biannual Conference of the International Association for the Study of People and Their Physical Surroundings, July 5-8, 1988, in Delft, The Netherlands. It is a compilation of articles from many of the current experts in the field. A good reader for someone interested in an overview of the building evaluation field, especially post-occupancy evaluation.

——— Harvey Z. Rabinowitz, and Edward T. White. 1988. *Post-Occupancy Evaluation*. New York: Van Nostrand Reinhold.
The background and process of post-occupancy evaluation as

well as three case studies. The process model shows three levels of effort for increasing time and cost involved.

Proshansky, Harold M., William H. Ittelson, and Leanne G. Rivlin. 1976. *Environmental Psychology: People and Their Physical Settings*, 2nd ed. New York: Holt, Rinehart and Winston.
A book of readings in environmental psychology by three of the mainstays of the Environmental Psychology Program at CUNY, NYC. It covers a broad range of topics of interest to architects. A good first reader.

Prussin, L., ed. 1984. *Gender-Related Design Issues: People in Living Space*. Seattle, Wash.: University of Washington, Northwest Center for Research on Women.

Rapoport, Amos. 1969. *House Form and Culture*, ed. Philip Wagner, Foundations of Cultural Geography Series. Englewood Cliff, N.J.: Prentice-Hall, Inc.
A thorough study of the influences on house form including socio-cultural factors, climate, materials, and technology. A good bridge between architecture and anthropology.

——— 1975a. An Approach to the Construction of Man-Environment Theory. In *Environmental Design Research*, vol. 1, ed. Wolfgang F. E. Preiser. EDRA 4. 124-35. Stroudsburg, Penn.: Dowden, Hutchinson and Ross.

——— 1975b. Toward a Definition of Density. *Environment and Behavior.* 7(2): 133-54.

Rea, M. S., et al. 1985. Design Considerations for Egress Signs Based Upon Visibility Through Smoke. In *Research and Design 85: Applications of Design and Technology Research*, 295-297, March 14-18, Los Angeles, Cal., Washington, D.C.: AIA Foundation.

Rock, Irvin. 1975. *An Introduction to Perception*. New York: Macmillan Publishing Co., Inc.

Sanoff, Henry. 1977. *Methods of Architectural Programming*. Stroudsburg, Penn: Dowden, Hutchinson and Ross.
A survey of research methods for architectural programming.

——— et al. 1979. *Senior Center Design Workbook*. Raleigh, N.C.: School of Design, N.C. State University.
A workbook developed as a research project with a group of design students to help people learn about designing senior centers.

——— 1991. *Visual Research Methods in Design*. New York: Van Nostrand Reinhold.
A good resource for more detailed information of research methodology for programming. Covers environmental measurement, imageability, environmental mapping, visual notation, environmental simulation, and planning and design methodological case studies.

Schatzman, Leonard, and Anselm L. Strauss. 1973. *Field Research: Strategies for a Natural Sociology*. Prentice-Hall Methods of Social Science Series, ed. Herbert L. Costner and Neil Smelser. Englewood Cliffs, N.J.: Prentice-Hall, Inc.
An introduction and how-to guide to field research from strategies for getting organized, watching, listening, recording, analyzing, and communicating the research.

Selltiz, Wrightsman, and Cook. 1981. *Research Methods in Social Relations*, 4th ed., ed. Louise Kidder, for the Society for the Psychological Study of Social Issues (SPSSI). New York: Holt, Rinehart and Winston.
A very thorough research text of great use to programmers. It covers research design, measurement, reporting, and ethical issues. It also has sections on analysis, experimentation, surveys, evaluation research, questionnaires and surveys, scaling, indirect assessment, observation, archival data and participant observation. Measurement issues included are reliability and validity.

Sergeant, John. 1976. *Frank Lloyd Wight's Usonian Houses: The Case for Organic Architecture*. New York: Whitney Library of Design.
This book is filled with plans, photographs, and details of Wright's Usonian houses. It is my all-time favorite Frank Lloyd Wright book.

Simonds, John O. 1983. *Landscape Architecture: A Manual of Site Planning and Design.* New York: McGraw-Hill, Inc.
A delightful volume that is filled with photographs and drawings to illustrate the principles of landscape architecture. It is a good place to start for any architect who wants to know more about landscape architecture.

Snyder, James C., and Anthony J. Catanese, eds. 1979. *Introduction to Architecture.* New York: McGraw-Hill, Inc.
A very good book for a survey course in architecture for non-architects. It covers all the bases and has bibliographies at the end of each chapter.

Sommer, Robert. 1969. *Personal Space: The Behavioral Basis of Design.* Englewood Cliffs, N.J.: Prentice-Hall, Inc.
One of the first books to take on the concepts of personal space in the context of specific architectural settings and research the implications for design. One of the set of basic books to be read by people wanting a basic understanding of the issues of environment and behavior.

——— 1974. *Tight Spaces: Hard Architecture and How to Humanize It.* Englewood Cliffs, N.J.: Prentice-Hall, Inc.
A look at institutional architecture and the fixed ideas that hold it in place. A call for social responsive and responsible architecture.

Spivack, Mayer. 1978. The Design Log: A New Information Tool. *AIA Journal.* Oct: 76-78.
The article illustrates the connection between the performance requirements and the hypothesis for people's behavior and points to the design of a new facility as a way to implement new philosophies or service delivery programs.

Steele, Fritz. 1981. *The Sense of Place.* Boston, Mass.: CBI Publishing Company, Inc.
An experiential examination of the sense of place and documentation that is easy to read. Great anecdotal examples rather than a dry scientific look at place and how designers might contribute to creating a sense of place.

Steinfeld, Edward, et al. 1979a. *Access to the Built Environment: A Review of the Literature.* Washington, D.C.: U.S. Government Printing Office.
Part of a research project that contributed to the updating of ANSI A117.1, *Making Buildings and Facilities Accessible to and Useable by the Physically Handicapped.* A good place to start for the useful information before 1979.

——— 1979b. *Accessible Buildings for People with Walking and Reaching Limitations.* Washington, D.C.: U.S. Government Printing Office.
The results of original research documented with photographs and charts. Very good for enlightening the novice designer about the real problems of people who are chair-bound or who have physical limitations caused by arthritis or other degenerative diseases.

——— 1979c. *Accessible Buildings for People with Severe Visual Impairments.* Washington, D.C.: U.S. Government Printing Office.
An analysis of the mobility problems of people who see poorly or not at all, with proposals and recommendations for solving these problems.

——— 1979d. *The Estimated Cost of Accessible Buildings.* Washington, D.C.: U.S. Government Printing Office.
Nine building types are analyzed for probable deficiencies in access to the mobility impaired and the design changes and their costs for making those buildings accessible are itemized in 1979 dollars.

——— 1979e. *Selected Bibliography on Barrier-Free Design.* Washington, D.C.: U.S. Government Printing Office.
126 basic references about barrier-free design. A good reference for pre-1979 information.

Van der Ryn, Sim H., and Murray Silverstein. 1967. *Dorms at Berkeley. An Environmental Analysis,* rev. ed., Monograph No. 11. Berkeley: Center for Planning and Development Research.

Wagner, Jon, ed. 1979. *Images of Information: Still Photography in the Social Sciences.* Beverly Hills, Cal.: Sage Publications, Inc.
A good introduction to the use of visual images in research — the benefits and the problems. Some of the insights might be applied to video work, but the emphasis is on the application of still photography to research questions.

Webb, Eugene J., et al. 1966. *Unobtrusive Measures: Non-reactive Research in the Social Sciences.* Chicago, Ill.: Rand McNally College Publishing Company.
A very insightful book into observational research that does not disturb the subjects of the investigation. A great resource for ideas about how to design research for architectural projects.

Weisman, Gerald D. 1985. Spatial Orientation and Way Finding, and Emergency Egress Behavior: Implications for Architectural Design and Life Safety Standards. In *Research and Design 85: Applications of Design and Technology Research,* 167-171. March 14-18, Los Angeles, Cal., Washington, D.C.: AIA Foundation.

White, Edward T. 1982. *Interviews with Architects About Facility Programming.* Tallahassee, Fla.: Graduate Program, School of Architecture, Florida A and M University.
A monograph recording results of interviews with architects from fifty-five firms about their attitudes toward programming and the needs for educating architects in programming. The two highest numbers of responses, regarding skills that programming students should have upon graduation, were communication skills and information processing (converting data into information).

———— 1972. *Introduction to Architectural Programming.* Tucson, Ariz.: Architectural Media.
An outline of the programming process with great check lists for research, facts, and general considerations in programming.

———— 1983. *Site Analysis: Diagramming Information for Architectural Design.* Tucson, Ariz.: Architectural Media.
Presents a wide variety of ways to deal with site data in a graphic manner. A thorough list of all the types of site information needed by designers.

———— 1986. *Space Adjacency Analysis.* Tucson, Ariz.: Architectural Media.
A thorough look at all the ins and outs of doing and presenting space adjacency analysis. Not for the complete novice, but a good tool for those wanting to expand and polish their skills.

———— no date a. *Learning Decision-Making for the Building Process.* Tallahassee, Fla.: Graduate Program, School of Architecture, Florida A and M University.
Fourteen page monograph on decision-making skills needed in programming and building design. "Good decision skills are never outmoded."

———— no date b. *Teaching Architectural Programming.* Tallahassee, Fla.: Graduate Program, School of Architecture, Florida A and M University.
A monograph that raises many issues of teaching and learning the skills of architectural programing. It is partially based upon an extensive survey of architects regarding their programming services.

Whyte, William H. 1979. *The Social Life of Small Urban Spaces* (movie). Washington, D.C.: Street Life Project. 57 minutes.
A must-see movie for all designers of public spaces. Great illustrations of research methods and the results of that research.

———— 1980. *The Social Life of Small Urban Spaces.* Washington, D.C.: The Conservation Foundation.
The definitive work on what makes good plazas. Research started in 1971 and the Street Life Project in New York City continues to function.

Wicker, Allan. 1979. *An Introduction to Ecological Psychology.* Cambridge, England: Cambridge University Press.
A very readable introduction to the ideas of ecological psychology from behavior settings to undermanning theory (which I think should be called understaffing theory). Looks at the psychological reasons why behaviors are congruent with environments and compares behavior in large settings and small settings.

Wright, Frank Lloyd. 1960. Frank Lloyd Wright: *Writings and Buildings.* In *Introduction to Architecture.* See Snyder 1979, 217.

Wurman, Richard Saul. 1989. *Information Anxiety.* New York: Doubleday & Company.
A fun-filled book about the information explosion and keys to getting the information you need when you need it. Chapters on performance, learning, understanding, and failure are all insightful and applicable to programming and designing.

Yin, Robert K. 1984. *Case Study Research: Design and Methods.* Applied Social Research Methods Series, vol. 5., ed. Leonard Bickman, Beverly Hills, Cal.: Sage Publications.
A great short book (146 pages) on doing case studies that is quite useful for anyone serious about using case studies as a method of gathering reliable data for architectural research. Yin starts with the design of a case study, moves through preparing for data collection, collecting the data, analysis and finally composing the report.

Zeisel, John. 1981. *Inquiry by Design: Tools for Environment and Behavior Research.* Basic Concepts in Environment and Behavior Series, eds. Irwin Altman, Dan Stokels, and Lawrence Wrightsman. Monterey, Cal.: Brooks/Cole Publishing Company.
A very good resource for designers to understand the interdependence of social scientists and designers in doing good architectural research. Also good for detailed methodologies for research study design including observing physical traces, observing behaviors, interviews, and questionnaires.

——— 1976. *Stopping School Property Damage: Design and Administrative Guidelines to Reduce School Vandalism.* Arlington, Va.: American Association of School Administrators and Educational Facilities Laboratories in collaboration with city of Boston Public Facilities Department.
A good example of social science research and its application to design in the form of design guidelines based upon behavior.

Ziglar, Zig. 1974. *See You at the Top.* Gretna, La.: Pelican Publishing Company, Inc.
A wonderfully homey and hokey book about success. A great section on goal setting — both personal and professional.

Index